Finance and Capital Markets Series

The Finance and Capital Markets series is designed to bring you high-quality, cutting-edge information on the latest issues and developments in the financial world. These authoritative yet accessible books, written by experts in their field, provide clear, practical guidance not only for industry professionals, but also serve as a framework of current analysis for scholars and form a comprehensive reference resource for libraries.

More information about this series at
http://www.palgrave.com/gp/series/13977

Tarsem Bhogal • Arun Trivedi

International Trade Finance

A Pragmatic Approach

Second edition

Tarsem Bhogal
London, UK

Arun Trivedi
London, UK

Finance and Capital Markets Series
ISBN 978-3-030-24539-9   ISBN 978-3-030-24540-5   (eBook)
https://doi.org/10.1007/978-3-030-24540-5

Cover illustration: Thatree Thitivongvaroon / GettyImages
Cover design by eStudio Calamar

This Palgrave Macmillan imprint is published by the registered company Springer Nature Switzerland AG.
The registered company address is: Gewerbestrasse 11, 6330 Cham, Switzerland

Preface

The global trading system is undergoing a period of transition. Shifting economic circumstances, major advances in technology and the emergence of new players on the global scene all underscore that we are on the cusp of big changes. Persistent imbalances, driven largely by macro-economic factors, continue to be a cause of concern in some major economies. Even in such a climate of uncertainty, one thing is certain: that there is a great need to strengthen the global trading system by making it more equitable and relevant for those who trade in the twenty-first century with Uniform Customs and Practice.

In retrospect we find that in 2005, the value of world merchandise exports rose by 13% to $10.1 trillion and the value of world commercial services export by 11% to $2.4 trillion. The volume and value of international trade is a testimony to make us believe that the world order has changed quite swiftly over the past ten years at a much faster pace than that of the previous 20 years. It is difficult to contemplate what the world trade/economies will look like in 2010. One thing is certain, however: Change is inevitable. Bankers and trading communities operating in such a climate will have to face challenges that are immense.

Technology has indeed opened up new markets, with geographic boundaries becoming non-existent to the web-enabled community. What we see today is the beginning of the reaction to this expansion as an outcome of globalisation and internationalisation, adding multi-complexities to the players in the international trade.

In this spectrum, industry practitioners will solicit solace by resorting to basics and learning the lesson of the laser. How to understand rather than find a solution from the ponderance? So we did, encouraged by these international interactive developments.

Based on our learning experience and working as practitioners facilitating international trade, in our capacity as bankers, we have worked on the treatise in your hands: *International Trade Finance: A Pragmatic Approach* (2007). In fact, we have been motivated to write this book in view of the urge from the beginners as well as industry practitioners to understand and grasp the type and nature of various documents in use in international trade and mechanisms of settlement of payments thereof.

The book is organised into 25 chapters endeavouring to address key topics relating to the gamut of international trade, letter of credit mechanism, collections, trade customs and practice, and so on. We do not pretend that all technical concerns are answered but we are confident that we have gone much further than any other published material on the subject. Dealing with complicated implementation issues in a forthright and comprehensive fashion and design, we have given a lucid account of provisions vis-à-vis trade customs and practice while protecting the interests of the parties involved in international trade. We have striven to present and explain transaction flow through diagrams, easing the job of a learner enabling to understand and grasp the hardcore subject matter.

We sincerely believe that this book will be regarded as an essential tool for both beginners and practitioners in international trade. We are hopeful that the readers will position this book within easy reach for navigating solutions to assorted trade-related issues and/or as a constant travel companion when in business across the world.

London, UK   Tarsem Bhogal
London, UK   Arun Trivedi

Acknowledgements

We are grateful to the following authorities for their permission to publish information in this book relating to their products and services. As the systems and procedures of international trade change with improvements of information technology and other developments, we request the readers to visit their websites to obtain the latest information:

1. Export Credit Guarantee Department—www.ecgd.gov.uk.
2. UK Export Finance—www.ukexportfinance.gov.uk
3. International Chamber of Commerce (ICC) Paris—www.iccwbo.org
4. Society for Worldwide International Financial Telecommunication— www.swift.com

Disclaimer: The authors have made reasonable efforts to ensure the accuracy of the information given in this book at the time but assume no liability for any inadvertent error or omission that may appear. The information may change from time to time and practical procedures may also differ from one bank to another; the authors do not accept any liability for the consequences of error or omission.

Tarsem Bhogal
Arun Trivedi

Praise for *International Trade Finance*

"This book is a welcome addition to the literature with details of both innovative concepts and professional practice. This book will be highly useful to academics, practitioners and banking officials all over the world."
—Professor Thomas Muthucattu Paul, *Professor of Economics and Finance, PNG University of Technology, Papua New Guinea*

"This topical book is essential reading suited to a wide range of readers interested in International Trade Finance. An armchair read for consultants and practitioners, it features useful background material for short duration or capsule programmes run by trainers. The extensive content qualifies this is as a good desk reference book for both bankers and shippers."
—Somya Mishra, *Assistant Vice-President, Risk COO, Deutsche Bank London, UK*

"This handy tool provides a comprehensive foundation for understanding all aspects of International Trade Finance in a global context, covering the key principles, concepts, infrastructures, practices, issues, and current developments. Definitely a must read for professionals in banking, commerce, trade and transport industry who want to gain a closer understanding of International Trade Finance pragmatically."
—Ankita Sethi, *freelance Socially Responsible Investment Consultant, analyst and writer*

"I appreciate the endeavours of the authors in bringing this informative, educational and self-training literature on this subject. The topics covered in the second edition will be appreciated by beginners and practitioners undertaking the demanding and complex international trade business."
—B.C. Bassi, *Former Non-workmen Director on the Board of State Bank of India (formerly known as State Bank of Patiala)*

Contents

About the Authors

Tarsem Bhogal was the Principal of the Staff Training Centre, Association of Indian Banks in the UK from 1990 to August 2006. Earlier, he was a senior faculty of an International Bank's Regional Staff Training and Development Centre in London. Bhogal set up a Regional Staff Training Centre of a public sector bank in northern India. Starting a banking career with The Standard Bank Limited, he has been a practical banker who has managed banking operations in Kenya, India and the UK. Bhogal is a fellow of The Institute of Financial Accountants, Fellow of the Institute of Public accountants, Member of Chartered Management Institute and ordinary member of the Chartered Institute of Bankers (now Institute of Banking and Finance), London, UK.

In his personal life, he is a poet, writer, thinker, General Secretary Panjabi Likhari Forum (UK), and formerly a governor of primary and secondary schools and six form colleges. Bhogal is a former elected Councillor in the London Borough of Waltham Forest and Mayor of the Borough, an important borough representing multi-cultural society with diverse faiths in his area of operation, and a philanthropist. He was a former Trustee of a Sikh Gurdwara (Temple), Chairman of Waltham Forest Citizen Advice Bureau and Vice Chairman of Waltham Forest Race Equality Council. He is a member of the Standing Advisory Council on Religious Education representing the Sikh faith. He lives in London, with his wife Amar Kaur.

Arun Trivedi is a thorough banker, thinker, researcher, author and an academic par excellence. Presently he is engaged as a business design consultant and a corporate governance coach, based in London, UK. He has engagements in Africa, Asia, Canada, Europe and the Middle East for human capital development, capacity building through seminars, specialised modular courses, mock-drills in areas such as behavioural sciences and provides functional knowledge viz. foreign exchange, international banking, trade finance and risk management, corporate governance/ethics and value system through behavioural applications. His practice includes banking, structured finance, financial strategy, innovation and corporate governance.

Trivedi has authored books on various subjects viz. "Forex and Risk Management" (2000), "Credit Risk Management" (2003), "International Trade Finance" (1996), "Behavioural Science—Scope and Uses" (1992) including a fiction *Dawn to Dusk* (2010).

Trivedi achieved his professional qualifications and experience in his early career in India, with State Bank of India (SBI)-(eSBP), Kotak Mahindra Bank (earlier Vysya ING), National Institute of Bank Management (Faculty on Deputation)—a prominent body of bankers, IndusInd Bank & Doha Bank, undertaking a number of roles—Chief Currency Dealer, Head Treasury, Chief of Global Banking Operations and also Vice President and Chief Representative office based at London, UK. He is a member of London Press Club. He has received numerous awards, titles and honours, to name a few Fellowship of the Indian Institute of Banking & Finance (IIBF), Chartered Fellowship of Chartered Institute for Securities and Investments (Chartered FCSI), Fellow of the Indian Society for Training and Development, and award for services in "Banking and Finance Management" from the International Biographical Centre, Cambridge, England,

He lives in London with his wife Madhvi.

List of Figures

List of Tables

1

International Trade and Inherent Risks

Background of International Trade

Ever since World War II there has been a considerable increase in world trade between independent sovereign states. In international trade, importers and exporters are quite often confronted with problems arising from the movements of goods from one country to another and are simultaneously subject to the different legislation, customs and practices of these countries. Importers and exporters have certain concerns such as:

Exporters want to be certain that they are paid when their goods have been shipped or dispatched because the goods will be out of their control.

Importers want to be certain that they receive goods that conform to what has been ordered.

Commercial banks play an important role in international trade; they act as intermediaries between importers and exporters. They have insight and wide practical experience in foreign trade coupled with legal knowledge of provision in different countries. Banks have correspondents in most countries, through whom they deal with the counter parties. Some banks may have their own branches in other countries.

As banks are major financial institutions they are trustworthy and can be relied upon by their customers. They provide advisory services on various subjects to their importing and exporting customers. They collect payment from overseas countries from importers in foreign countries and also remit funds to the exporters abroad on behalf of their customers.

© The Author(s) 2019
T. Bhogal, A. Trivedi, *International Trade Finance*, Finance and Capital Markets Series,
https://doi.org/10.1007/978-3-030-24540-5_1

Banks offer various types of services to local and international business communities. These services include financial facilities to exporters and importers by way of loans and overdrafts, discounting and purchasing of bills of exchange. There are many more inherent risks in buying and selling goods overseas than locally. Some of the risks in foreign trade are explained in brief hereunder.

Exporters' Risks

Arrangements for selling goods abroad are often more complex than those connected with home market sales due to the following reasons:

Geographical Factors: The exported goods are sold to buyers who, for geographical reasons, are likely to be less known to the seller's own country.

Legal System: The buyer will often be subject to a different legal system and trade customs from those in the exporter's country.

Language: The languages of the exporters and importers may be different, and thus there would be need to translate the basic text and its related implications.

Non-Payment: Exporting tends to entail a greater risk of non-payment than domestic sales. This risk is known as the buyer's risk.

Importers' Risks

Delay in delivery of goods and settlement of funds: The time taken for goods to pass from the seller to the buyer is generally longer for exports than for goods sold to buyers at home. This poses a problem because buyers prefer not to pay until the goods have been inspected, while suppliers want payment on or before shipment. What actually happens is often a compromise—the result of the relative bargaining powers of the two parties to trade.

Exchange Risks: Export trade involves a financial transaction in a foreign currency either to the buyer or to the seller, or sometimes to both, and hence entails exchange risks.

Exchange Control: Export trade may involve exchange control regulations, both in the seller's and the buyer's country, and a variety of further risks for the seller.

Political Risks: There are risks in the event of war or national disaster between countries. These risks are also known as country risks.

Manufacturing Risks: The buyer cancels or modifies the order unilaterally. In such a case the exporter has to find an alternative buyer who is willing to buy the goods. The exporter might be forced to accept a substantially lower price. A system well-developed by international banks ensures that contracts signed between two parties in the United Kingdom (UK) are adhered to and that the parties fulfil their delivery or payment obligation.

The buyer/importer has concerns about the quality and quantity of goods. The buyer/importer should therefore be aware of the types of documents that are required to protect against these risks.

Export/Import Facilities: The sophisticated arrangements which surround exporting trade stem from the various risks, and a wide range of the available facilities and how to avoid these risks are described later in this book.

2

Services Offered by Commercial Banks

The finance of international trade forms an important part of any major bank's services package. Many banks have specialised departments to handle the various aspects involved, comprising experienced staff able to cope with the demands of customers with overseas business to transact.

Trade Enquiries: Banks with overseas branch networks or correspondent banking relationships are able to identify potential markets for their exporting customers, and assist to an extent with the introduction to their importing customers overseas.

Credit Information: By using the standard form of bank-to-bank status enquiry it is possible for banks based in the UK to obtain information on importers, for example in respect of their creditworthiness, from banks overseas.

Economic and Political Reports: Many large international banks employ economists who provide reports on a number of countries, which are useful to exporters, particularly if the country concerned is politically unstable or its economy is weak.

Travel Services: In addition to the usual services available to the travelling business executive, such as travellers cheques and foreign currency, the banks may also be able to provide a letter of introduction addressed to their overseas branch or correspondent. This letter introduces the customer and requests that all possible assistance is given so that local trading terms and conditions may be fully understood.

Exchange Control Regulations: Many countries have restrictions on the amount of local and/or foreign currency that can be taken into and out of the country at any one time. Consequently, an exporter who is unaware of the current situation may export goods to a country and then find that the

© The Author(s) 2019
T. Bhogal, A. Trivedi, *International Trade Finance*, Finance and Capital Markets Series,
https://doi.org/10.1007/978-3-030-24540-5_2

importer is unable to transfer the funds due in settlement without the sanction of the Central Bank. Banks are able to provide their customers with advice to avoid such problems.

Exchange controls were lifted in the UK during October 1979, and UK residents are now free to transfer and receive funds as they see fit, without the approval of the Regulators, provided money laundering and terrorist activities are not involved.

Sale and Purchase of Foreign Currencies/Exchange Contracts: Banks sell and purchase foreign currencies to and from their customers/non-customers and travellers. An exporter may find that before payment in foreign currency is received the exchange rate has reduced, thus reducing profit on the transaction. It is possible for an exporter to enter into a forward exchange contract with a bank, which enables the bank to fix the exchange rate at which the currency will be converted on a specified date/period in the future. The exporter can then price goods safe in the knowledge that the rate will not change whatever happens in the foreign exchange markets. The bank covers its own commitment by matching deals in the market.

Collection of Bills: A British exporter who has drawn a bill of exchange on an overseas buyer is able to obtain reimbursement by asking their bank to send the bill to the importer's bank, that is, an exporter's bank will "collect" the proceeds.

If the bill/cheque or draft is sent without any attached documents it is known as a "clean" collection. More often, documents of title to the goods concerned are enclosed with the bill and it then becomes a "documentary" collection. Unlike a documentary credit there is no guarantee of payment when the bill is presented for payment. Thus the bill routed through the bank remains at risk of non-payment.

When a bank is asked to collect a bill of exchange, with or without other documents, it acts as agent to the exporter. Careful note is taken of any instructions that the exporter may give, particularly concerning what action the bank is to take if the bill is not accepted (if usance) or unpaid. The risk of non-payment can be reduced if the documents are handed over against payment of the bill (a Documents against Payment [D/P] bill). If an element of trust exists between the exporter and importer and the bill is a usance bill, documents may be released against the importer's acceptance (a Document against Acceptance [D/A] bill). The importer's bank in another country will be acting as an agent to the bank in the UK and will remit the proceeds to the UK when payment is made. The exporter's account will then be credited less the bank's charges for the collection, unless otherwise agreed.

In a manner similar to documentary credits, collections are subject to International Chamber of Commerce Uniform Rules for Collections (ICC Publication URC 522).

Finance for Exports

Banks finance exporters in a number of ways, including the following:

Advances Against Shipping Documents: Often when handling bills and documents on a collection basis, banks are willing to allow overdrafts to the exporters subject to the bank's satisfaction with the financial standing of the parties. The documents of title can be used as a form of security pending receipt of the collection proceeds.

Formerly known Export Credit Guarantee Department (ECGD): Insurance cover may be required. The exporter pays an insurance premium for the cover. The bank is then guaranteed by the ECGD for the repayment should the importer default. The ECGD policy is assigned to the bank so that any proceeds under the policy are paid directly to the bank and not to the customer. New organisation UK Export Finance offer various policies to support exporters instead of ECGD.

Negotiation of Bills of Exchange: Bills drawn on, and usually accepted by, the importer can be "negotiated" by the exporter's bank. The bank buys the bill from the exporter paying over the proceeds before maturity, in return for an interest charge rather like discounting a bill. Negotiation is "with recourse" that allows the bank to claim the amount paid back from the exporter if the bank is unable to collect the bill proceeds.

3

Methods of Trade

In international markets the situation is often more complex than in local markets. In local markets it is possible that the parties may have known each other for some time and have built a certain level of trust. Trading risk in local markets is much less than in international markets. There are a number of methods of trade and settlement of trade accounts. Details of various methods of trade that are available to buyers and sellers for trading indicating the risks involved and the benefits are discussed in the following pages. Before importers and exporters decide to do business with each other they need to understand and adopt a method suitable to meet their specific needs.

The contract between buyer and seller will specify the way in which payment is to be made. The seller will ask: How will I be paid, when will I be paid and how can the risk of non-payment be minimised?

Certain methods of payment are less risky than others. It is up to the buyer and seller to agree on a method that suits them both.

Cash on Delivery

This is a system where goods and all shipping documents are sent directly to the buyers who pay on delivery or after an agreed period. The system does not offer any security to the seller/exporter. The seller can face risks of non-receipt of payment, or goods may be left in a distant port due to non-payment by the buyer/importer. A high degree of mutual trust and confidence must exist between the two parties.

© The Author(s) 2019
T. Bhogal, A. Trivedi, *International Trade Finance*, Finance and Capital Markets Series,
https://doi.org/10.1007/978-3-030-24540-5_3

Advance Payment

This is the safest way for an exporter to receive payment for goods shipped abroad because the funds are received before the goods are released. The risk has been transferred to the importer who must trust the exporter to actually deliver the goods paid for. The method of payment is usually by cheque, bank draft, mail transfer or telegraphic transfer/SWIFT (Society for Worldwide Inter-bank Financial Telecommunications). Due to various implications of this system, advance payments are rarely used. More common is the payment in advance of a cash deposit by the buyer, with the balance being paid in one of the following ways.

Open Account

When the exporter and importer trust one another implicitly, perhaps because they have traded together for a number of years, they may agree to trade on open account terms. Goods are shipped to the importer and the documents of title are sent directly by the exporter. A set date for payment is given and the importer merely remits the necessary funds to the exporter as agreed. In transactions involving regular shipments the importer often makes payments at set intervals, paying for goods received during that particular period. The exporter has no control over the goods and cannot be guaranteed payment, so an open account is perhaps the riskiest method of trade available.

Collections

Promissory Notes: A promissory note is simply a promise to pay. It is written out by the buyer, promising to pay the exporter (or bearer) an amount of money at a specified time. A bill of exchange is an instrument drawn by a seller on a buyer. The promissory note provides a degree of security similar to that afforded by an accepted bill of exchange.

Bills of Exchange: Another method of payment for exports is by means of bills of exchange which are drawn on the buyer by the seller. Bills of exchange provide a very flexible and popular method of settling international trade transactions. Such trade bills may be at sight or a term/at usance. In the former case, the drawee of the bill (the buyer) has to pay cash on presentation of the bill with a term/usance bill. A credit period (known as the tenor or usance bill) is allowed to the buyer, who signifies agreement to pay on the due date by writing an acceptance across it.

A British exporter who has drawn a bill of exchange on an overseas buyer is able to obtain reimbursement by asking his bank to send the bill to the importer's bank, that is, the exporter's bank will 'collect' the proceeds.

Letters of Credit

Payment through the medium of a bill of exchange can be made still more secure by the use of a letter of credit (although a bill of exchange is not always necessarily required under a letter of credit, it is frequently called for under its terms).

A letter of credit is issued by the buyer's bank at the buyer's request in accordance with the payment terms of the underlying contract, and is a guarantee of payment by that bank. The beneficiary would be well advised to seek the advice of his own bankers on the value of the issuing bank's guarantee, as there may be exchange control problems, political risks or even a question about the credit standing of the issuing bank.

If the credit is made irrevocable, the issuing bank is unable to amend or cancel its terms without the consent of all the parties, including the beneficiary. A further security can be obtained by the exporter by making it a confirmed irrevocable letter of credit, where the bank through which the letter of credit is transmitted to the exporter adds confirmation.

Methods of Payment/Settlement of Account

Cheque

The buyer could draw a cheque payable at his own domestic bank and forward it to the exporter. It may take some weeks for such a cheque to be cleared through the banking system, though it is sometimes possible for the exporter to obtain funds against the cheque by having it purchased by his own bank.

Bank Draft

This is an instrument drawn by the buyer's bank, normally on a correspondent bank in the exporter's country. The buyer sends the draft to the exporter, who then obtains payment via his own bank. It is possible for the buyer's bank to draw a draft on itself, which is less convenient to an exporter in the UK if payment is required in GB pounds, and, in any case, will not finally be paid until it is presented to the bank on which it is drawn.

Mail Transfer (MT)

In this case, the buyer's bank sends instructions by airmail to a correspondent bank, asking it to credit the exporter or his bank with GB pounds or foreign currency. Bank charges for remitting funds by MT are met by either the buyer or the exporter depending on what the parties have agreed. This method is slower than the other methods of transfer of funds between the banks in two different countries.

SWIFT

Swift Transfer: This is identical to Mail Transfer except that the instructions are conveyed by telex or cable or electronically. Transfers can also be made via the SWIFT network.

CHAPS

Clearing House Automated Payment System is a private telecommunication and payment system for inter-bank clearing of British pound payments, operated since 1984 by the Bankers' Clearing House of London.

CHIPS

Clearing House Inter-bank Payment System (CHIPS) is a computerized funds transfer system for international dollar payments linking over 140 depository institutions with offices or subsidiaries in New York. Funds transfers through CHIPS, operated by the New York Clearing House Association, account for over 90% of all international payments relating to international trade. Final settlement occurs through adjustments in special account balances at the Federal Reserve Bank of New York.

Direct Debit

This is a pre-authorised payment system used in collecting recurring bills by electronic means. Generally, the borrower signs a pre-authorisation agreement giving his bank the right to debit an account for the amount due on a designated day.

EFT

Electronic Funds Transfer (EFT) transfers funds between accounts by electronic means rather than conventional paper-based payment methods such as writing a cheque.

Fedwire

Fedwire is a high-speed electronic communication network linking the Federal Reserve Board of Governors, the 12 Federal Reserve Banks and 24 branches, the U.S. Treasury Department and other federal agencies.

4

Foreign Exchange Rates

Introduction

Both the importer and the exporter need to know what means are available to make payments overseas and to receive payments from foreign buyers. They may have the option to decide whether to trade in GB pound or a foreign currency. Before they look at these important points, it would be better to consider the international financial system as this will help in the selection of the appropriate method of payment and/or settlement of funds due.

Foreign Currency Transactions

When payments are made between countries there is no physical movement of currency notes, and instead the transactions are accounted for and recorded in the books of accounts of the banks. Almost all the commercial banks operating in one country maintain accounts with other banks operating normally in the main cities of foreign countries.

Bank's Accounting System

For example, if a payment is to be made to a British exporter by a German buyer, depending upon the method of payment adopted, either the euro account of the British (exporter's) bank will be credited or a GB pound account of the German (importer's) bank will be debited. The exporter will be

© The Author(s) 2019
T. Bhogal, A. Trivedi, *International Trade Finance*, Finance and Capital Markets Series,
https://doi.org/10.1007/978-3-030-24540-5_4

paid the value of the exports in GB pound, or in the GB pound equivalent of the euros by the exporter's bank in the UK.

Commercial banks are involved in thousands of foreign currency transactions each business day on behalf of their customers, in respect of visible and invisible trade. They maintain a careful check on the transactions made on their Nostro and Vostro accounts, and buy/sell foreign currency in the foreign exchange market as per their and their customers' need.

Foreign Exchange Market

In the UK there is no foreign exchange market by way of physical structure or a building. Rather the foreign exchange market comprises the foreign exchange departments of a large number of banks and other authorised dealers. They have an efficient telecommunication network between one another and are able to maintain an up-to-date exchange rate.

Exchange Rates Quotation

The exchange rate of a currency is in fact the price of one unit of currency against the other. In London this price is quoted or expressed as so many units of a foreign currency per pound, that is, on an indirect basis. The prices (rates) are quoted, one for buying and the other for selling currency. The dealer, that is, the bank, will buy at the higher quotation and will sell at the lower quotation, so as to receive as many units as possible of foreign currency for every pound, and when selling the dealer will want to give as few units of foreign currency as possible for every pound. The maxim of foreign exchange dealers is "BUY HIGH, SELL LOW", but for the customer the opposite is true.

GB Pound Spot and Forward Rates

As an example, Table 4.1 presents spot and forward market exchange rates for some of the world currencies on a particular date at close of market against GB pound, extracted from *The Times* newspaper of 31 October 2018.

The left-hand column shows the currency of the country. Column "A" gives the range of movement of the exchange rate of a currency during the day. Column "B" indicates the exchange rate at the close of business of the exchange market. The closing exchange rates become the opening rates of

Table 4.1 Example of exchange rates spot/forward against GBP

City/Currency	"A" Range	"B" Close	"C" 1 month	"D" 3 months
Copenhagen	8.3471–8.3996	8.3522–8.3572	108ds	350ds
Euro	1.1259–1.1189	1.1199–1.1196	10pr	32pr
Montreal	1.6692–1.6808	1.6694–1.6704	14pr	51pr
New York	1.2699–1.2812	1.2711–1.2713	17pr	63pr
Oslo	10.675–10.739	10.688–10.692	7pr	58pr
Stockholm	11.634–11.715	11.646–11.651	141ds	470ds
Tokyo	143.22–144.38	143.41–143.42	13ds	45ds
Zurich	1.2758–1.2837	1.2765–1.2771	18ds	59ds

Premium = pr; Discount = ds

exchange when the foreign exchange market opens the following business day. Columns "C" and "D" indicate forward exchange margins for one month and three months, respectively.

Sterling Spot and Forward Rates

Market Rates for 30 October 2018.

As an example, a table of spot and forward exchange rates of US dollars against GB pound is given below.

Spot Exchange Rates

The spot exchange rate is a rate of exchange at a particular moment in time in the day. The exchange rate may fluctuate during the day as shown in Column "A" of Table 4.1. The settlement of these transactions takes place within 48 hours, that is, two working days.

Let us assume the above rates are at the close of business; they are the rates that would apply as the market opens on the following business day. If a large transaction of a currency is involved, an up-to-date/latest rate should be obtained from the bank dealer.

Forward Exchange Rates

Forward rates apply to transactions for completion at an agreed future date beyond two working days. The forward exchange rates can be "Fixed Forward Rate" or "Option Forward Rate".

Fixed Forward Exchange Rates

Fixed forward rate is for receipt or delivery of a foreign currency at a fixed date sometime in the future, that is, after one month, three months, six months and so on.

Option Forward Exchange Rates

Option forward exchange rate is for the receipt or delivery of a foreign currency sometime in the future between two agreed dates. For example, an importer has to pay for goods in foreign currency and wishes to enter into a three-month forward contract with a one-month option. Here the customer has the option to buy the foreign currency any time during the third month. In this case the two dates in the future are after the end of the second month and before the end of the third month from the date of the forward contract.

For example, the spot rate is quoted (at close of business from Table 4.1, Column "B") in the London Foreign Exchange Market, as U.S. $1.2711–1.2713 = £1, which means that the foreign exchange dealer will buy from its customer(s) US$ 1.2713 for a pound and will sell US$1.2711 for a pound to the customer(s). The difference between two rates (1.2713–1.2711), that is, 0.0002 points, denotes the profit margin of the foreign exchange dealer.

How Exchange Rates Are Determined

The price of a currency is determined by the rate of exchange of another currency. This rate of exchange is determined on the basis of demand and supply of a currency in the foreign exchange market. If the demand of a currency increases, its value will rise, and if the demand of the currency decreases, its value will fall. For example, let us take the value of GB pound against US dollar. If on a particular day the rate of exchange £/US$ is 1.27139603 and the demand for sterling pound increases, then the rate might go up to US$ 1.2725. This means that the pound is now worth more US dollars than before. If the demand for the pound falls then the rate might move down to US$ 1.2700. This means the GB pound is now worth fewer US dollars than it was earlier. This will indicate that the value of the US dollar has increased in comparison to the GB pound.

Factors Influencing Exchange Rate

There are many factors that influence the exchange rates and also demand and supply for a particular currency.

Balance of Payment: If the balance of payment of a country is in deficit, for example if the UK's imports are more than its exports, payments for the imports have to be made in GB pound. The foreign exchange market will be flooded by GB pound. The increased supply of GB pound will depress its value; this means the exporters to the UK will get fewer US dollars and exporters in the UK will get more GB pounds.

Capital Transactions: In addition to commercial transactions, the demand and supply situation in the foreign exchange market is affected by capital transactions in respect of short-term and long-term investment, both in the UK and from overseas government loans and the International Monetary Fund.

Confidence in a Currency: The confidence in a currency influences exchange rates. The confidence will be affected by the political and economic conditions of a country.

Forward Exchange Rates

When a person intends to make a transaction in a foreign currency at a future date, he may enter into a forward exchange contract with a commercial bank or an authorised dealer in foreign currency. You will notice in the table that Japanese yen is quoted at discount, which means yen is cheaper to buy forward than immediate delivery (spot). Every pound will buy more units of yen. Therefore, the rate of exchange margin quoted as discount must be added to the spot rate. Where a currency is quoted at a premium (pm) rate, the pound sterling will buy fewer units of foreign currency. Therefore, the premium rate quoted must be deducted from the spot rate of exchange.

In the case of currencies at premium, the exchange margin figure is higher on the left-hand side and for currencies at discount the exchange margin figure is higher on the right-hand side. The dealer will buy high and sell low; the left-hand spot quotation is the dealer's selling rate and the right-hand spot quotation is the dealer's buying rate. The dealer will deduct the premium margin when buying and selling currencies at premium in future and will add discount margins when buying and selling currencies at discount in future.

Foreign Exchange Spot Transaction: Mechanism

Let us take as an example a case where a British importer XYZ & Company has imported goods from the United States (US) and receives an invoice for the value of the goods in US dollars. The importing customer XYZ & Co. does not maintain a bank account in US dollars with their bank. Therefore, the company will have to request their bank to buy US dollars to make payment for the imports and sell the equivalent amount in GB pounds. Theoretically, the bank does not have dollars available and in turn it will have to go to the foreign exchange market dealer to buy US dollars.

Example 1 Foreign exchange transaction—mechanism

Foreign Exchange Dealer's selling rate of US $ against GB Pounds is	US$1.9598
Bank will make profit 5 points (margin) by giving less amount	0.0005
	1.9593

A UK importer wishes to make payment in US dollars to an American exporter.

A UK importer imports goods from the US and receives an invoice in US dollars. To pay in US dollars the importer sells GB pounds to his bank and buys US dollars.

As mentioned earlier, the bank would like to make some profit from each foreign exchange transaction. If the bank makes a profit of 5 points as before, the bank will give 5 points less of US dollars to the customer. This figure is calculated as: shown in Figs. 4.1 and 4.2.

Example 2 Foreign exchange transaction—mechanism

A UK exporter receives payment in US dollars from an American importer.

A British exporter ABC & Company has exported goods to the US. The company agreed to sell in US dollars (Figs. 4.1 and 4.2) and sends an invoice for the value of the goods in US dollars. ABC & Co. receives payment in US dollars. The company does not maintain a bank account in US dollars with the bank in the UK. Therefore, the company will have to request their bank to sell the amount of dollars to convert the amount in GB pounds. Theoretically, the bank will have to buy those dollars and sell them to the foreign exchange dealer on the foreign exchange market to receive GB pounds.

The bank's foreign exchange dealer wants to make some profit on each transaction. The dealer will sell a lower amount of US dollars to the bank, keeping a margin of two points. Whenever a bank dealer buys and sells foreign

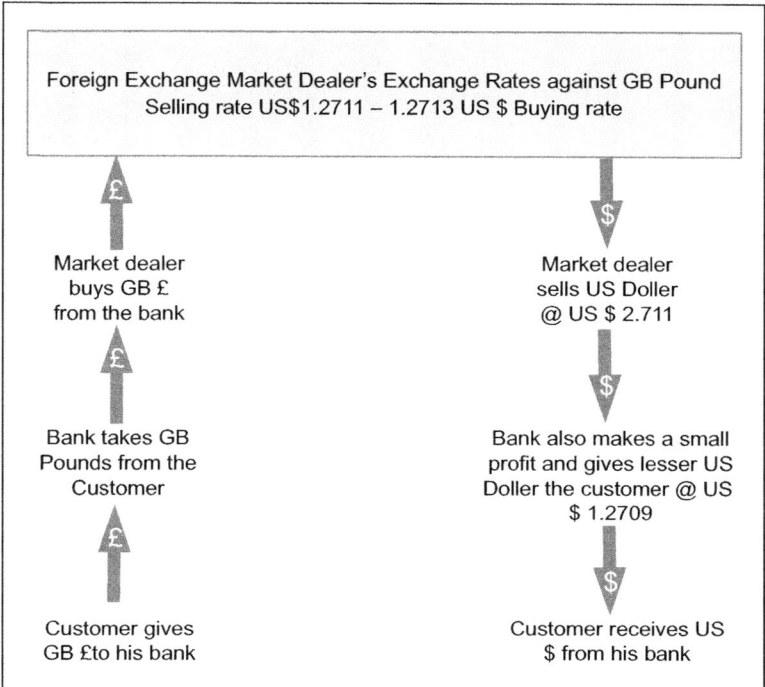

Fig. 4.1   Action flow diagram customer sells GBP against USD

currencies he also keeps some margin as profit. Therefore, the bank's rate of exchange in the above examples is 1.2713–1.2715, that is, the bank sells US dollars at 1.2709 and buys US dollars at 1.2715 against one GB pound. The bank dealer's exchange rate in the examples above will be US $ 1.2709–1.2715 against one GB pound.

Forward Exchange Contract

A forward exchange contract is entered into between a bank and a customer; the bank fixes the rate of exchange at which a foreign currency will be bought or sold. The exchange rate may fluctuate during and at the time of maturity but this will not have any effect on the forward contract agreed between the bank and the customer. Through forward exchange contracts, both the importer and exporter know the exact amount of their payables and receivable in foreign currency, thereby covering against fluctuation of any exchange rates during the period. A forward exchange contract is a legal contract to receive or deliver foreign currency on the agreed date.

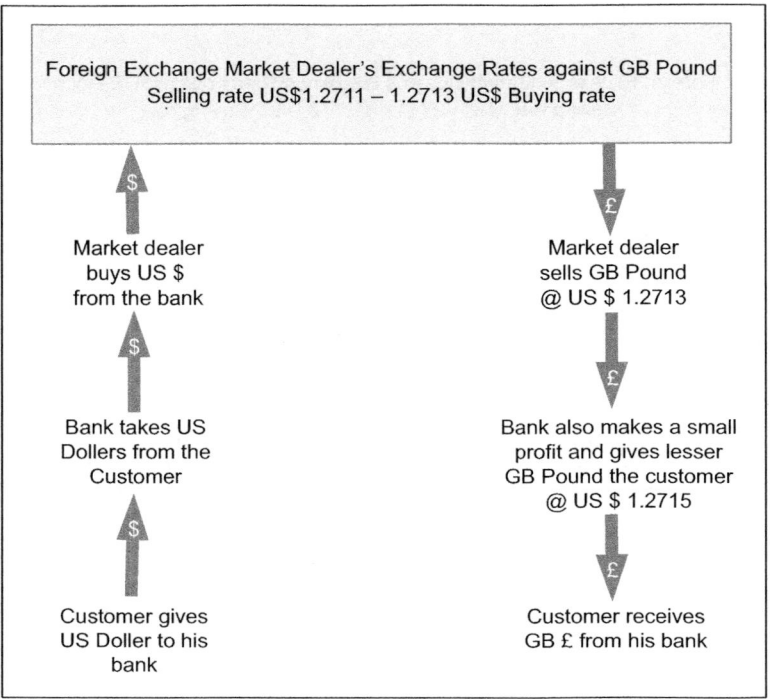

Fig. 4.2   Action flow diagram customer sells USD against GBP

How the Forward Exchange Rate Is Calculated

If the foreign currency is at premium the exchange margin for the period is deducted from the spot rate of exchange, because the foreign currency will be stronger in future. If the foreign currency is at discount in future, the exchange margin is added to the spot rate. This is because the foreign currency will be weaker in future and the pound will be able to buy more foreign currency.

A forward exchange contract may be a "fixed forward contract" or "option forward contract". In case of a "fixed forward contract" foreign currency will be delivered or received on a fixed date in future, for example at the end of one month, two months, three months or more as agreed. This is shown in Fig. 4.3.

If a forward contract for three months is entered on 1 December it will mature on 1 March. The agreed amount of foreign currency must be delivered or received on the agreed fixed date, that is, 1 March.

Option forward contract: In an "option forward contract" the bank agrees to receive or deliver foreign currency any time between two different dates

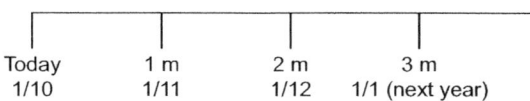

Fig. 4.3 Fixed forward contract

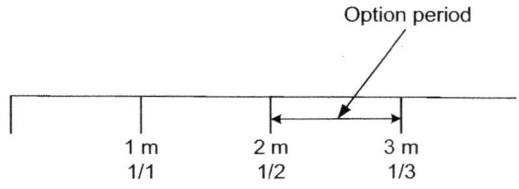

Fig. 4.4 Forward contract with option over third month

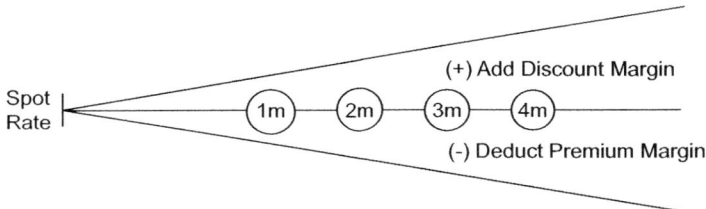

Fig. 4.5 Exchange margins: premium and discount in forward contract

both in future. For example a customer enters into a three-month "option forward contract" with a one-month option. The option is in the last month of the option period. The customer will have the option to buy or sell foreign currency any time during the third month, that is, between the end of the second month and the end of the third month, as shown in Fig. 4.4.

An option forward contract for three months entered on 1 December with an option of one month will have an option period between 1 February and 1 March. The foreign currency may be delivered or received any time during the option period but it will definitely mature on 1 March. The agreed amount of foreign currency must be delivered or received on the agreed fixed date, that is, 1 March (Fig. 4.5).

For example, 3-month forward rate will be calculated as follows:

Spot Rate GB £ = US $	1.2713–1.2711	
	0.0063–0.0063	Plus 3-month exchange margin
	1.2648–2.2650	

Exchange margin is added to the spot rate as the currency in future is at discount. The bank will buy US $ 1.2650 and sell US $ 1.2648 against £1, three months forward. The gap between the buying and selling rates forward will never narrow unless an aggressive dealer with speculative instinct quotes a "choice price", meaning one can buy or sell at the same price. This phenomenon is sometimes observed in a highly competitive market.

5

Bills of Exchange, Collections, Purchasing and Discounting

Bill of exchange: Bills of exchange are widely used in international trade, partly since they are convenient methods of debt collection from traders abroad. Finance may be arranged in a number of ways against bills of exchange, both for the buyer (drawee) and for the seller (drawers). If a bill of exchange has been dishonoured the holder may sue the other parties to the bill.

Definition of a Bill of Exchange

"A Bill of Exchange is an unconditional order in writing addressed by one person to another signed by the person giving it requiring the person to whom it is addressed to pay on demand or at a fixed or determinable future time a sum certain in money to or to the order of a specified person or to bearer" (Sec 3, The Bills of Exchange Act 1882).

To ease understanding the definition is broken down into small segments and each segment considered individually:

1. "An unconditional order": The order to pay should not be subject to the fulfilment of any condition(s). It should simply say "Pay". If a condition is set, for example, "Pay John Clark when he marries my daughter" it is not a bill of exchange but a conditional order. "In writing": It is not possible to have an oral bill of exchange. Evidence must be available, in writing, of its existence. What the bill is actually written on, or written with, is not important;
2. "Addressed by one person";

© The Author(s) 2019
T. Bhogal, A. Trivedi, *International Trade Finance*, Finance and Capital Markets Series,
https://doi.org/10.1007/978-3-030-24540-5_5

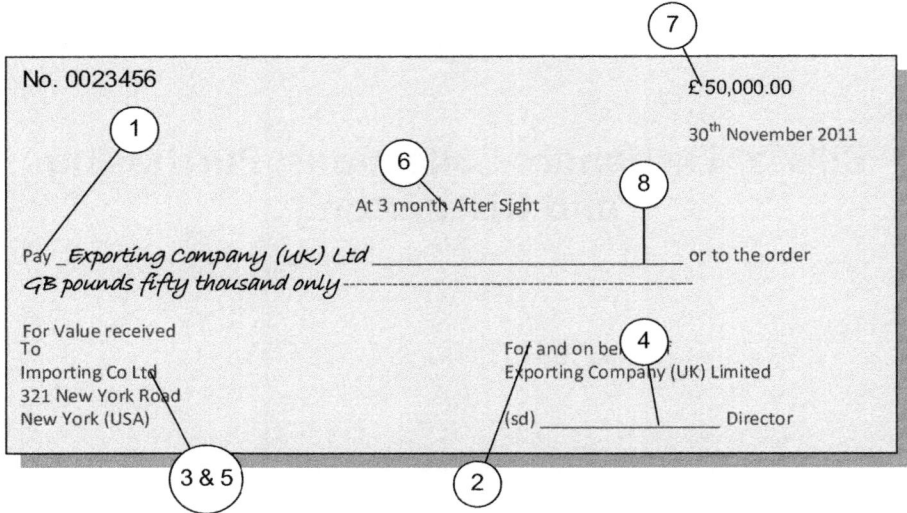

Fig. 5.1 Bill of exchange: specimen

3. "To another person" (the drawee): A bill of exchange is usually written by the person selling goods or services (the drawer) and addressed to the person who is required to pay (the drawee);
4. "Signed by the person giving it": It is signed by the person who is owed money (the drawer);
5. "Requiring the person to whom it is addressed to pay": It is self-explanatory (the drawee);
6. "To pay on demand": The bill would say "at sight" requiring immediate payment to be made. "Or at a fixed or determinable future time": If the bill is not payable immediately then it may be payable "at 90 days sight" meaning that it is due 90 days from the day it is seen by the person to whom it is addressed. A bill payable "90 days from the date of docking of the S.S. Titanic" would not be valid, because the ship may sink!
7. "A sum certain in money": The exact amount must be stated. "About £1000" would not be acceptable, although "£1000 plus interest at 10%" would be because the extra amount can be calculated;
8. "To or to the order of a specified person (the Payee) or to bearer": An order bill payable to a specific person can be easily transferred to another by endorsement. A bearer bill is payable to the holder of the bill at the date of maturity (payment).

Most bills of exchange are written on specially printed forms available from all good business stationers. Such bills often have "for value received" printed on them to establish "valuable consideration", usually essential if legal action is proposed under contract law.

Parties to a Bill of Exchange

There are three main parties to a bill of exchange:

The Drawer is the person who gives an order to pay the amount of the bill of exchange.

The Drawee is the person on whom the bill is drawn, that is, the person who is required to pay the amount of the bill of exchange.

The Payee is the person to whom the amount of the bill is payable. The drawer and payee of a trade bill are often the same person.

Other Parties to a Bill of Exchange

The Endorser: When a person (the payee) transfers the bill of exchange to another person the payee writes his signature together with a statement on the reverse of the bill and is known as the endorser.

The Endorsee: The name of the person to whom the bill of exchange is transferred. The endorsee's name is written in the endorsement.

The Acceptor: An acceptor is the person (the drawee) who gives consent to comply with the order of the drawer to pay by signing across the face of the bill of exchange.

The Holder: The payee or any other person who for a valid reason or legally comes into actual possession of a bill of exchange.

The Holder for Value: A person who gives "consideration" to obtain actual possession of the bill.

The Holder in Due Course: A person who obtains actual possession of the bill of exchange:

1. When it is complete and regular on its face (i.e. properly completed with all information required);
2. Before it is overdue, that is, before its maturity date;
3. Without notice that it has been previously dishonoured (unpaid);
4. In good faith and without notice of defect in the title of the person from whom obtained;
5. After giving "consideration" for it.

Types of Bills of Exchange

Sight Bill of Exchange

A sight bill of exchange is one which is payable on sight, demand or presentation to the drawee. Acceptance of a sight bill is not required because the bill is payable on demand, that is, immediately after the drawee has "seen" it.

Usance Bill of Exchange

A usance bill of exchange is one which is payable sometime in future, that is, after a number of days, months or years, for example "90 days sight". It needs to be accepted by the drawee to make him liable for the bill. The drawee accepts the bill by signing on the face of the bill, that is, the drawee agrees to make payment on maturity. A usance bill is also known as a Term or Tenor bill.

Clean Bills of Exchange

A clean bill of exchange is one that is not accompanied by the shipping documents. When the goods are shipped the documents are sent directly to the importer so that he can take delivery of the goods and the bill of exchange is handed over by the seller to his bank for collecting the payment from the importer.

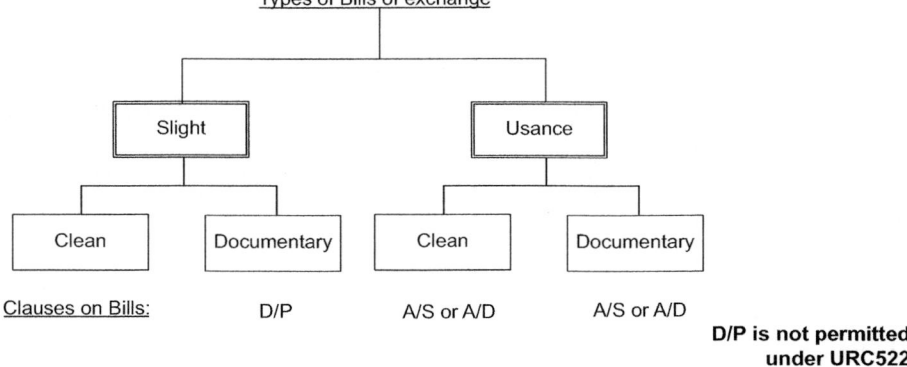

Fig. 5.2 Types of bills of exchange (Note: the term D/P is not permitted on "Usance bill of exchange" under URC522)

Documentary Bill of Exchange

A bill of exchange accompanied by shipping documents, that is, invoice, bill of lading, insurance policy and other documents, is called a documentary bill of exchange.

Accommodation Bill of Exchange

A bill to which a person, called an accommodation party, puts his name to oblige or accommodate another person without receiving any consideration for so doing. The position of such a party is, in fact, that of a surety or guarantor. Bills of this type are called "kites" or "windmills" or "windbills". "A" may accept a bill for the accommodation of "B" the drawer, who is in need of money. "A" receives no consideration and does not expect to be called upon to pay the bill when due.

Banks discourage the use of accommodation bills by the customers who may request finance against such bills.

Clauses on Bills of Exchange

- D/P—The drawer/seller gives instructions to the remitting bank to deliver documents relating to the goods against payment of the bill. The remitting bank instructs the agent bank, that is, collecting bank, to follow the same instructions. These instructions are in the case of a sight bill of exchange. The buyer makes payment and takes delivery of the documents, which need to be presented to the carrier for delivery of the goods.
- A/S—This clause is used in the case of usance bill of exchange. The seller sells goods on a credit basis. The drawer/seller gives instructions to the remitting bank to deliver documents relating to the goods after the bill has been sighted, that is, accepted. This means the buyer agrees with the terms and conditions of the sale contract and undertakes to pay on the maturity date. The maturity date is calculated after the date of acceptance of the bill of exchange. The remitting bank instructs the agent bank, that is collecting bank, to follow the same instructions.
- A/D—This is another clause also used in the case of usance bill of exchange. The seller sells goods on a credit basis. The drawer/seller gives instructions to the remitting bank to deliver documents relating to the goods after the bill has been sighted, that is, accepted, and the maturity date is calculated,

as instructed by the seller, for example after the date of the bill of exchange or the bill of lading. This means the buyer agrees with the terms and conditions of the sale contract and undertakes to pay on the maturity date. The remitting bank instructs the agent bank, that is, collecting bank, to follow the same instructions.

The use of D/P clause on usance documentary bills of exchange is not allowed under the URC 522.

Acceptance of a Bill of Exchange

Meaning of Acceptance—Acceptance is a promise to pay the creditor when the drawee of a usance or time bill of exchange writes the words "accepted" above their name and signature across a bill.

A bill may be accepted:

1. Before it has been signed by the drawer, or while otherwise incomplete;
2. When it is overdue or after it has been dishonoured by a previous refusal to accept, or by non-payment.

Importance and Requisites of Acceptance

1. The acceptance of a bill is signification by the drawee of his assent to the order of the drawer;
2. An acceptance is invalid unless it complies with the following conditions, namely

   (a) It must be written on the bill and signed by the drawee. The mere signature of the drawee without additional words is sufficient.
   (b) It must not express that the drawee will perform his promise by any other means than the payment of money.
   (c) The acceptance must be completed by delivery of the bill or notification that it has been accepted.

A holder with a "general acceptance" bill may present it to the acceptor, but if there is a place of payment mentioned on the bill it must be presented at that place, otherwise the holder will lose recourse against all other parties to the bill.

Liability of Acceptor

The acceptor of a bill, by accepting it, engages that he will pay it according to the tenor of his acceptance. It precluded the acceptor from denying his obligation to make payment to a holder in due course on the due date of the bill of exchange

(a) The existence of the drawer, the genuineness of his signature, and his capacity and authority to draw the bill;
(b) In the case of a bill payable to drawer's order, the then capacity of the drawer to endorse, but not the genuineness or validity of his endorsement;
(c) In the case of a bill payable to the order of a third person, the existence of the payee (the third party) and his then capacity to endorse, but not the genuineness of the third party or validity of his endorsement that may require confirmation by his banker.

Presentation for Acceptance

Presentation of a bill of exchange for acceptance is legally necessary:

1. Where the bill is payable after sight. Presentment for acceptance is necessary in order to fix the maturity of the instrument.
2. Where a bill expressly stipulates that it must be presented for acceptance, and
3. Where a bill is drawn payable elsewhere than at the residence or place of business of the drawee. Except in these three cases, it is not obligatory to present a bill for acceptance. The holder may await the maturity of the bill and then present it for payment. As a rule, however, it is presented for acceptance to secure the liability of the drawee. If the drawee refuses to accept the bill, the holder then has an immediate right of recourse against the drawer and endorsers, if the appropriate steps are taken.

Types of Acceptances

There are two principal types of acceptance of a usance bill of exchange:

General Acceptance—to confirm the drawee's liability and agreement to the terms of the bill.
Qualified Acceptance—where the drawee, upon accepting bill, varies or alters its terms, for example by partial acceptance of the amount. The holder's agreement to any alteration may discharge the liability of any previous parties to the bill.

Types of qualified acceptances

1. Qualified as to a certain event: A conditional acceptance, which makes payment dependent upon the fulfilment of a stated condition for example on arrival of a ship, or the goods themselves;
2. Qualified as to amount: A partial acceptance, an acceptance to pay part of the amount for which the bill is drawn, for example a bill drawn for £10,000 but the drawee accepts for a lesser amount, that is, £7000 only;
3. Qualified as to tenor: Where the usance period on the bill is changed, for example extended from 90 to 180 days;
4. Qualified as to place of payment: An acceptance to pay at a particular specified place but unless the words "and not elsewhere" or "and there only" or their equivalent are inserted the acceptance is a general acceptance.

Endorsement of Bills of Exchange

Many bills are payable to a specific person "or order". This means that title to the bill can be transferred, or "negotiated" by the payee to another person. This is achieved by endorsement and delivery to the person concerned.

By law, a bill is an order bill when:

• It is expressed to be payable to order, or
• It is payable to the order of a particular person, or
• It is payable to a particular person and does not contain words prohibiting any transfer.

Endorsement is not required to transfer the title of a bearer bill, as it may be negotiated by mere delivery to the other person.

Types of Endorsements

There are four common types of endorsement.

Note: Under the Cheques Act 1992 these endorsements do not apply to cheques in the UK, but may apply to cheques in other countries.

1. Blank Endorsement: This is where the payee simply signs his name on the reverse of the bill without stating the name of any particular endorsee. The cheque becomes payable to bearer.

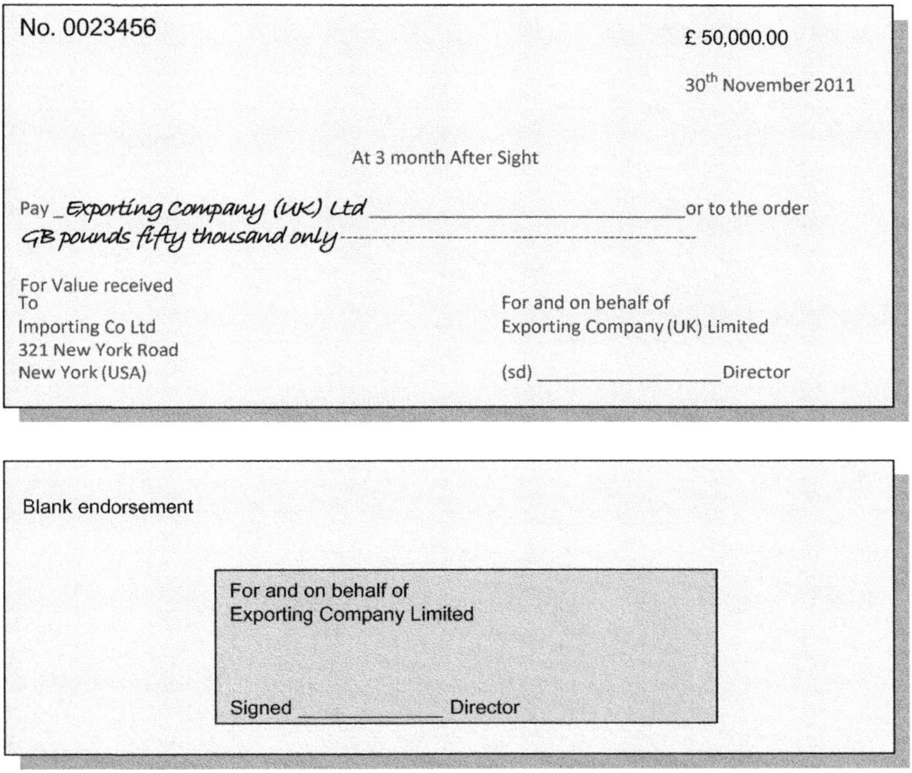

No. 0023456

£ 50,000.00

30th November 2011

At 3 month After Sight

Pay _Exporting Company (UK) Ltd _____ or to the order
GB pounds fifty thousand only ---

For Value received
To
Importing Co Ltd
321 New York Road
New York (USA)

For and on behalf of
Exporting Company (UK) Limited

(sd) _____ Director

Blank endorsement

For and on behalf of
Exporting Company Limited

Signed _____ Director

Fig. 5.3   Example of a blank endorsement of a bill of exchange

2. Special Endorsement: The payee, on signing his name, specifies the endorsee. The endorsee can either collect the proceeds of the bill or sign his own name, that is, blank endorse the bill, to make it payable to bearer. Similarly, a blank endorsement can be converted into a special endorsement by any holder signing it and stating the name of the person to whom it is to be payable.

No. 0023456

£ 50,000.00

30th November 2011

At 3 month After Sight

Pay _Exporting Company (UK) Ltd_____ or to the order
GB pounds fifty thousand only--

For Value received
To   For and on behalf of
Importing Co Ltd   Exporting Company (UK) Limited
321 New York Road
New York (USA)   (sd) _____ Director

Special endorsement

Pay XYZ Bank Limited

For and on behalf of
Exporting Company Limited

Signed _____ Director

Fig. 5.4   Example of a special endorsement of a bill of exchange

3. Restrictive Endorsement: A restrictive endorsement, as the name implies, prevents further endorsement of the bill. The payee specifies the name of the endorsee and writes "only" at the end, for example, "Pay XYZ Bank Limited only".

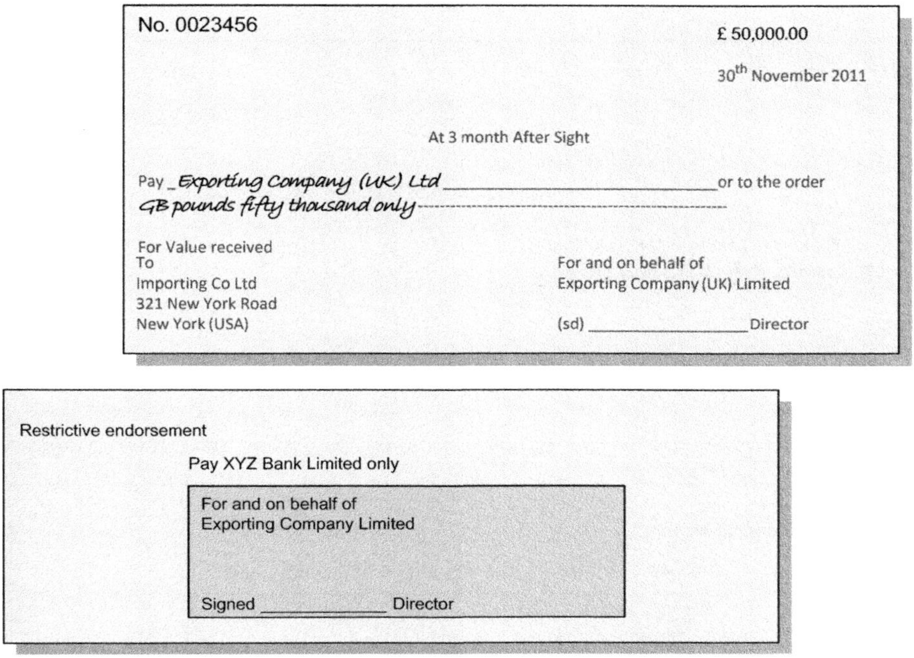

Fig. 5.5 Example of a restrictive endorsement of a bill of exchange

4. Conditional Endorsement: The least important of the four, the payee states a condition that has to be fulfilled before negotiation, for example "Pay XYZ Bank Limited after arrival of goods". In practice, banks will ignore any conditional endorsement as they presume the condition has been satisfactorily fulfilled.

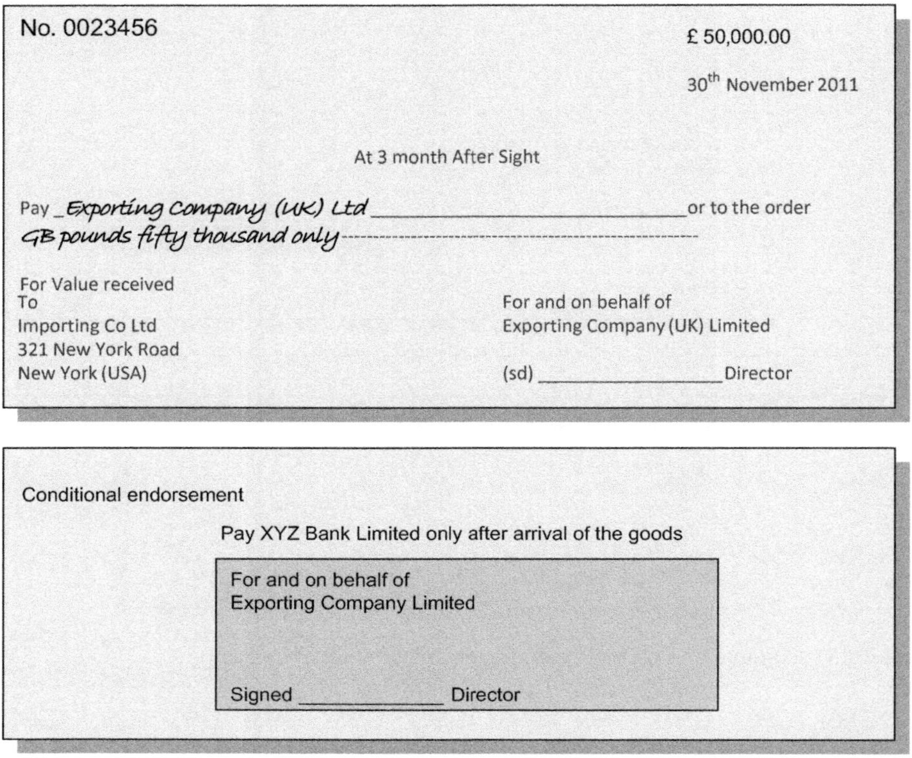

No. 0023456

£ 50,000.00

30th November 2011

At 3 month After Sight

Pay _Exporting Company (UK) Ltd_____or to the order
GB pounds fifty thousand only--

For Value received
To   For and on behalf of
Importing Co Ltd   Exporting Company (UK) Limited
321 New York Road
New York (USA)   (sd) _____ Director

Conditional endorsement

Pay XYZ Bank Limited only after arrival of the goods

For and on behalf of
Exporting Company Limited

Signed _____ Director

Fig. 5.6 Example of a conditional endorsement of a bill of exchange

Negotiability of Bills of Exchange

An instrument which is legally considered as "negotiable" has the following characteristics:

- It is transferable by delivery, or by endorsement and delivery.
- The legal title passes to the person who takes it in good faith, for value, and without notice of any defect in the title of the transfer.

- The legal holder can sue in his own name.
- Notice of transfer need not be given to the party liable on the instrument.
- The title passes free of all equities or counterclaims between previous parties of which the transferee has no notice.

When a negotiable instrument, for example a bill, is passed from one person to another all prior parties are liable to the final holder if the instrument is dishonoured. The last person in the chain is deemed to be a "holder in due course" if he can prove that he has fulfilled the requirements of s.29 of the Bills of Exchange Act 1882, that is,

- He has taken the bill in good faith;
- The bill is complete and regular on the face of it;
- For value;
- Before it is overdue;
- Without notice of any defect in the title of the transferor or any prior dishonour of the bill.

It follows that before giving value the new holder may look to see who has previously endorsed the bill and assess his creditworthiness in case the bill should be dishonoured. This is in line with the practice of the Acceptance Houses who add their own names to various bills, effectively guaranteeing payment to any future holder, charging commission in return.

Discharge of Bills of Exchange

The Bills of Exchange Act states that any liability on the bill is discharged:

- When the bill is paid by the acceptor on the due date;
- Where the acceptor becomes the holder of the bill at or before maturity;
- Where any material alteration has been made to the bill without the agreement of all parties liable on the bill. If the bill is altered without consent those liable prior to the alteration (but not after) will be discharged;
- Where the holder gives up his right to receive payment, cancelling the bill itself;
- Where the bill becomes statute-barred under the Limitations Acts, for example the holder usually has only six years to take legal action in recovery of the debt.

The majority of bills are properly accepted and subsequently paid on maturity. However, bills may be dishonoured by non-acceptance where the drawee refuses to accept liability, or dishonoured by non-payment when the acceptor refuses to pay.

In the UK, presentation of a dishonoured bill to the court is usually considered sufficient proof of dishonour when taking legal action. For foreign bills, that is, those drawn in this country payable abroad, or bills drawn overseas and payable in the UK, certain legal steps must be taken immediately in the country of dishonour to preserve the liability of previous parties to the bill. Any delay could result in their being discharged.

The first step is the "noting" of the bill, which is official evidence that the bill has been dishonoured. A local legal official, called a "notary public", represents the bill for acceptance or payment as required. If the request is refused the bill is noted.

The next step is formal "protest", which is a document sealed by the notary public confirming that the bill has been dishonoured. The protest document is accepted in most countries as evidence of dishonour.

On occasion, a "notary public" may not be available, so a householder may, with the aid of two witnesses, issue a certificate attesting the dishonour of the bill. The "householder's protest" is considered the same as a formal protest document.

Collection of Bills

A seller sells the goods to a buyer and asks his banker to collect money on his behalf from the buyers. So the bank acts as agent of the seller in collecting money from the buyer. In this respect the seller must give clear instructions to the bank.

The seller/exporter hands over the bill of exchange together with the relative documents for collection of payment by giving the instructions to his bank (by completing the application form for collection of bills) from the buyer/importer through the banking system/channel. The remitting bank records the information in its books and forwards the bill with the documents to the collecting bank with its schedule for collection with instructions as requested by the seller.

When the seller asks his bank to collect money against a clean/documentary bill on his behalf, this instructs the bank to release documents against acceptance of the bill; the bill is known as a D/A bill. If the documents are to be released against payment the bill is known as a D/P bill. If a sight bill is drawn the documents will be handed over to the buyer against payment only.

To avoid misunderstandings/difficulties and delay that might arise through acting as an agent to the customer, a set of rules has been developed by ICC called Uniform Rules for Collections, International Chamber of Commerce Publication (URC 522). The Rules are the basis on which the customer should instruct the bank. Banks use formats (application for collection of bills of exchange) given on the next page. This is required to be completed before accepting requests for collection of bills. The seller gives instructions to his bank (remitting bank) on the format by marking (✓) against the appropriate statement/instructions.

From: Our Reference _____

                                         Account No. _____

                                         Date   _____

Dear Sir,

Bills for collection drawn on _____ Amount _____

We enclose the first and second of exchange of our bill for collection/negotiation with recourse to us, subject to Uniform Rules for Collection (1995 (revision)) Publication number 522. Please follow instructions marked "√":

☐ Documents to be released against payment/acceptance.

☐ Please airmail advice acceptance stating maturity date. Retain the accepted draft for presentation on due date.

☐ Payment/acceptance may be deferred at drawee's request pending arrival of the relative goods.

☐ In case of non-payment/non-acceptance on presentation please advise us by AIRMAIL/TELEX stating reasons.

☐ If unpaid/unaccepted, please Note/Protest the drafts and advise us by AIRMAIL/TELEX stating reasons.

☐ On arrival of goods, if documents remain unpaid/unaccepted, please attend to the warehousing and insurance of the goods and advise us by TELEX.

☐ Recover all charges, including your charges from drawees. Charges may not be waived.

☐ Please collect interest ---- % p.a. from the date of draft to approximate arrival of return remittance in London. Interest may not be waived.

☐ If unpaid on due date, overdue interest to be charged @ ---- % p.a. from due date to approximate arrival of return remittance in London. Interest may not be waived.

☐ In the event of foreign currency cover not being available at the time of maturity of the Bill, you may instruct your correspondent to accept deposit in local currency to the full equivalent of the value of the draft amount together with interest and charges at the rate ruling on the date of deposit and remit the same when foreign currency cover is provided by the Central Bank.

☐ Please obtain an undertaking from the drawees to hold themselves responsible for any difference due to fluctuations in exchange rates which may arise between the date of deposit in local currency and foreign currency allocation by the Central Bank.

☐ Please disburse the proceeds as under

☐ Credit our account with you under advice to us.

☐ Send us your cheque for the amount due.

☐ Details of documents enclosed.

Documents	Draft	Invoice	Bill of lading/ air waybill	Insurance	Packing list	Cert. of origin	Others		
Original									
Duplicate									

☐ In case of need refer to:

                                         _____
                                         Authorised Signature

Yours faithfully

Fig. 5.7 A specimen of customer's instructions for collection of bills of exchange

Mechanism: Sight Bill for Collection

1. Negotiations between the seller and the buyer;
2. The buyer places an order;
3. The seller makes goods ready and despatches through transporters/shippers;
4. The seller prepares shipping documents and hands over to his bank (remitting bank) with instructions to collect money from the buyer;
5. The seller's bank (remitting bank) records in its books and sends the documents to its agent's bank (collecting bank) in the place of the buyer with instruction to collect money from the buyer and remit to them;
6. The collecting bank sends advice of receipt of documents to the buyer and asks for payment;
7. The buyer makes payment;
8. The buyer collects documents from the bank;
9. The buyer presents the transport document to the transporters/shippers;
10. The buyer collects the goods;
11. The collecting bank remits funds to the (remitting bank) seller's bank;
12. The remitting bank credits the seller's account and sends payment advice to the seller.

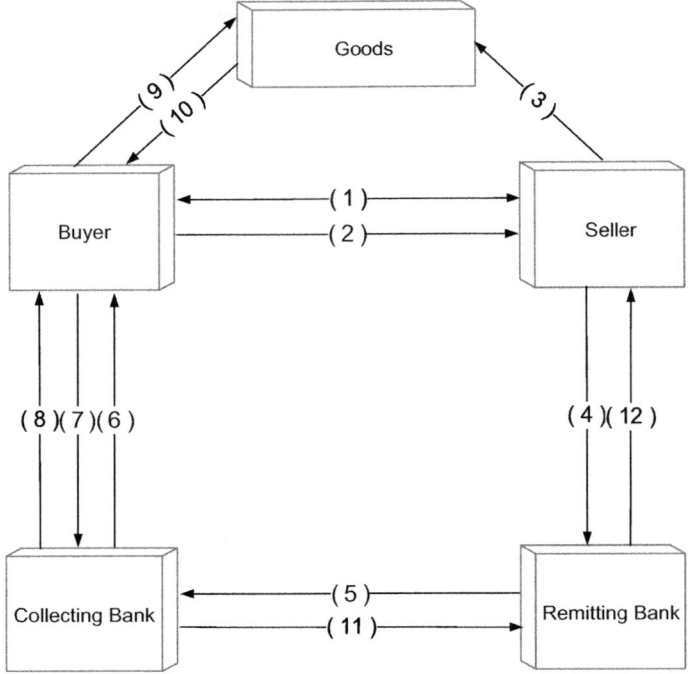

Fig. 5.8 Mechanics of a sight bill for collection

Mechanism: Documentary Usance Bills for Collection

Action steps—collection of bill of exchange.

Once the buyer and seller have negotiated and agreed terms and conditions of sale, then

1. The buyer places an order to the seller.
2. The seller makes goods ready, despatches them to the buyer through transporters and forwards the bill of exchange together with the relative documents to his bank, known as remitting bank (e.g. 1 January).
3. The remitting bank receives the documents, records them in its books/registers, and prepares a collection schedule on the basis of instructions received from the seller (e.g. on 5 January). The remitting bank forwards the collection schedule with the bill and the documents to the collecting bank.

4. The collecting bank records the details in its books/registers and advises to buyer of having received the documents (e.g. on 10 January).
5. The buyer (if it is a usance bill) accepts the bill and takes the documents. The buyer then presents the transport document to the transport agent and collects the goods.
6. The collecting bank sends advice of acceptance and maturity date to the remitting bank.
7. The remitting bank makes note of maturity date against the original entry made in its register and forwards an advice to the seller.
8. On maturity (1 April) the buyer makes payment to the collecting bank (if the buyer is a customer of the collecting bank it debits the buyer's account).
9. The collecting bank remits funds to the remitting bank through their bank's accounting system/arrangements.
10. The remitting bank records payment in its register, credits the seller's account and sends payment advice to the seller (1 April).

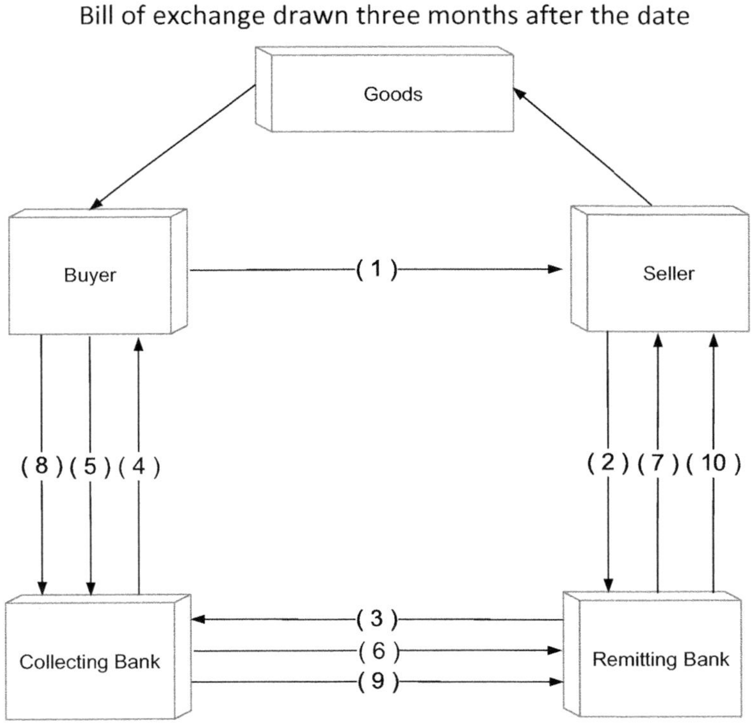

Bill of exchange drawn three months after the date

Fig. 5.9 Mechanics of a documentary usance bill for collection

Bills Purchased

The bills which are purchased by banks are usually Sight/Demand trade bills drawn on sound parties and the banks have up-to-date status reports on the drawees of bills of exchange.

Table 5.1 Bill of exchange indicative processing cost

Activity	Scale of charges	Amount
Outward bills		
Documentary bills	0.25% minimum £20/US$ 5, maximum £100/US$160. Exclusive of postage	
Clean bills/foreign currency bills/cheques/travellers cheques	0.25% minimum £20/US$35 maximum £50/US$80	
Postage/courier charges—	Courier charges—UK/Europe £10/US$20 Charges other countries	
SWIFT/telex charges	Maximum £20/US$35. Per collection	
Inward collections		
Documentary bills	0.2%—Minimum £20/US$35 Maximum £100/US$160. Exclusive of postage, etc.	
Clean bills	0.2%—Minimum £20/US$35 Maximum £100/US$160 Exclusive of postage, etc. per collection schedule	
Handling charges	Sight bills 1 per mile on the bill amount Minimum £20/US$35 per month, or part thereof, if bill not paid within 30 days if intimation Usance bills 1 per mile on the bill amount Minimum £20/US$35 per month, or part thereof, if bill not paid within 30 days if intimation	
Issue of delivery order	£25/US$40 per order	
Issue of delivery order for taking delivery of pledged goods	£5/US$10	
Advise of due date/status/ payment	£20/US$35 postage/telephone per bill	
Postage/courier charges	UK and Europe: £10/US$20 Other countries $20/US$35	
Any other out of pocket expense		
Total	(Total cost can be arrived at based on the above factors)	

The face value of a bill is credited to the customer's account at the time of purchase (some banks keep an x% margin of the amount). Interest on the amount is deferred until receipt of payment from the drawee or the collecting bank is received. The interest on the amount is calculated for the period from the date of purchase of the bill until receipt of payment (funds) by the bank.

Bills Discontinued

Banks discount trade bills which are drawn on financially sound parties. The discount (interest) and commission (postage, etc.) are deducted from the face value and the net amount is credited to the customer's account. The bank's assets for Local Bills Discounted (LBD) and for Foreign Bills Discounted (FBD) account is debited with the face value of the bill. The bank's income accounts are credited with the appropriate amounts. On maturity/receipt of payment (funds) from the drawee or the collecting bank, the Bills Discounted account is credited and the appropriate (Cash or Agency account) account is debited.

Precautions to Be Taken

- The bills must be genuine trade bills.
- The drawers and the drawees must be of sound financial position.
- Bank must obtain status reports periodically (quarterly) on parties.
- Facility amount must not exceed credit limits.
- Finance must not be provided against bills for longer periods.
- The bills must not be accommodation bills.

Accommodation Bill: A bill of exchange to which a person, called the accommodation party, puts his name to oblige or accommodate another person without receiving any consideration for doing so. Bills of this type are also called "windmills" or "windbills" or "kites". It is risky to provide a finance facility against these types of bills. Banks therefore do not provide finance facility against such bills.

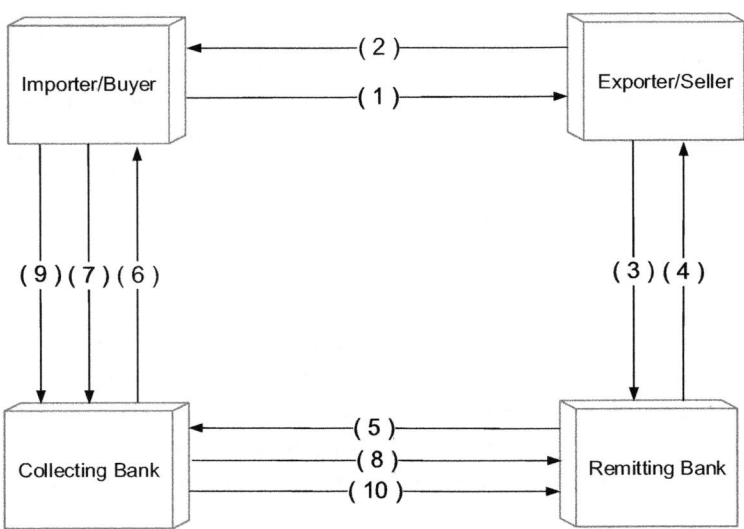

Fig. 5.10 Mechanics of a bill discounting

Bills Processing Cost (Indicatives)

The following is an example of the cost of processing of bills for collection. The scale of charges may vary from one bank to another (Table 5.1).

6

Documentary Letters of Credit

There is always an underlying agreement between the principal parties to a trade transaction, often a buyer and a seller. The agreement may be verbal or written in a formal or informal language. Its terms may be simple or complex, as the parties may feel necessary. Such an underlying agreement is referred to as a "sale contract".

A bank may grant a credit facility against a tangible security or without it. This depends on various factors. Sometimes banks may fix limits on various types of uses, such as term loan, overdrafts and letters of guarantee. This helps the banks to monitor the use of each type of facility utilised by the customer. A letter of credit is also a credit facility like a loan or overdraft but its nature of operation is different from a loan or overdraft facility.

Genesis: This is the safest and probably the fastest method of obtaining payment for goods exported. The documentary credit achieves a commercially acceptable compromise between the conflicting interests of buyer and seller by matching time of payment for the goods with the time of their delivery. It does this, however, by making payment against documents representing the goods rather than against the goods themselves.

A letter of credit is not only a method of obtaining payment but it also assures buyers of receiving documents relating to goods through their bank, provided they ask for the required type of documents.

Definition of Letter of Credit: (UCP 600 Articles 1 and 2) "For the purposes of the Article, the expressions 'Documentary Credit(s)' and 'Standby Letter(s) of Credit' (hereafter referred to as 'Credit(s)'), mean any arrangement, however named or described, whereby a bank (the 'Issuing Bank')

© The Author(s) 2019
T. Bhogal, A. Trivedi, *International Trade Finance*, Finance and Capital Markets Series,
https://doi.org/10.1007/978-3-030-24540-5_6

acting at the request and on the instructions of a customer ('the Applicant') or on its own behalf

1. is to make a payment to or to the order of a third party ("the Beneficiary"), or is to accept and pay bills of exchange (Draft(s)) drawn by the Beneficiary,

   or

2. authorizes another bank to effect such payment, or to accept and pay such bills of exchange (draft(s)),

   or

3. authorizes another bank to negotiate, against stipulated document(s), provided that the terms and conditions of the Credit are complied with.

For the purposes of these articles, branches of a bank in different countries are considered another bank".

An irrevocable documentary credit (especially a confirmed one) is therefore an excellent instrument of payment. Also, if appropriate documents are called for and provided reliance can be placed on the integrity of the seller—it is an effective means of obtaining delivery of the goods.

It is nevertheless a precision instrument, and must be properly handled by all concerned. Thus, both buyer and seller should observe certain rules of common sense and understand their responsibilities.

It is an important instrument for the exporter to secure payment.

Parties to a Letter of Credit and Their Responsibilities

1. Applicant's/Buyer's Responsibilities: The applicant to a letter of credit is a buyer or importer of goods. The applicant makes a request in writing to their bank to issue a letter of credit in favour of the seller/exporter of the goods or beneficiary. Their instructions to the issuing bank must be clear and precise and free from excessive detail. The bank cannot be expected to guess what is wanted, nor can it check complicated, and often technical, specifications and so on.

The purpose of the credit is to pay for the purchase, not to "police" the commercial transaction. Its terms and conditions, and the documents called for, should therefore be in agreement with the sales contract on which it may be based.

Any examination of the goods prior to or at the time of shipment must be evidenced by a document. The precise nature and issuer of such document must be stated in the credit. The credit should not call for documents that the seller cannot provide, nor set out conditions that cannot be met. (This is particularly important with changes in traditional documentation resulting from trade facilitation developments and changes in transport technology.)

2. The Issuing Bank: The issuing bank is the opening bank of a letter of credit on behalf and at the request of the applicant, the buyer/importer of the goods. A letter of credit is a legal contract between the seller/beneficiary and the issuing bank. It is an independent undertaking of the issuing bank to pay or accept the bill of exchange and make payment, on presentation of the documents according to the terms and conditions stated in the letter of credit. If the documents do not satisfy the requirements of the letter of credit the issuing bank is not liable to act in any way, that is, to pay or accept the bill of exchange and make payment.

Letters of credit may be issued by mail, telex, cable or SWIFT in accordance with the requirements of the applicant and the beneficiary. Using the SWIFT system is becoming more popular these days. Authentication of the letter is the responsibility of the advising bank by verifying authorised signatures on the letter, in case of mail, test key number in case of telex and cable and so on.

3. The Advising Bank: The advising bank is an agent bank of the issuing bank in the country of the exporter. The advising bank forwards the letter of credit to the beneficiary in accordance with the instructions of the issuing bank. Being an agent of the issuing bank, it has a list of signatories of the issuing bank. Therefore, it is the advising bank's responsibility to ensure that the letter of credit is signed by the authorised signatories of the issuing bank before forwarding it to the beneficiary.

If the advising bank forwards the letter without any undertaking on its part it must say clearly when advising the letter of credit to the beneficiary, that is, it (the advising bank) is under no obligation to make payment or incur any liability to make deferred payment and so on.

4. The Seller's/Beneficiary's Responsibilities: Although considerable time may elapse between the receipt of a credit and its utilisation, the seller should not delay studying it and requesting any necessary changes, if required.

The seller should satisfy him that the terms, conditions and documents called for are in agreement with the sales contract. (Banks are not concerned with such contracts. Their examination of the documents will take into consideration only the terms of the credit and any amendments to it.)

When it is time to present the documents the beneficiary should:

(a) Present the required documents exactly as called for by the credit. The documents must be in accordance with the terms and conditions of the credit and not on their face inconsistent with one another.
(b) Present the documents to the bank as quickly as possible and in any case within the validity of the credit and within the period of time after the date of issuance of the document specified in the credit or as applicable under Article No.14 (c) U.C.P. 600.
(c) Remember that non-compliance with the terms stipulated in the credit or irregularities in the documents oblige the bank to refuse settlement.

5. A confirming bank: A confirming bank is the one which adds its independent guarantee to the letter of credit. It undertakes the responsibility to make payment/acceptance of bills of exchange and pay on maturity or negotiate under the letter of credit in addition to the issuing bank. A confirming bank is usually the advising bank. If the issuing bank requests the advising bank to add its confirmation to the credit the advising bank does so. If the advising bank does not wish to do so, it must advise the issuing bank immediately of its intention of not doing so. Once the advising bank adds it confirmation, it is known as a confirming bank. The confirmation is an independent undertaking between the confirming bank and the beneficiary.
6. Nominated Bank: A nominated bank is the bank authorised by the issuing bank to pay, incur deferred payment liability, to accept bill of exchange and pay on maturity, or to negotiate the letter of credit.
7. Reimbursing Bank: A reimbursing bank is a bank authorised by the issuing bank to honour the reimbursement claim made by the negotiating/paying bank in settlement of negotiation/payment under a letter of credit. This is the bank with which the issuing bank has agency/accounting arrangements.
8. The Carrier: The carrier is the company which takes possession of the cargo with an undertaking to transport and deliver it safely at a place of destination agreed by the buyer and the seller. The cargo carrier is a shipping company, an airline or another type of transporter by road that is, lorries and so on. The cargo carrier supplies a transport document indicating receipt of goods and the terms of carriage of the goods.

9. The Insurer: The insurer is an insurance company with prime responsibility for insuring the cargo as required under the terms and conditions of the letter of credit. The insurer indemnifies the holder of the insurance document, that is, insurance policy or insurance certificate against any loss or damage to the cargo.

Who Does What?

The buyer and the seller conclude a sales contract for payment by documentary credit. The buyer requests his bank, the "issuing bank", to issue a letter of credit in favour of the seller/beneficiary specifying the instructions according to the agreed terms and conditions with the seller.

The issuing bank issues a letter of credit incorporating the terms and conditions agreed with the seller and asks another bank, usually the bank of the seller or another bank which is the correspondent of the issuing bank, to advise and/or confirm the credit, if so requested by the buyer/applicant.

The advising or confirming bank checks the authenticity of the letter of credit and informs the seller that the credit has been issued in their favour.

As soon as the seller receives the credit and is satisfied that he can meet its terms and conditions, he is in a position to load the goods and dispatch them. The seller then sends the documents evidencing the shipment to the bank where the credit is available (the bank). It may be the issuing bank, or the confirming bank, or any bank named (nominated bank) in the credit as the paying, accepting or negotiating bank, or it may be the advising bank or a bank willing to negotiate under the credit.

The advising bank/confirming bank carefully scrutinises the documents received under a credit. If the documents are in conformity with the terms of the credit it will process them accordingly. Any other bank, including the advising bank if it has not confirmed the credit, may negotiate, but with recourse to the beneficiary.

The bank, if other than the issuing bank, sends the documents to the issuing bank.

The issuing bank also scrutinises the documents and, if the documents are found as per terms of letter of credit, it:

1. Effects payment in accordance with the terms of the credit, either to the seller if he has sent the documents directly to the issuing bank or to the bank that has made funds available to the beneficiary in anticipation, or

2. Reimburses in the pre-agreed manner the confirming bank or any bank that has paid, accepted or negotiated documents under the credit.

When the documents have been scrutinised by the issuing bank and found to meet the credit requirements, they are released to the buyer upon payment of the amount due, or upon other terms agreed between the buyer and the issuing bank.

The buyer will present the transport document to the carrier who will then release the goods.

Advantages and Disadvantages of Letters of Credit

Advantages to Exporter

Assurance of Payment: The beneficiary is assured of payment as the issuing bank is bound to honour the documents drawn under the letter of credit.

Ready Negotiability: The exporter, if he needs money immediately, can secure payment by having the documents, drawn under the letter of credit, discounted (post shipment advance).

Compliance with Regulations: Letter of credit is evidence that the exchange control regulations, if applicable in the country of the importer, have been complied with.

Pre-shipment Facility: The exporter can secure an advance from his bank against a letter of credit received for export of goods (pre-shipment advance).

Advantages to Importer

Credit Facility from the Issuing Bank: The issuing bank lends its own credit facility to the importer against a letter of credit, if the importer cannot avail any credit facility from the exporter.

Assured Delivery of Goods: The issuing bank honours the documents drawn under a letter of credit only when all the terms and conditions of the credit have been complied with. Therefore, the importer is assured not only of obtaining the goods, but also, if proper care is taken, obtaining the specified goods in time. In this respect the buyer and seller should negotiate the date of shipment of the goods from named ports of shipment and destination.

Disadvantages to Applicant/Importer

Fraudulent Documents: The beneficiary wants to sell goods against a letter of credit and lays down the terms and conditions, regarding payment for the goods, suitable to him. He is going to supply certain documents as evidence of shipment of goods and, if bent upon defrauding, he may succeed in obtaining payment by supplying poor-quality goods or falsifying the documents.

Expensive: Issuing banks charge fees for issuing a letter of credit and such fees are not required to be paid in case of an open account system. The charges recovered by banks under an open account system are much lower than under a letter of credit.

Credit Line: A certain amount/portion of the buyer's/applicant's credit line with their bank gets tied up in an outstanding letter of credit. It will not be available for any more pressing credit needs which may develop in the applicant's business operations.

Cash flow: The applicant may have to tie up his cash as collateral security against the letter of credit, which will cause deficit in his cash flow.

Documents Delayed: It often happens that the documents of title to goods do not reach the importer on time because these are processed by different banks in different countries.

Goods Delayed: Sometimes the goods are delayed in transit because of various reasons. If the importer had committed himself to another party to supply those goods on or before a pre-determined date, delay may cause damage to his reputation and/or financial loss.

Disadvantages to the Beneficiary

Discrepancies in Documents: If the exporter is not familiar with the proper procedures for processing documents, the documents may be presented with discrepancies and the bank will send those on collection basis.

Difficult Terms and Conditions of Letter of Credit (L/C): Terms and conditions relating to certain documents may not be easy to fulfil or the documents may be difficult to obtain.

Different Language: Letters of credit may be received in the importing country's language and may not be understood by the exporter. It will be costly to get the documents translated.

Competitive Terms: Letters of credit payment terms are so restrictive that sellers may lose sales to competitors who quote less restrictive terms.

Documents Delayed: It often happens that the documents of title to goods do not reach the importer on time because documents have been processed by different banks in different countries.

Goods Delayed: Sometimes the goods are delayed in transit because of various reasons. If the exporter has committed by issuing a performance bond and so on in favour of the importer to supply those goods on or before a predetermined date, the delay may cause damage to his reputation and also financial loss if a claim is made by the importer.

Letter of Credit Mechanism

1. Proforma invoice;
2. Firm order placed by importer;
3. L/C application;
4. Foreign currency forward contract;
5. L/C. Advice sent through AB/CB;
6. L/C. Confirmation advice to beneficiary;
7. L/C. Confirmation advice;
8. Exporter hands goods to the carrier;
9. The carrier issues bill of lading/transport document;
10. Insurance company issues insurance policy;

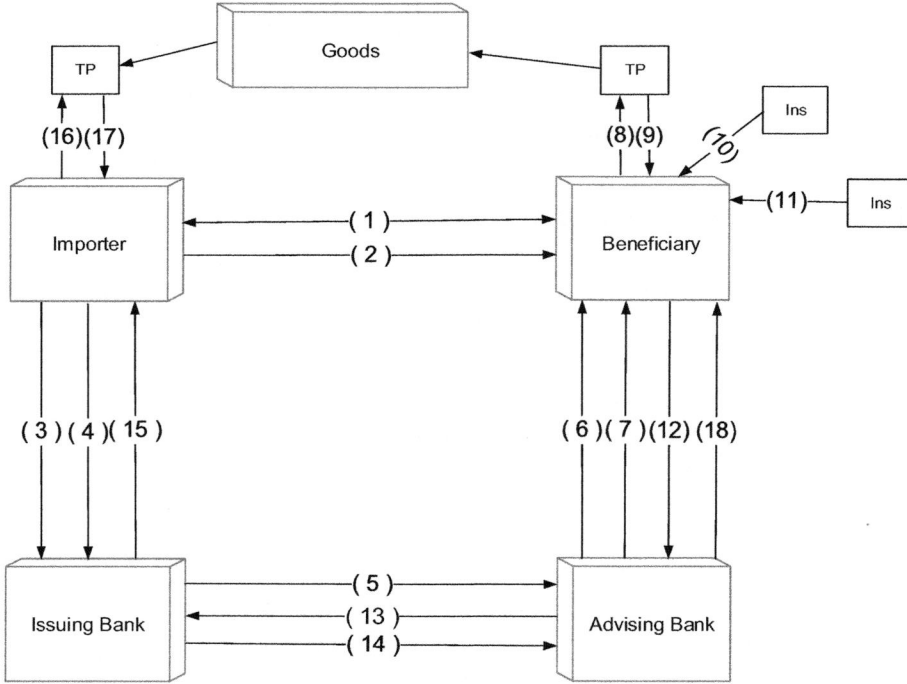

Fig. 6.1 Letter of credit: mechanism

11. Other documents as required;
12. Documents forwarded by the beneficiary to AB/CB and documents checked and/or negotiated by AB/CB/NB;
13. Documents forwarded by the AB/CB/NB to the issuing bank in accordance with reimbursement clause;
14. The issuing bank provides reimbursement to the AB/CB/NB;
15. Payment/acceptance of documents/bills of exchange and other documents forwarded to the importer;
16. The importer hands transport documents to the carrier;
17. The carrier delivers goods to the importer;
18. Funds credited to the beneficiary's account.

Letter of Credit Contracts and Regulations

Contracts and Regulations

1. Sale contract between buyer and seller;
2. L/C. Contract between the importer and the issuing bank;
3. Foreign currency forward contract between the importer and the issuing bank;
4. L/C. Contract between the issuing bank and the beneficiary;
5. L/C. Contract between AB/CB/NB;
6. L/C. Contract between the exporter/beneficiary and AB/CB/NB;
7. Pre-shipment finance contract between AB/CB/NB and the beneficiary;
8. Counter indemnity between AB/CB and the beneficiary—performance bond;
9. Performance bond between the AB/CB and the importer;
10. Contract of freightment—the exporter and the carrier company;
11. Contract of insurance—between the beneficiary and the carrier company;
12. Risk cover contract—between the exporter and the carrier company;
13. Export finance guarantee—NCM and ECGD and so on;
14. Seller's indemnity for negotiation of documents under reserve—between the beneficiary and the negotiating bank;
15. Loan contract for L.I.M. between the importer and the issuing bank;
16. Shipping guarantee—between issuing bank and carrier company;
17. L/C. confirmation contract between IB and CB.

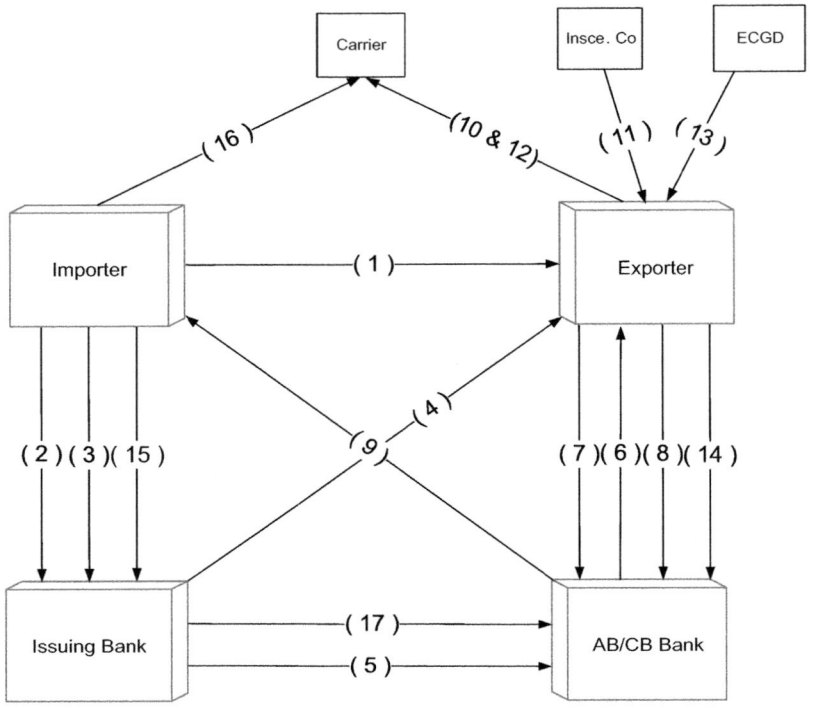

Fig. 6.2 Letter of credit: contracts and regulations

Sale Contract

What Is a Sale Contract?

A sale contract is an agreement between the buyer and the seller in which various terms and conditions of the transaction are specified. One need not get confused between the terms "sale contract" and "letter of credit". Credits, by their nature, are separate transactions from sales or other contract(s) on which they may be based, and banks are in no way concerned with or bound by such contracts, even if any reference whatsoever to such contracts is included in the credit (UCP. 600 Art. 4(a)).

The sale contract, in its simplest form, is an accepted order to buy or offer to sell a certain commodity or service that has been negotiated between the buyer and the seller.

The agreement between the buyer and the seller may be made orally or in writing. Although an oral contract is in general legally binding, it may cause some problems due to different understandings of its provisions by different parties. Therefore, to avoid misunderstanding, a verbal contract is required to be confirmed in writing.

Contents of a Sale Contract

A properly negotiated sale contract should include the following points:

- Description of goods;
- The price of the goods;
- Payment terms, that is, sight/usance (term period);
- Trade terms;
- Packing and marking;
- Shipping instructions, that is, date shipment;
- Ports of shipment and discharge;
- Insurance of goods;
- Inspection and warranties;
- Methods of payment;
- Additional documents or conditions.

The terms used will determine which party is to bear the costs involved in shipping the goods abroad, and are subject to international rules for their interpretation. They are known as "Incoterms" and are published by the International Chamber of Commerce, commonly known as ICC Publication "Incoterms 2010".

7

Letters of Credit: Types

Let us understand letter of credit and its various types with the help of a grid as in Fig. 7.1.

Types of Letters of Credit

Clean Letter of Credit

A clean letter of credit does not specify the documents of title to goods or terms and conditions to be complied with before effecting payment. In such cases goods are sent directly to the importer (buyer) and payment is made without the production of financial documents. It is not safe for a bank to establish such a type of letter of credit as neither the goods nor the documents of title to goods come into the possession of the bank and the bank issuing a clean letter of credit may suffer a loss if the applicant fails to make the payment. Such types of letters of credit could only be established where both parties, that is, the importer and exporter, are of undoubted integrity.

Documentary Letter of Credit

A documentary letter of credit is one which specifies certain terms and conditions to be satisfied in respect of documents of title to goods and other documents required together with the bill(s) of exchange if required to be drawn under a letter of credit. The interest of the issuing bank is safeguarded as the

© The Author(s) 2019
T. Bhogal, A. Trivedi, *International Trade Finance*, Finance and Capital Markets Series,
https://doi.org/10.1007/978-3-030-24540-5_7

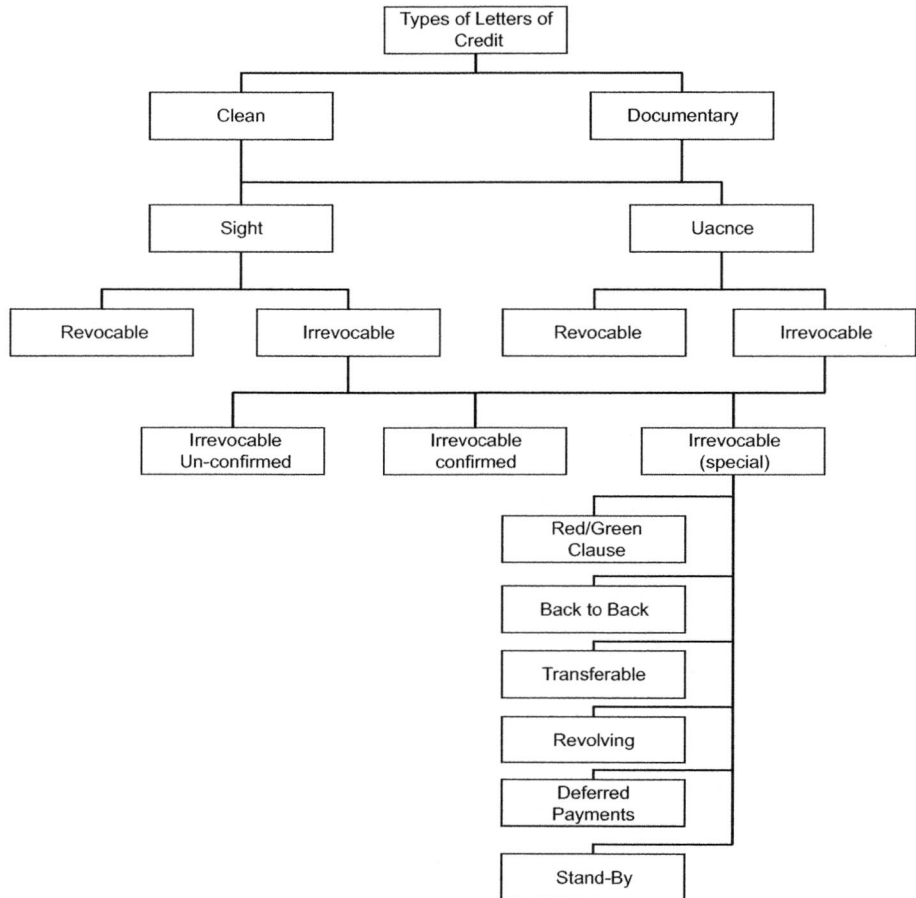

Fig. 7.1 Types of letters of credit

documents of title to goods remain in the bank's possession. The importer cannot take the delivery of the goods unless the importer (applicant) accepts the bill of exchange or makes payment there-against.

Circular or Traveller Letter of Credit

It is risky for travellers to carry cash when they wish to visit several places. It was the practice among banks to issue a letter called a circular letter of credit, requesting their branches, agents and correspondents to pay, up to a certain amount of money by a fixed date (date of expiry of the letter), to the person named in the letter. Another letter called a letter of introduction was also issued, addressed to their branches, agents and correspondents bearing the specimen of signature of the beneficiary, that is, applicant. Both of these documents were required to be presented to the bank/agent making the payment against the letter.

Revocable Letter of Credit

All letters of credit issued by banks are irrevocable unless specifically mentioned as revocable. A revocable letter of credit can be amended or cancelled by the issuing bank at any moment and without prior notice or notification to the beneficiary.

* The buyer (importer) has maximum flexibility as he/she is able to amend or cancel the credit without prior notice to the seller up to the moment of payment, acceptance or negotiation by the bank at which the issuing bank has made the credit available.
* The seller is at risk because the credit may be amended or cancelled while the goods are in transit and before the necessary documents have been presented.
* The seller may face the problem of obtaining payment direct from the buyer.
* However, the issuing bank must:
  – Reimburse another bank with which a revocable credit has been made available for sight payment, acceptance or negotiation for any payment, acceptance or negotiation made by such bank prior to receipt by it of notice of amendment or cancellation, against documents which appear on their face to be in compliance with the terms and conditions of the credit;
  – Reimburse another bank with which a revocable credit has been made and proceeds available for deferred payment, if such bank has, prior to receipt by it of notice of amendment or cancellation, taken up documents which appear on their face to be in compliance with the terms and conditions of the credit.

The beneficiaries, usually, do not like this type of L/C. This type of L/C may be used by the parties having utmost trust or to complete a legal formality of a country to transfer funds. It is important to note that there is no mention of a revocable letter of credit in the UCP 600.

A revocable L/C does not carry a definite undertaking of the issuing bank and is advised by the advising bank without any undertaking on its part. It does not carry the issuing bank's request for confirmation. The advising bank is required to verify and ensure legality of the signature appearing on a letter of credit.

Irrevocable Letter of Credit

An irrevocable letter of credit cannot be amended or cancelled without the agreement of the applicant, issuing bank, confirming bank (if a letter of credit has been confirmed) and beneficiary (UCP 600 Article No. 10).

An irrevocable credit constitutes a definite undertaking of the issuing bank, provided that the stipulated documents are presented and that the terms and conditions of a credit are complied with:

1. If a credit provides for sight payment to pay, or that payment will be made;
2. If a credit provides for deferred payment—to pay, or that payment will be made, on the date(s) determinable in accordance with the stipulations of the credit;
3. If a credit provides for acceptance—to accept drafts drawn by the beneficiary if a credit stipulates that they are to be drawn on the issuing bank, or to be responsible for their acceptance and payment at maturity if a credit stipulates that they are to be drawn on the applicant for the credit or any other drawee stipulated in a credit;
4. If a credit provides for negotiation—to pay without recourse to drawers and/or bonafide holders, draft(s) drawn by the beneficiary, at sight or at a tenor, on the applicant for the credit or on any other drawee stipulated in the credit other than the issuing bank itself, or to provide for negotiation by another bank and to pay, as above, if such negotiation is not effected;
5. Note: Under a letter of credit the bill of exchange should not be drawn on the applicant but must be drawn on the issuing bank. This is because a letter of credit is an undertaking of the issuing bank with the beneficiary. If a bill of exchange is required to be drawn on the applicant, then it will be considered as an additional document required under a credit.

Examples of "Irrevocable Clauses" on a letter of credit:

1. "We undertake to honour such draft(s) on presentation provided that they are drawn in conformity with the terms of a credit" and
2. "We hereby engage that payment(s) will be duly made against documents presented in conformity with the terms of a letter of credit".

It may be advised to the beneficiary directly, if appropriate, or through an advising bank. When it is advised through an advising bank:

- The advising bank may add its confirmation, if required by the beneficiary.
- The issuing bank may request the advising bank to add confirmation. If the advising bank is not prepared to add its confirmation it must inform the issuing bank without delay unless otherwise specified by the issuing bank.
- When the advising bank adds its confirmation to it, it is called "Irrevocable Confirmed Letter of Credit".

Irrevocable Confirmed Letter of Credit

An irrevocable letter of credit may be advised to the beneficiary through another bank without any undertaking on its part, but where the issuing bank requests or authorises another bank to add its confirmation to the credit and the other bank does so, then the letter with this additional clause of confirmation is called a "confirmed" letter of credit: this confirmation is a definite undertaking of the bank doing so in addition to the undertaking of the issuing bank. Provided the terms and conditions of a letter of credit are complied with, such confirmation or undertaking cannot be cancelled or amended without the consent of all parties to the letter of credit.

Where a letter of credit bears a confirmation of another bank it will assume the same liabilities as the issuing bank.

When an issuing bank authorises or requests another (advising) bank to confirm its irrevocable credit and the latter has added its confirmation, such confirmation constitutes a definite undertaking of that bank (known as confirming bank) in addition to that of the issuing bank, provided that the stipulated documents are presented and that the terms and conditions of the letter of credit are complied with.

Example of "confirmation clause".

"This credit bears our confirmation and we engage to:

1. Pay—if the credit provides for sight payment to pay, or that payment will be made;
2. if the credit provides for deferred payment—to pay, or that payment will be made, on the date(s) determinable in accordance with the stipulations of the credit;
3. if the credit provides for acceptance, to accept drafts drawn by the beneficiary if the credit stipulates that they are to be drawn on the confirming bank, or to be responsible for their acceptance and payment at maturity if the credit stipulates that they are to be drawn on the applicant for a letter of credit or any other drawee stipulated in a letter of credit;
4. if a letter of credit provides for negotiation—to negotiate without recourse to drawers and/or bona fide holders, draft(s) drawn by the beneficiary, at sight or at a tenor, on the issuing bank or on the applicant for a letter of credit or on any other drawee stipulated in a letter of credit other than the confirming bank itself".

If a bank is authorised or requested by the issuing bank to add its confirmation to a credit but is not prepared to do so, it must inform the issuing bank without delay. Unless the issuing bank specifies otherwise in its confirmation authorisation or request, the advising bank will advise a letter of credit to the beneficiary without adding its confirmation.

Such undertakings can neither be amended nor cancelled without the agreement of the issuing bank, the confirming bank (if any) and the beneficiary. Partial acceptance of amendments contained in one and the same advice of amendments is not effective without the agreement of all the above named parties.

An irrevocable letter of credit which has been confirmed by another independent bank (confirming bank) gives the seller a double assurance of payment as a bank in the seller's country has added its own undertaking to that of the issuing bank.

Silent Confirmation

The request to confirm a letter of credit is made by the issuing bank to the advising bank on behalf of the applicant. This is a separate contract between the issuing bank and the advising/confirming bank.

Silent confirmation: Sometimes the issuing bank does not ask the advising bank to add confirmation but for some reason the beneficiary approaches the advising bank to add its confirmation to a letter of credit without the knowledge of the issuing bank. This is known as silent confirmation. This is a separate contract between the beneficiary and the confirming bank. Under these circumstances, the issuing bank takes no liability in this respect. The issuing bank will have no obligation to inform the confirming bank of:

- any amendment to the letter of credit or
- in case of instances of fraudulent or falsified documents presented, the issuing bank will refuse to honour its commitments under the letter of credit.

Revolving Letter of Credit

A revolving letter of credit is one where, under the terms and conditions thereof, the amount is renewed or reinstated without specific amendment to the letter of credit being needed.

A revolving letter of credit may be revocable or irrevocable. It can revolve in relation to time or value.

Revolving Letter of Credit: Mechanism

A revolving letter of credit is used when the same goods are to be imported or purchased on a repeat basis over a period of time without any changes/amendments to the terms and conditions of a letter of credit:

- The amount of the credit is available again for the stated credit amount after each drawing.
- The credit may revolve in either time or value.
- Time is the most common.
- Credit revolving in time, for example monthly, means that the credit is available every month until the expiry date.
- It may be automatically re-available or subject to the receipt of the issuing bank's instructions at each cycle.

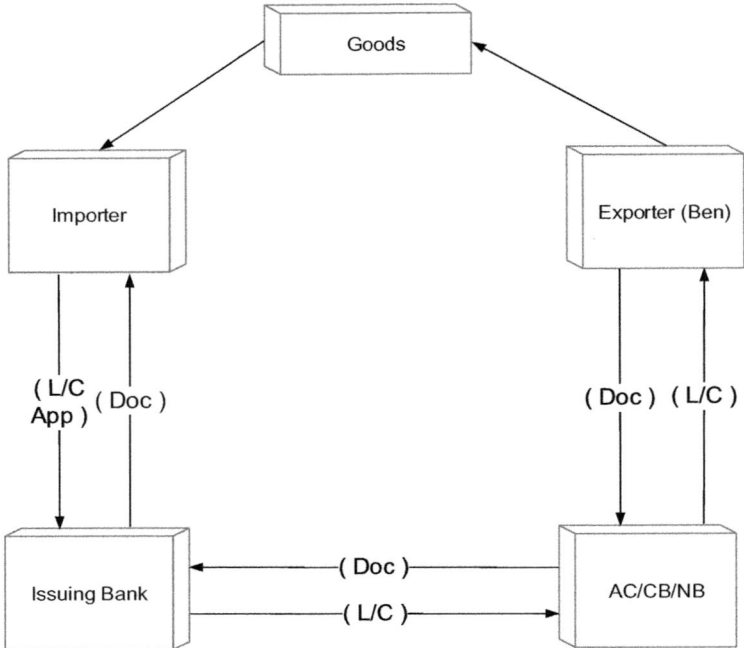

1. Once the transaction under the Original L/C is completed in terms of time or amount
2. The same L/C is reinstated with the same terms and conditions as many times as agreed

Fig. 7.2 Revolving letter of credit: mechanism

A revolving credit may be cumulative or non-cumulative. Cumulative means shipment missed in one cycle can be carried forward into the next cycle and non-cumulative means shipment missed in one cycle cannot be carried forward into the next cycle.

This type of credit permits the beneficiary to ship the good and make periodic drawing up to the value of the credit until the expiry date of the revolving letter of credit. If such a credit revolves in time it is also called a "periodic letter of credit".

Red Clause Letter of Credit

A red clause letter of credit is a credit with a special clause incorporated into it that authorises the advising bank to provide a credit facility by way of advance against the letter of credit for the purchase of raw material or for working capital, for example preparation of the goods to be exported by the beneficiary. The clause also stipulates the cover, that is security, for such advance and is incorporated at the specific request of the applicant.

To draw the attention of the beneficiary this clause was written in red or green ink. Thus it derived the name "red clause" letter of credit.

The red clause: This is a special clause added (see mechanics of red clause for an example of wording of red clause), at the request of the importer, in red ink or a red border to the clause, to an irrevocable credit to draw attention to the special clause on the credit. The clause contains an authorisation by the issuing bank to the advising or confirming bank to make funds available to the beneficiary before presentation of documents.

It is often used as a method of providing the seller with funds prior to shipment of goods. Therefore, it is of great value to middlemen that require pre-shipment finance where the buyer would be willing to meet this special request from the seller/beneficiary. It originated, for example, so that a wool importer in England could enable a wool shipper in Australia to obtain funds to pay the actual suppliers (either by direct purchase or through the wool auctions) by obtaining a loan from the Australian bank, either on an unsecured basis or against the security of interim documents.

The finance facility is arranged between the buyer and the seller. The advising or confirming bank provides the beneficiary loan or overdraft facility up to the amount authorised or percentage of the value of the credit, and would get repayment of the facility plus interest from the proceeds due to the beneficiary when the goods are shipped and documents presented in accordance with the terms and conditions of a letter of credit. If the seller fails to ship the merchandise, the advising or confirming bank recovers the amount advanced plus interest from the issuing bank, which in turn recovers from the buyer (applicant).

The issuing bank ensures to take cash deposit or mark a lien on the applicant's deposit to protect itself from any loss for claim made by the advising/confirming bank in case the beneficiary fails to ship the goods and submit the documents under a letter of credit, as it is the liability of the applicant to pay for such a facility to the exporter.

Red Clause Letter of Credit: Mechanism

Example of a Standard Red Clause Addressed to the Advising/Confirming Bank

You are authorised to advance up to ------ % of the credit amount to the beneficiary, and we undertake to repay on demand any amounts so advanced with or without presentation of shipping documents called for in this credit.

Example of Advance Payment Red Clause (RC)

The negotiating bank is hereby authorised to make advance to the beneficiary to the extent of £ --- or the unused balance of this credit, whichever is less, against the beneficiary's receipt for the amount advanced which must state the advance to be used to pay for the purchase and shipment of the merchandise for which this credit is opened and accompanied by the beneficiary's written undertaking to deliver documents in conformity with the credit terms to the negotiating bank on or before the latest date for negotiation. The advance, with interest, is to be deducted from the proceeds of the draft(s) drawn under this credit. We (the issuing bank) hereby undertake the repayment of such advances, with interest, should they not be repaid to the negotiating bank by the beneficiary on or before the latest date for negotiation.

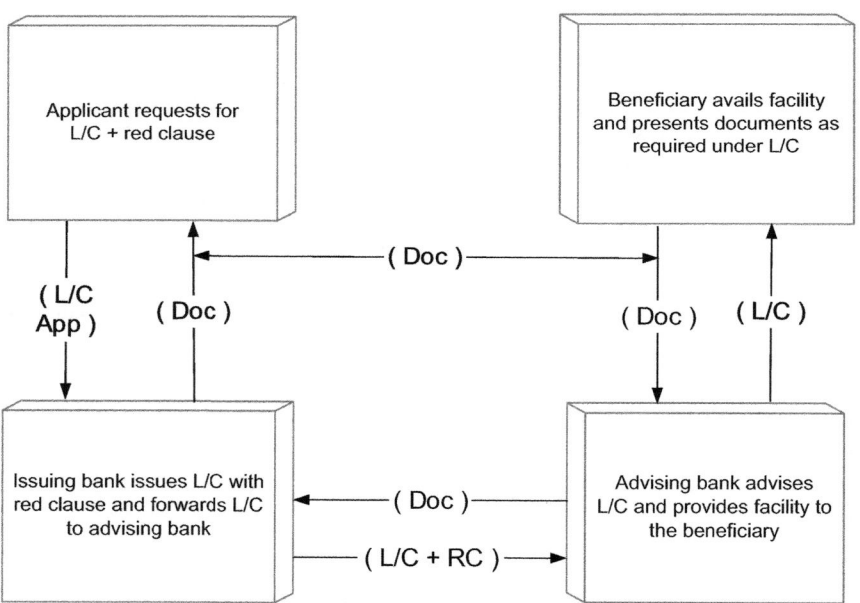

Fig. 7.3 Red clause letter of credit: mechanism

Example of Anticipatory Drawing Red Clause

You are authorised to draw clean sight draft(s) on the issuing bank to the extent of £ --- accompanied by your signed statement that the amount drawn to be used for the purchase and shipment of the merchandise for which this credit is opened and your written undertaking to deliver documents in conformity with the credit terms to the negotiating bank on or before the latest date for negotiation.

Risk Factors: A foreign exchange risk may accrue to either party, depending upon the currency of a letter of credit. If payment is to be made in the currency of the beneficiary, the buyer will incur the foreign exchange risk. If a letter of credit is in the buyer's currency, the foreign exchange risk will accrue to the seller/beneficiary. Before the beneficiary avails this facility from the advising/confirming bank he will be required to give two undertakings in writing to the bank:

1. That the amount drawn or advanced under a letter of credit will be used only for the purchase and/or shipment of the merchandise for which the credit is opened;
2. That the documents in conformity with requirements of a letter of credit will be delivered to the bank on or before the latest date for negotiation.

Example of Red Clause Payment at Maturity

The negotiating bank is hereby authorised to make advance to the beneficiary to the extent of £ --- of the amount of this credit, against the beneficiary's receipt for the amount advanced, which must state that the advance is to be used to pay for the purchase and shipment of the merchandise under the credit and written undertaking to deliver the documents in conformity with the credit terms to the negotiating bank on or before the latest date for negotiation. The advance, with interest, is to be deducted from the proceeds of the draft drawn under this credit. We (the issuing bank) hereby undertake the payment of such advances, with interest, should they not be repaid by the beneficiary or by negotiation/payment on presentation of the documents strictly in terms of this credit at maturity.

Green Clause: This clause is distinct from the Red Clause and primarily covers in a degree to which each one ties up the applicant's funds and exposes the applicant to a foreign exchange risk. The merchandise is taken as collateral security against the advance of funds allowed by this clause. The advance funds may be given against warehouse receipts. Such clauses are not common these days and are of academic interest.

Transferable Letter of Credit

A transferable letter of credit is a credit under which the beneficiary (first beneficiary) may request the bank authorised to pay, incur a deferred payment undertaking, accept or negotiate (the "transferring bank"), or in the case of a freely negotiable credit, the bank specifically authorised in a letter of credit as a transferring bank, to make the credit available in whole or in part(s) to one or more other beneficiary(ies) (second beneficiary(ies)) (UCP 600 Article 38).

Transferable Letter of Credit: Mechanism

Transferable Letter of Credit: A transferable credit is one that can be transferred by the original (first) beneficiary to one or more second beneficiaries.

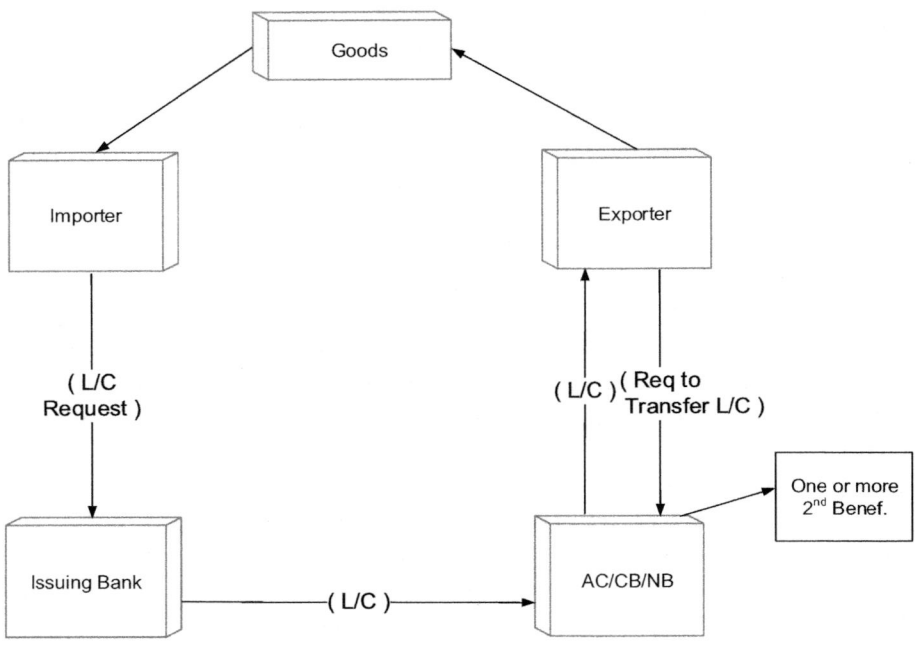

Fig. 7.4 Transferable letter of credit: mechanism

(Article 38 UCP 600). It is normally used when the first beneficiary does not supply the merchandise himself, but is a middleman and thus wishes to transfer part, or all, of his rights and obligations to the actual supplier(s) as second beneficiary(ies).

It should be noted that a letter of credit would only be issued as a transferable one on the specific instructions of the applicant. This would mean that both the credit application form and the credit itself must clearly state that the credit is transferable. (Only an irrevocable credit would be issued in this form and a letter of credit can be transferred once only.) A suggested format in this regard is given on the next page.

Transferable Credit: Limitations

This type of letter of credit can only be transferred once, that is, the second beneficiary(ies) cannot transfer to a third beneficiary. The transfer must be affected in accordance with the terms of the original credit, subject to the following exceptions:

- The name and address of the first beneficiary may be substituted for that of the applicant for the credit.
- The amount of the credit and any unit price may be reduced: this would enable the first beneficiary to allow for profit.
- The period of validity and the period for shipment may be shortened.
- The transfer is affected on the instructions of the first beneficiary by the bank where the credit is available (the advising bank).

Thus, it permits a letter of credit to be arranged by the first beneficiary in favour of one or more second beneficiaries, while allowing the first beneficiary to substitute his invoices for those presented to the bank by the second beneficiary or beneficiaries. The bank must, of course, correlate and check both invoices with the other documents called for and ensure that all documents are in accordance with the terms of the original (prime) credit.

It is normally used when the first beneficiary does not supply the goods himself and requests to transfer part or all of his rights and obligations to the actual suppliers of the goods.

The transfer must be made by a named bank, and effected using exactly the same wording as the original credit, with only three possible exceptions:

The transferee's name and address is substituted for the beneficiary's.
The amount of the credit may be reduced (by the beneficiary's profit).
The expiry date may be brought forward to allow movement of documents between the transferring and the issuing banks.

The issuing bank must be informed of the transfer(s), name(s) of the second beneficiary and the amount(s).

Limitations

- Goods obtained must be the same as those required by the original credit.
- Only one level of transfer can be made (from first beneficiary to second beneficiary(ies).

- If "partial shipment" is not permitted it cannot be transferred to more than one transferee (second beneficiaries).
- Total value of transfers cannot exceed the value of an original letter of credit.

The Manager,
Bank _____
Address _____

Dear Sir/Mdam,
Re: Transferable Irrevocable Credit No. _____ for £ _____ in our
favour. We refer to the above letter of credit issued by _____ and request you to
transfer the benefit of the credit to: _____
64 INTERNATIONAL TRADE FINANCE of _____ to the
extent of £ _____ upon the same terms and conditions, with the following
variations:

The transferred credit is to be available until _____ and we shall be glad if you will
advise the transferee(s) of this and the above variations by / cable/
swift or letter accordingly. No amendment of the terms of the original credit
may, however, be advised to them without reference to us. The original credit is
enclosed for endorsement, together with our cheque for £ _____ being your
commission @ _____% for effecting the transfer, correspondents charges, if any, being
for our account.

In consideration of your so transferring the credit we undertake to deliver to
you, on or before your payment/negotiation of drafts drawn under the transferred
credit, our own drafts, invoices for amounts equal to or exceeding
those of the transferee(s) and other documents (if any) as required by and
drawn in accordance with the original credit.

On our compliance with the above undertaking you will deliver the transferees
invoices to us and will pay us the amount, if any, by which the total of our invoices
exceeds theirs but if we should fail to deliver to you our drafts or invoices or any other
requisite document forthwith, as agreed above, you are hereby authorised at your
discretion and without notification to us to forward the transferees documents to your
principals and without responsibility for any consequential disclosure of the
transferee's names and prices or any other particulars.

It is understood that neither you nor your correspondents shall be under
any responsibility for the description, quality, quantity or value of the merchandise
covered by the documents against which you have paid/negotiated in accordance with
the transferred letter of credit or for the correctness, genuineness or validity of the
documents themselves, nor shall you be under any obligation to notify us of the failure
of the transferees to tender any documents to you: and we hereby indemnify you in
respect of all loss, damage and expense of any kind which you may incur as a direct;
or indirect result of your acting on these instructions.

Yours faithfully,

AUTHORISED SIGNATURE
(Authorised signature should be confirmed by the beneficiary's bank

---

Fig. 7.5 Suggested specimen of request to transfer transferable L/C (Note: Amend to suit the Bank's … requirement)

Procedure for Effecting Transfer of a Letter of Credit

A transferable letter of credit usually attracts the attention of the advising bank. The advising bank, before forwarding such a letter of credit to the beneficiary, will attach its usual covering letter and any forms which the beneficiary may need to complete to effect the transfer, if so wished.

The beneficiary of the original letter of credit may decide:

1. Not to use the option to transfer a letter of credit;
2. To transfer a part of a letter of credit amount; or
3. To transfer the whole amount of a letter of credit to one or more second beneficiaries.

If the original beneficiary decides to transfer a complete or partial letter of credit the beneficiary must complete the appropriate form, as required under a letter of credit. The beneficiary's signatures on the transfer form need to be verified by his bank before informing the issuing bank of the transfer. The advising bank will transcribe appropriate (full) details of the transfer(s) from the original letter of credit on its own letter(s) and forward to the second beneficiary(ies).

On receipt of the completed transfer form(s) the issuing bank will make note of the changes in the name(s) of the beneficiary(ies) and the amounts, as necessary.

Back-to-Back Letter of Credit

It may happen that the credit in favour of the seller is not transferable, or, although transferable, cannot meet commercial requirements by transfer in accordance with Article 38 of UCP 600 conditions. The seller, however, is unable to supply the goods and needs to purchase them from another supplier. The other supplier of the goods is prepared to sell to him on the basis of a letter of credit. In this case, it may be possible to use a "back-to-back credit". This concept involves the issue of a second credit by the seller in favour of his supplier.

Under the back-to-back concept, the seller, as beneficiary of the first credit, offers it as "security" to the advising bank for the issuance of the second credit. As applicant for this second credit the seller is responsible for reimbursing the bank for payments made under it, regardless of whether or not payment has been received under the first credit. There is, however, no compulsion for the bank to issue the second credit, and, in fact, some banks may not do so.

In the case of a counter credit, the procedure is the same except that the seller requests his own bank to issue the second credit as a counter to the first one. The seller's bank may agree to issue such a credit if the transaction falls within the seller's existing credit line or if a special facility is granted for the purpose. The bank will, of course, have rights against the seller in accordance with the term of a credit line or special facility.

With both the back-to-back credit and the counter credit, the second credit must be worded so as to produce the documents (apart from the commercial invoice) required by the first credit—and to produce them within the time limits set by the first credit—in order that the seller, as beneficiary under the first credit, may be entitled to be paid within those limits.

It is usually a domestic letter of credit issued on the strength of a foreign letter of credit, by the bank notifying/negotiating a foreign letter of credit. A back-to-back letter of credit is issued in favour of the suppliers of raw materials or finished products/goods to the beneficiary of a foreign letter of credit, which are to be exported under a foreign letter of credit.

It may happen that the credit in favour of the seller is not transferable, or, although transferable, cannot meet commercial requirement by transfer in accordance with Article No.38 of the UCP 600 conditions. The seller, however, is unable to supply the goods and needs to purchase them from, and make payment to, another supplier.

Under the above circumstances the beneficiary of a letter of credit (foreign letter of credit is also known as prime letter of credit) offers it as "security" to the advising bank for issuance of a second letter of credit matching the commercial requirements. The second letter of credit is known as "back-to-back" L/C.

Banks have special preference for trade-related business. In order to develop such business, they keep on exploring different avenues, and back-to-back letter of credit is one of them.

It is, however, imperative that before focusing on back-to-back credit business, banks should be fully aware of the inherent risks involved in this type of business. The objective of these guidelines is to assist banks in exercising proper care in developing back-to-back letter of credit business, so that the banks' interest is safeguarded.

Back-to-Back L/C: Salient Features

Certain aspects of back-to-back transactions requiring further clarification are:

- Overall Risk;
- Issuing Bank of Prime Letter of Credit;
- Credit Check on Letter of Credit Openers;
- Assignment of Prime Letter of Credit;
- Cash Margin;
- Pricing;
- Technical details;
- Prime Letter of Credit;
- Bank's Appropriate Credit Approval.

Back-to-Back Transactions Risks

If the advising bank of the original credit does not add its confirmation to the original credit, it does not become a party to such credit and will thus be unable to reject an amendment that the opening bank of the original credit will issue.

The bank will therefore stipulate in its credit agreement with the intermediary that amendments will have to be approved by the bank.

If the advising bank of the original letter of credit does not wish to add its confirmation to the original credit, it has to be certain about the credit standing of the bank issuing that credit and the situation in the country of that bank. After all, this credit serves as collateral for the issuance of the back-to-back credit. Normally, the bank issuing the back-to-back credit will be prepared to accept the credit without confirmation if the issuing bank is a first-class bank located in a reputable or low- or no-risk country. In all other cases, the bank will insist on adding its confirmation. In any case, the bank will have the credit exposure to the opening bank no matter whether it confirms the credit or not. After all, the credit serves as security for the commitment it enters into. This means that the overall commissions charged to the client should be identical. If the credit is confirmed, the bank will charge a confirmation commission and a lower issuance fee for a back-to-back letter of credit. If the credit is not confirmed, the issuance commission will be higher, as it has to compensate for the credit risk of the opening bank.

In transactions with different purchase and sale terms, for example Free on Board (FOB) purchase and CFR (cost and freight) or CIF (cost, insurance and freight) sale, there are additional risks involved relating to transportation and/or insurance.

It is important that the freight is paid and insurance is effective. So there should be sufficient cash and a credit line in place to cover the freight and insurance charges.

Risk Factors

It is important to understand that a back-to-back letter of credit is essentially a self-liquidating transaction. A bank opening back-to-back credit sometimes may not have collateral security or comfort to rely upon, except prime letter of credit.

Inherently, back-to-back credit is a straightjacket transaction, which requires extreme precision in handling. Prime letter of credit is not collateral as it has no intrinsic value, but it is a perfect source of repayment, provided its terms are respected in back-to-back letter of credit. In case of even a slight variation, a back-to-back letter of credit opening bank could be left to bear the loss without any support from the opener of the prime letter of credit.

Consequently, back-to-back letter of credit can be a safe and rewarding business if the terms of the prime letter of credit are strictly adhered to, and could be disastrous if proper care is not taken.

Back-to-Back Letter of Credit: Mechanism

Important Points to Consider

The customer (beneficiary) requests his bank to take the foreign (prime) L/C as security for another (back-to-back) L/C that he wishes to be issued.

Certain terms and conditions of the back-to-back (second) L/C must be modified according to the circumstances.

The back-to-back L/C should have an early expiry date to allow the customer time to:

1. Manufacture goods;
2. Make goods ready for despatch;
3. Substitute his own shipping documents.

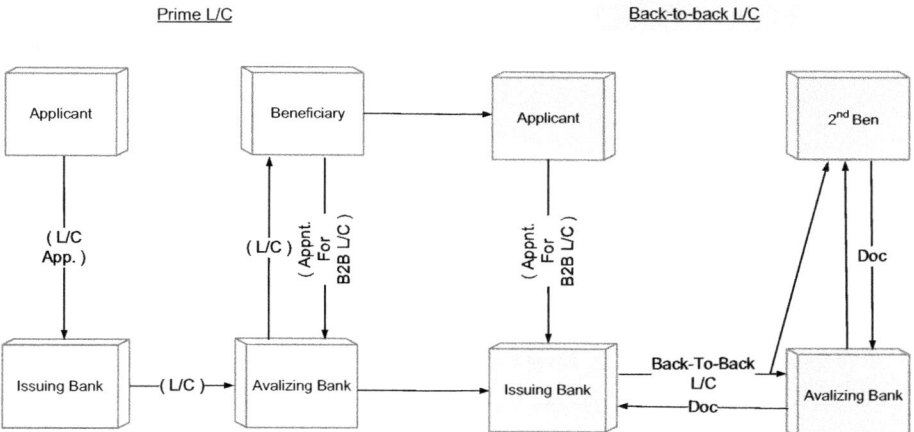

Fig. 7.6   Back-to-back letter of credit: mechanism

Back-to-back L/C must be for a smaller amount because the supplier wants to make a profit on the transaction.

The supplier (beneficiary of prime L/C) must substitute documents showing his own name. If the beneficiary of back-to-back (second) L/C is to be paid before the beneficiary of prime L/C receives payment the bank must consider the credit limit (credit worthiness) of the customer (first beneficiary) carefully.

The issuing bank should not permit the advising/negotiating bank to negotiate documents against second L/C with discrepancies, however minor those discrepancies may be.

Intermediary supplier's and ultimate buyer's names must not be disclosed. If any amendments to the prime (first) L/C are received, it must be checked whether such amendments affect the back-to-back (second) L/C in any way. If necessary, appropriate amendments must be made in time.

If any amendments are to be made to back-to-back L/C the terms and conditions of the prime L/C must be checked for whether such amendments affect the prime L/C in any way. If necessary, appropriate amendments must be made before any amendments to the back-to-back L/C.

The bank which issues back-to-back L/C is responsible for scrutinising the documents in respect of both L/Cs.

The bills of lading under back-to-back letter of credit should be to the order of the bank issuing back-to-back L/C.

The bank issuing back-to-back L/C must take care of the accounting aspect of liabilities and record necessary entries.

First or prime L/C must be assigned to the bank issuing back-to-back L/C. The bank must create a charge on the customer's stock and book debt (i.e. General Letter of Pledge or Hypothecation).

Table 7.1 Transferable and back-to-back credits: comparison

Transferable L/C	Back-to-Back L/C
Involves one credit	Involves two separate credits
Credit only transferable at the applicant's request	Credit may be used as security to create a back-to-back credit without the knowledge of the applicant of prime L/C
Subject specifically to UCP. 600 Art. 38	No specific article of UCP 600

Status of Issuing Bank of the Prime Letter of Credit

As the entire transaction is structured on the basis of prime letter of credit it is important to establish the credentials of the issuing bank, and also the genuineness of the instrument. In this connection, the following points require special attention:

- The issuing bank should be reputable.
- The bank handling back-to-back credit must be holding and control documents vis-à-vis test keys and specimen signatures of the prime letter of credit issuing bank so that genuineness of the instrument can be established.
- It is suggested that before getting involved in serious negotiations, the bank should know the status of the bank issuing prime letter of credit. It is also equally important to clearly understand the country risk of the country where the prime letter of credit issuing bank is domiciled. Once the status, risks and relationship with the bank and country involved are cleared, detailed negotiations should be undertaken.
- Even a prime letter of credit opened by banks in locations of high-risk area countries requires prior clearance for undertaking cross-border risks, and should be referred to the competent authority of the bank before making any commitments.

Credit Check on Letter of Credit Applicant

The nature of back-to-back letter of credit transactions is such that at times, the bank is required to deal with a new customer without having the benefit of a previous track record. It is therefore important that before undertaking the transaction, the bank should check the credit worthiness of the applicant.

It is also more important to check the credit worthiness of the applicants of back-to-back letter of credit as they are usually middlemen/brokers, who undertake transactions which may be far in excess of their capacity, and may be unknown to the dealing bank.

However, if the back-to-back letter of credit applicant is a regular customer of the bank or a known entity in the market with an established track record, then the bank may exercise its own judgement.

A satisfactory credit report on the beneficiary of the back-to-back letter of credit to be opened by the bank should be obtained.

Assignment of Prime Letter of Credit

Sometimes the prime letter of credit may be a final source of repayment of the bank's obligations under their back-to-back letter of credit. It is important to perfect their interest in the prime letter of credit. The following steps will be useful.

- When back-to-back letter of credit is opened, a lien should be marked on the prime letter of credit, showing details of the back-to-back letter of credit.
- Where prime letter of credit is restricted for negotiation to another bank or confirmed by a third bank, it is necessary to obtain a Letter of Authorisation from the beneficiary assigning the proceeds of negotiation under the prime letter of credit to the bank (issuing back-to-back L/C), which must be reported to the letter of credit advising/confirming bank and their acknowledgment obtained.
- If this assignment request is addressed to the advising/confirming bank of the prime letter of credit, it should be obtained before establishing the back-to-back letter of credit.
- The assignment must be obtained for the total amount of the prime letter of credit, and if this is not possible, at least for an amount sufficient to cover the back-to-back letter of credit including estimated bank charges.
- Prime letter of credit should be held in custody, together with the assignment of letter of credit duly completed.

Cash Margin: The back-to-back credit usually resists the idea of providing a cash margin. However, the issuing bank should endeavour to negotiate a cash margin, especially where the opener is a newly established company and/or is a relatively unknown party.

In this respect, it is important to understand that cash margin will not provide any comfort if there is a problem in carrying out the transaction caused by negligence of the bank opening back-to-back credit.

Cash margin is always desirable as it ensures a continued commitment and involvement of the applicant of the letter of credit.

There is no rule of thumb regarding the margin amount, but there has to be a stake by way of a reasonable cash margin. It varies between 20 to 30% or more of the face value of back-to-back letter of credit.

Pricing: As discussed earlier, a back-to-back letter of credit is a self-liquidating transaction. Therefore, pricing of each transaction should depend on the risk and complexities involved.

Besides applying a regular schedule of charges for a letter of credit, a bank may negotiate a handling fee, depending upon the market practice in their area of operation.

In the case of the prime letter of credit opening bank being domiciled in a country of high risk, branches of the bank should get clearance from the competent authority, as the transaction may require confirmation of prime letter of credit at a fixed price, which will be advised on a case-by-case basis. Hence, the bank's charges will include:

- Confirmation commission;
- Handling fee;
- Regular schedule of charges for letter of credit.

It is always advisable to negotiate pricing before undertaking the deal as the parties are inclined to know and accept or otherwise pricing before initiating the transaction.

Technical Details: It is not possible to provide exhaustive guidelines on technical details as to the accurate opening and handling of back-to-back credit. However, a few points are given hereunder:

Prime letter of credit should first be examined thoroughly to ensure that the terms and conditions could be honoured under back-to-back letter of credit. However, if there is any clause in the prime letter of credit which could not be transcribed in back-to-back credit, a suitable amendment/deletion should be obtained from the bank issuing the prime letter of credit before opening a back-to-back letter of credit.

A letter of credit containing clauses providing for reimbursement on receipt of documents or on inspection at the port of discharge is not acceptable as prime letter of credit.

The amount of a back-to-back letter of credit should always be less than the amount of a prime letter of credit.

The shipping and negotiation dates of back-to-back credit should expire earlier than the corresponding expiry dates of the prime letter.

The issuing bank may incorporate a clause in back-to-back credit as "documents must be presented for negotiation within (x number of) days after the date of issuance of the transport document, but within the validity of the expiry date of a Letter of Credit". In this case it must be ensured that the date for presentation of documents be reduced accordingly when issuing back-to-back credit. Negotiations, in any case, must be within the validity period of the back-to-back letter of credit.

If for any reason the time limit is not sufficient in the prime letter of credit to cover back-to-back letter of credit, it must be ensured that a suitable amendment extending its validity is received before issuing a back-to-back letter of credit.

In some cases, a prime letter of credit may require certain documents, such as an Inspection Certificate or Certificate of Origin or Sanitary Certificate, to be issued by a particular organisation, for example a government agency, and consequently back-to-back letters of credit require exactly the same documents.

Since quality and specification of goods to be shipped under prime letter of credit are of utmost importance, the bank should incorporate a suitable inspection document, if such requirement was not provided for in the prime letter of credit.

In the case of CIF shipments, the prime letter of credit requires insurance policy/certificates. It must be ensured that the insurance coverage and value of both letters of credit are identical. If, for example, prime letter of credit calls for the coverage of "invoices value plus 10%", and in view of the lesser value of the relative back-to-back letter of credit, it would not be possible to comply with the identical terms of the prime letter of credit.

Where prime letter of credit is advised through another bank, it is important to ensure that complete control over all subsequent amendments is maintained. The beneficiary should not accept any amendment in the prime letter of credit without the bank's knowledge and consent.

In cases where prime letter of credit is restricted to the bank (issuing back-to-back letter of credit), it must be ensured that all subsequent amendments are suitably matched with back-to-back letter of credit, after obtaining written consent to this effect from the beneficiary. Where a particular amendment cannot be honoured, it is necessary that the prime letter of credit opening bank be informed immediately after obtaining written consent from the applicant.

Once a prime letter of credit has been advised to the beneficiary (your customer), amendments thereto can be effective only if accepted by the beneficiary and the bank. Banks should ensure that their customers do not accept any amendments without their approval. Before accepting any amendments to the prime letter of credit it should be ensured that the corresponding amendments to the back-to-back letter of credit are acceptable to the beneficiary of the letter of credit.

To identify a back-to-back letter of credit transaction from any other regular letter of credit, it is necessary to mark a "Cross Reference Caution" on the related files, that is, prime letter of credit and back-to-back letter of credit, so that the transaction can be carefully monitored and the possibility of an amendment being advised without reference to the prime letter of credit is avoided.

The back-to-back credit must be made restricted, as far as possible, for negotiation at the issuing bank's counters. In this way, the bank would be able to ensure that negotiation takes place within a reasonable time before the expiry date of the prime letter of credit.

However, if it is not possible, then a suitable clause should be incorporated in the back-to-back letter of credit instructing negotiating bank to send all shipping documents in one lot through a reputable courier service, as well as to advise the issuing bank by a tested telex the details of negotiation including the name of the courier service, airway bill number and date documents were despatched. In this way, the bank could monitor movement and the timely delivery of the documents.

In back-to-back transaction, drafts and commercial invoices are commonly replaced before the documents are presented at the counter of the prime letter of credit issuing bank. In this connection it is suggested that the bank obtain pre-signed documents before opening a back-to-back letter of credit. It is important to observe this procedure where the branch is dealing with a relatively unknown or new customer and also if the cash margin is not provided by the applicant of the back-to-back letter of credit. If blank documents are obtained beforehand, then prime letter of credit would be negotiated even if the letter of credit opener declines to co-operate or is unable to provide the documents when required.

A letter of assignment must be obtained from the applicant of back-to-back letter of credit before a credit is established.

Documents under back-to-back letter of credit bearing discrepancies must not be accepted. Any request from the back-to-back letter of credit applicant for accepting documents with the discrepancies should not be entertained unless secured by 100% plus bank charges and so on as cash margin.

Shipping guarantees should under no circumstances be issued for shipment made under back-to-back letter of credit. Once a shipping guarantee is issued, the bank will be obliged to accept documents regardless of discrepancies.

Prime letter of credit: While considering proposals for opening letters of credit against the cover of a prime letter of credit, it is necessary to take additional safeguards as follows:

Where prime letter of credit is on CIF terms, and back-to-back letter of credit is on Cost and Freight (C&F) terms, a corresponding insurance cover of adequate value should be obtained from the customer, identical to that of the support letter of credit.

Where prime letter of credit is on CIF terms and back-to-back letter of credit is required on FOB terms, in addition to the insurance requirement specified above, it should be ensured that the back-to-back letter of credit provides for the bills of lading to evidence "Freight Prepaid".

Similar terminology would apply in the case where a prime letter of credit calls for C&F terms whereas back-to-back letter of credit is on FOB basis, except that the requirement of insurance coverage would not apply.

A prime letter of credit may call for a particular "Transport Document" whereas the customer may require the bank to issue a back-to-back letter of credit. This sort of transaction evolves either when a customer cannot arrange with his proposed buyer to have the goods shipped on similar terms and conditions as arranged with the ultimate buyer, or the customer would not like to disclose the name of the actual buyer.

To illustrate, a support letter of credit may call for "Marine Bill of Lading", while the back-to-back letter of credit may require "Truck Bill of Lading". Alternatively, a support letter of credit may call for shipment of goods from Toronto to Egypt, while a back-to-back letter of credit may call for despatch of goods from the US to Toronto.

Safeguards

Considering the involvement of two modes of carriage in these transactions, the following safeguards are suggested:

The related goods must be under the bank's control, at all times.

- The documents, when received, should be handed over only to the clearing agent/shipping company approved by the bank for this purpose.
- The clearing agent/shipping company would be responsible for ensuring that the goods are cleared and shipped under their supervision, and that proper documentation is made out strictly in terms of prime letter of credit and is delivered directly to the bank.
- While handing over documents to the clearing agent/shipping company, it should be ensured that they are accompanied by a proper letter giving detailed and specific instructions regarding documents required, such as what date should appear on the transport document, the exact descriptions of merchandise, and proof of shipment and port of discharge.
- The letter must clearly stipulate that these documents will be delivered to the bank directly. The documents must correspond with the requirements as called for in the prime letter of credit.
- Proper insurance with "bank" clause should be obtained before a back-to-back letter of credit is opened.
- Trans-shipment must not be allowed. Such transactions may delay delivery under prime letter of credit.
- Proper documentation required for customs clearance must be incorporated in the back-to-back letter of credit wherever necessary.
- Since goods under the support letter of credit would involve payment of customs duty, sales tax, ocean freight (if applicable), inland freight and so on, it should be ensured that prime letter of credit amount will cover all these costs.
- The back-to-back letter of credit must also include a clause requiring an inspection certificate so as to evidence that the merchandise conforms with specification, quality, quantity and so on as stipulated in the prime letter of credit. To inspect the goods the Inspection Agency required to be approved by the bank and any cost invoiced would be on the account of the customer.

In handling back-to-back letter of credit transactions, it must always be borne in mind that prime/support letter of credit is only a source of repayment, provided of course the documents there-under are absolutely in order. Otherwise the prime/support letter of credit does not form a security.

Credit approval by the competent authority, as per internal guidelines of the bank, may be required in dealing with this type of letter of credit.

Third Country or Transit Letter of Credit

Mechanics of Third Country or Transit Letter of Credit

Sometimes a London bank may be asked by a bank overseas to open letters of credit in favour of beneficiaries in another overseas country. The exporter may request the importer to have a letter of credit issued by a bank in a country other than the country of the importer. This is done through an overseas correspondent bank. The bank in London may be requested to issue a letter of credit by an overseas bank for various reasons such as:

- The importer and exporter would like to settle in a currency which is acceptable to both parties, for example in GB pounds. Nosto and Vostro are the titles of accounts through which the banks' settle their financial transactions in their books of accounts (internal financial settlements).
- The financial standing of UK banks and financial stability of the UK in the eyes of the world as regards integrity, experience/expertise in handling documentary letter of credit transactions with absolute impartiality;
- The UK government is most unlikely to declare a moratorium;
- Finance under the letter of credit may be arranged in London from time to time, exchange control regulations permitting, where local finance in either of the two countries is more expensive or not available (e.g. by term drafts drawn on and accepted by the London bank and then discounted by them on the London money market at the fine rate for bank bills);
- Where the opening bank is unknown in the seller's country (i.e. its signatures cannot be verified). Where direct communication between the buyer's and seller's countries is not possible for political reasons.

Additionally, sellers sometimes require a credit to be confirmed by a bank in the UK and passing the credit through such a bank (provided they have arranged a credit line) is a convenient way of providing such confirmation. This occurs more frequently when the buyer's country is considered by the seller to be politically unstable, or its currency to be weak, or the buyer's bank to be other than first class. The London bank's confirmation, in such cases, makes the credit as good as that of the London bank.

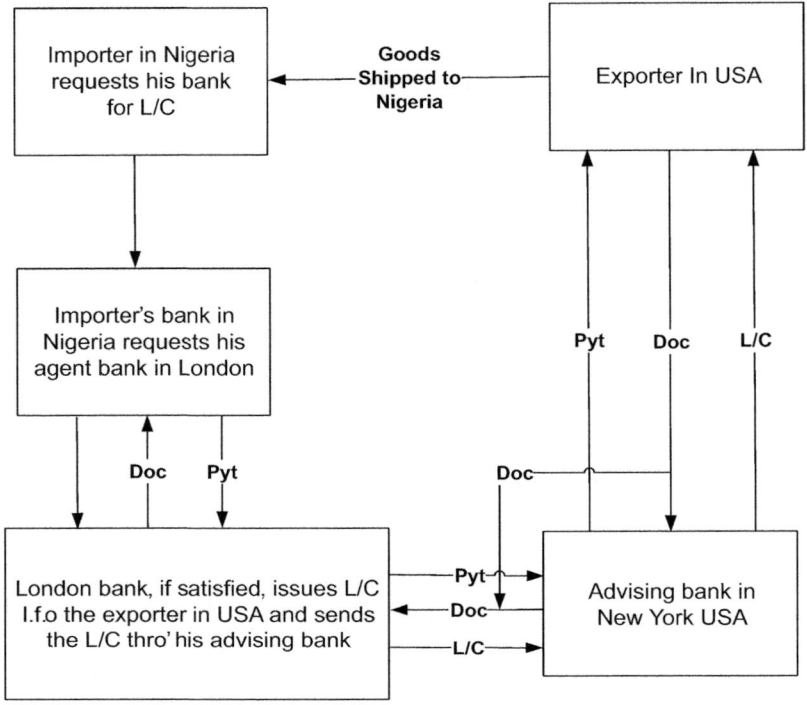

Fig. 7.7 Third country/transit letter of credit: mechanism

Banks in the UK are requested to advise or open transit credits for various reasons, such as:

1. Settlement being effected in GB pounds, a major trading currency often acceptable to both buyer and seller, which can conveniently be arranged through the GB pound (Vostro) accounts maintained by UK banks for the hundreds of different banks abroad; transit credits need not be expressed in GB pounds since settlement may be arranged by UK banks in other currencies.
2. The opening bank may be unknown in the seller's country (i.e. signatures appearing on a letter of credit cannot be verified).
3. There may not be direct communication between the buyer's and seller's countries. This may be due to political reasons.
4. The settlement may be effected easily in most trading currencies like GB pounds and US dollars.

Additionally, sellers sometimes require a credit to be confirmed by a bank in the UK and passing the credit through such a bank (provided they have arranged a credit 'line') is a convenient way of providing such confirmation. This occurs more frequently when the buyer's country is considered by the seller to be politically unstable, or its currency to be weak, or the buyer's bank to be other than first class. The London bank's confirmation, in such cases, makes the credit as good as that of the London bank.

Deferred Payment Letter of Credit: Mechanics

Deferred Payment L/C: The deferred payment letter of credit was developed in the early 1950s in the Far Eastern Trade practice, where a negotiable instrument was not commonly used. The goods are delivered to the buyer before the date or receipt of payment. If the goods prove defective the buyer may resort to any appropriate legal action. When documents under the credit are received, they are to be checked as the normal practice of banks but no bill of exchange is drawn under deferred letter of credit.

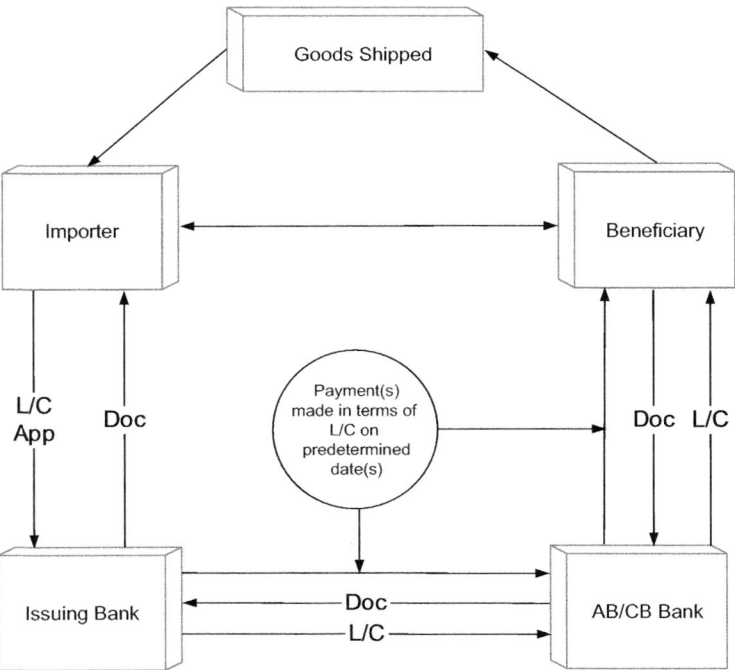

Fig. 7.8 Deferred payment letter of credit: mechanism

Under this type of letter of credit the payment to the beneficiary is made at pre-agreed future date which may be after a specified number of days or months from the date of shipment or presentation of documents. Sometimes this type of credit is referred to as deferred sight letter of credit. The issuer of this letter of credit undertakes to the beneficiary on pre-agreed date(s). Payment may be made in periodic instalments.

UCP 600 Article 2(b) states if a credit provides for deferred payment to pay on the maturity date(s) determinable in accordance with the stipulations in the credit.

This deferred credit should not be confused with a usance letter of credit. In the case of a usance credit there must be a bill of exchange but in the case of a deferred payment letter of credit a bill of exchange is not drawn.

Standby Letter of Credit

The role of the traditional documentary credit (commercial credit), issued at the request of the buyer in favour of the seller, has been to enable the seller to obtain the payment due from the buyer when he, the seller, has fulfilled his part in the commercial contract and "evidenced" this fact by presenting "stipulated documents".

The role of a standby credit is different, although it possesses all the elements of a documentary credit subject to UCP 600. It is often used in lieu of the performance guarantee, for example in respect of major construction contracts or major long-term sales. But it may sometimes be used for other purposes, such as a form of guarantee by, for example, a parent company's guarantee of loans granted to a subsidiary. A standby letter of credit may be issued in favour of the seller to ensure that if payment is not received under some other pre-agreed method it will be made under a standby credit upon the seller fulfilling his part of the standby credit.

A standby credit may be issued at the request of the applicant (usually seller or contractor) directly in favour of the beneficiary (usually buyer or employer), or it may be issued in favour of a bank in the beneficiary's country to cover a guarantee issued by that bank in favour of the beneficiary.

A standby letter of credit is one whose value is held in reserve or only paid as a penalty for non-compliance with some other contract, or on failure of other payments to be forthcoming. Standby letters of credit are mostly used to prove a commitment to honour a contract.

Basically, however, a standby credit is intended to cover a "non-performance" (default) situation instead of a "performance" situation, as with the traditional documentary credit. This affects both the position of the issuing bank and the type of documentation called for. Even if the applicant has claims that he "performed", the bank must pay under the terms of the credit if the specified documentation is presented—usually a sight draft on the issuing bank accompanied by a statement of claim issued by the beneficiary. (This position has been upheld in a number of cases where the courts have ruled against an applicant seeking an injunction to prevent the issuing bank from honouring its undertaking.)

The type of documentation referred to above gives some indication of the "extent to which they may be applicable" to standby credits. Thus, many articles dealing with "Documents" would seem likely to not be applicable.

A standby letter of credit operates just like any other letter of credit except that:

- It is not secured by goods in trade.
- Its value will be paid out only on non-performance.
- Its purpose is to prove financial ability and commitment to honour a contract, not to pay for specific goods/services, because it is used to secure contracts, not for payment in full for anything.
- Value of standby letter of credit rarely exceeds more than 10% of the value of the contract.

Standby Letter of Credit: Mechanism

This type of credit was first mentioned under UCP regulations in the 1983 revision of ICC and since then it is recognised under ICC regulations. It performs a similar function to a "performance bond". It provides a "guarantee" that payment will be made by the issuer (via the opening bank) if the buyer fails to render payment or performance to the beneficiary. The payment may be evidenced by documentation or, possibly, by a simple demand from the beneficiary.

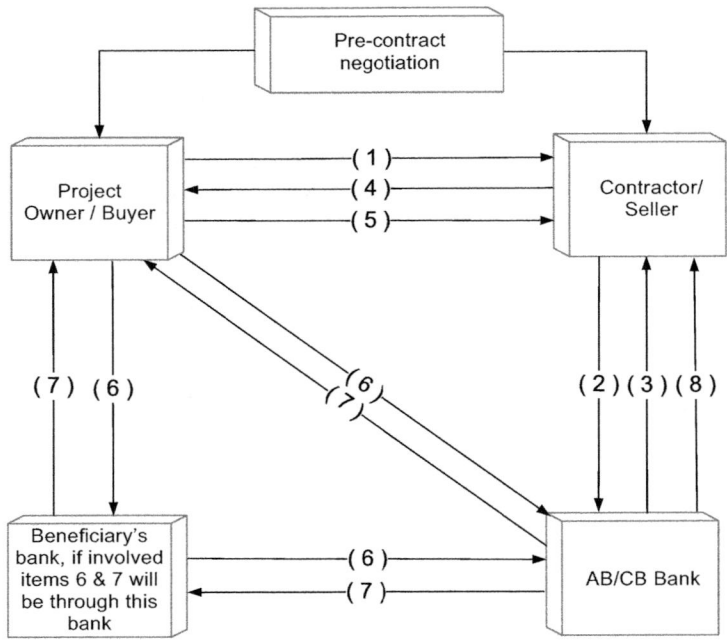

Fig. 7.9 Standby letter of credit: mechanism

1. Invitation for Bid. The project owner sends a tender to bid on a project to a contractor. The tender requires a bid bond and permits the bid bond to be in the form of a standby letter of credit.
2. The contractor applies to the bank for the issuance of a bid bond.
3. The contractor's bank (issuing bank) issues a bid bond and forwards it to the contractor.
4. The contractor forwards his bid together with the bid bond to the project owner.
5. The project owner accepts the contractor's bid and sends a contract to the contractor.
6. If the contractor fails to sign the contract or fails to obtain and forward to the project owner a performance bond, the project owner will demand payment under the bid bond.
7. When the contractor has signed the contract and obtained a performance bond, or whatever else the contract may require, the project owner will return the bid bond to the contractor to be cancelled.
8. The issuing bank informs the contractor of his action.

Distinction between a commercial letter of credit and a standby letter of credit.

Table 7.2 Comparison of commercial and standby letter of credit

Basic concept	Commercial L/C	Standby L/C
Performance	It is a payment device	It is a security instrument
Documentation	All parties expect the beneficiary to draw documents	Does not expect the beneficiary to draw documents. Claim is made only if something goes wrong
	Involves third-party's documents, that is, B/L, insurance and other commercial documents	May involve only a declaration
Security	Third-party documents of title provide security to bank	No inherent security; an additional security or margin may be required by the bank

A Specimen of Standby Letters of Credit

Specimen 1

Name and full address of Issuing Bank

Name and full address of the beneficiary

Gentlemen,

Date:

OUR IRREVOCABLE STANDBY LETTER OF CREDIT NO _____ FOR GB POUNDS _____
IN YOUR FAVOUR _____

In consideration of your having entered into an agreement with _____ (*Full name and address)* hereinafter referred to as the applicant to supply a consignment of _____ for a total value of GB Pounds _____ *(amount in words)*

We, the Bank _____, hereby issue our Irrevocable Standby Letter of Credit No:_____ in your favour, which is available to you _____ days after the date of Bill of Lading/Airway Bill upon your written demand which must be accompanied by the following documents and must reach us at our Counter, _____ within the validity of this Standby Letter of Credit.

1. Our written statement signed by your two authorised signatories, whose signatures must be certified by your bankers, stating that the goods as detailed herein above have been shipped to _____ in accordance with your agreement with _____ and you have not received payment for the same _____ after _____days from the date of Bill of Lading/Airway Bill.

2. Copy of the unpaid invoice made out to _____ evidencing the shipment of the abovementioned goods, consigned to _____ and the amount due from the applicant.

3. Copy of the Clean on Board Bill of Lading/Air Waybill evidencing the shipment of the above mentioned goods consigned to _____

4. This original Standby Letter of Credit expires on _____ in London, UK

We undertake that documents drawn under and in strict compliance with this Standby Letter of Credit shall be duly honoured upon presentation to us at our counter in London on or before the expiry date.

This Standby Letter of Credit is subject to the Uniform Customs and Practice for Credits (2007 Revision) International Chamber of Commerce No.600.

Fig. 7.10 Specimen of standby letters of credit (Specimen 1)

Specimen 2

FROM: XYZ BANK PLC

We herewith issue our irrevocable standby letter of credit No._____ which is subject
to the Uniform Customs and Practice for Documentary Credits (2007 Revision) ICC Publication
No. 600, as follows:

Applicant:	Name and address of the buyer
Beneficiary:	Name and address of supplier
For an amount of:	(Currency and amount)

Date/Place of expiry: (Latest date of credit validity) _____(Place)_____

Available with XYZ BANK PLC, London at sight, but not prior to 30 days after shipment date,
against presentation of the following documents:

1.   Beneficiary's statement, purportedly signed by an authorised/signatory, reading to the
     effect that:

     a.   Goods have been delivered in accordance with the contractual terms

     b.   The invoice and any relevant payment documents have been presented to the
          applicant

     c.   The amount claimed has not been paid and is now past due by the applicant in
          accordance with the contract terms;

2.   Copy of unpaid invoice addressed to the applicant by beneficiary.

3.   Copy of bill of lading covering: Goods

The amount available for drawing under this standby letter of credit will be automatically
reduced by the amount of any payment(s) made in favour of (beneficiary) whether under and/or
outside this standby letter of credit, if such payment is effected by XYZ Bank PLC and if
reference is made to this standby letter of credit.

Special Conditions: Documents presented later than 21 days after the issuance date of the
transport document(s) are acceptable.

Bank charges: All banking charges outside of the Issuing Bank are for the beneficiary's
account.

Method of Reimbursement: After receipt of strictly credit conform documents at our counters
in London we will remit funds to the presenting bank in accordance with their instructions.

Instructions to the Advising Bank: Please advise the beneficiary without adding your
confirmation.

Date: _____

_____   _____

Authorised Signature   Authorised Signature

Fig. 7.11   Specimen of standby letters of credit (Specimen 2)

Skeleton Letter of Credit

This type of letter of credit does not specify the goods to be shipped but states "General Merchandise", which allows the beneficiary freedom to ship any goods up to the amount of the credit. It is particularly important when a transferable credit is issued to agents of the applicant company allowing them freedom to shop around while abroad.

Omnibus Letter of Credit

This type of credit does not specify the port of loading, which implies the applicant's acceptance of specific goods from any port or anywhere in the world.

Straight Letter of Credit

This is a letter of credit which expires for payment or acceptance at the counters of the issuing bank. The issuing bank gives the following type of undertaking, "We engage with you that the drafts drawn under and in compliance with the terms and conditions of this credit will be honoured upon presentation of documents to us as specified not later than Date)".

8

Methods of Payment Settlement

There are different methods of payment settlement. The following statement is made by the issuing bank: "We hereby engage that payment will be duly made against documents presented in conformity with the terms of this credit".

Payment L/C

The following action steps take place:

1. The seller/beneficiary sends the documents evidencing the shipment of the goods to the bank where the credit is available (issuing bank or advising/confirming bank)
2. The bank examines the documents and, if the documents meet with the requirements of the letter of credit, makes payment.
3. This bank, if other than the issuing bank, then sends the documents to the issuing bank and claims reimbursement in accordance with the bank's agreed settlement procedures.

Channels of Payment Settlement

Payment

1. Requires only two parties—buyer and seller;
2. May or may not involve a bill of exchange;

© The Author(s) 2019
T. Bhogal, A. Trivedi, *International Trade Finance*, Finance and Capital Markets Series,
https://doi.org/10.1007/978-3-030-24540-5_8

3. Where a bill of exchange is involved it must be a sight bill of exchange;
4. Payment is always without recourse.

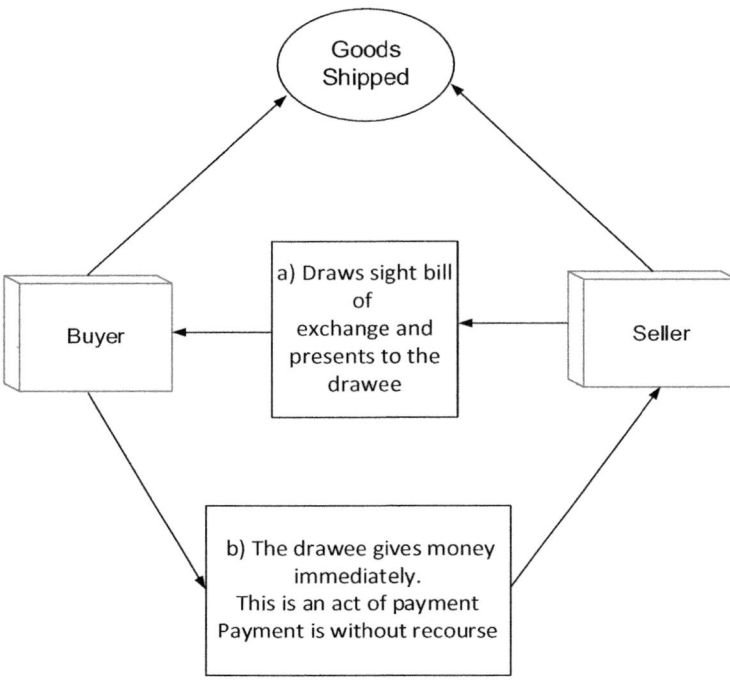

Fig. 8.1 Channels of payment settlement

Payment L/C: Bill on Issuing Bank

Payment Settlement: Method/Acceptance Letter of Credit

The issuing bank usually gives the following undertaking: "We hereby engage that drafts drawn in conformity with the terms of this credit will be duly accepted on presentation and duly honoured at maturity".

The following action steps take place:

1. The seller/beneficiary sends the documents evidencing the shipment of the goods to the bank where the credit is available (issuing bank or advising/confirming bank) accompanied by a usance bill of exchange drawn on the bank with the specified tenor.

2. The bank examines the documents and if the documents meet with the requirement of a letter of credit, the bank accepts the bill of exchange and returns it to the seller/beneficiary.
3. This bank, if other than the issuing bank, sends the documents to the issuing bank, stating that it has accepted the bill and maturity date. At maturity reimbursement will be made in accordance with the banks' agreed procedures

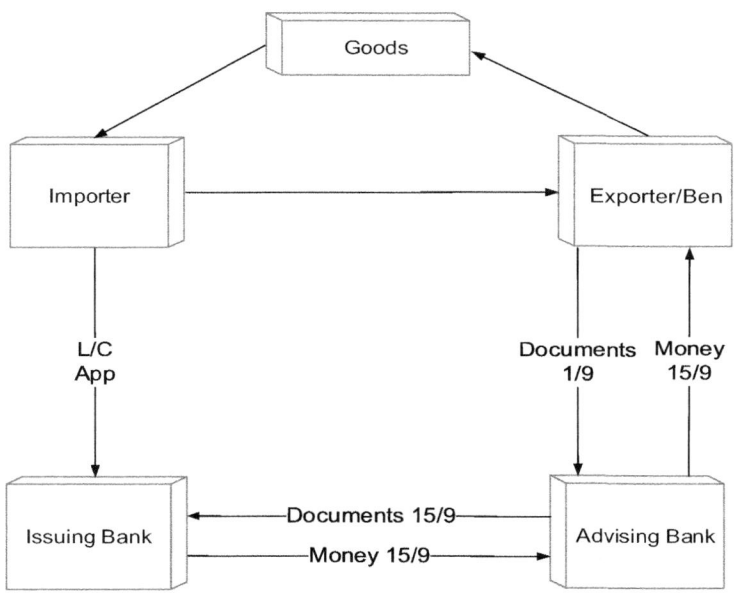

Fig. 8.2   Payment letter of credit: bill on issuing bank

Mechanism of Settlement: Acceptance L/C

Acceptance

Involves 2 stages
  Stage 1. Requires minimum of two parties

1. Requires a bill of exchange;
2. It must be a usance bill of exchange;
3. Acceptance is an undertaking of liability of the drawee to pay on maturity.

Stage 2.

1. Presentation of the bill of exchange on maturity;
2. Money is given at maturity Act of Payment (without recourse).

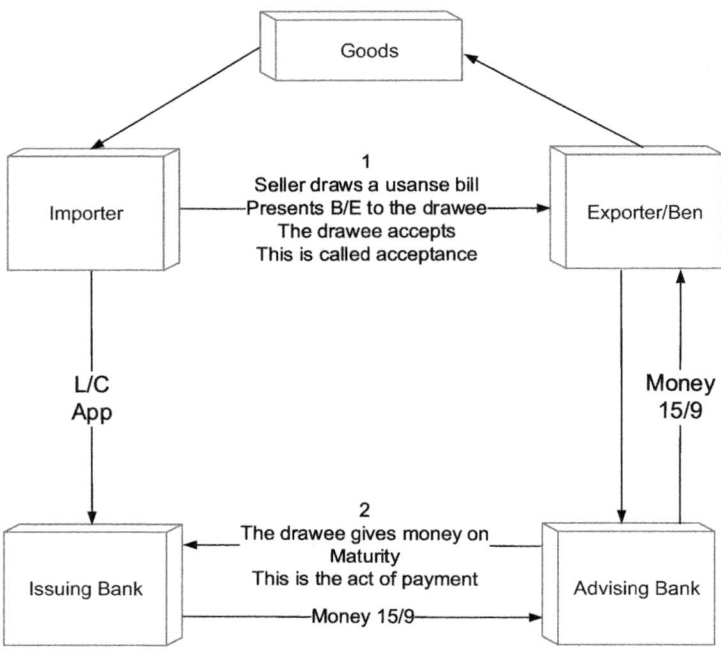

Fig. 8.3 Acceptance letter of credit: mechanism of settlement

Method of Settlement: Usance Bill on Issuing Bank

Bankers' Acceptances

The rules under UCP 600 Article No. 2(c): "if the credit provides for acceptance:

1. By the issuing bank—to accept Draft(s) drawn by the Beneficiary on the Issuing Bank and pay them at maturity. Or
2. By another drawee bank—to accept and pay at maturity Draft(s) drawn by the Beneficiary on the Issuing Bank in the event the drawee bank stipulated in the Credit does not accept Draft(s) drawn on it, or to pay Draft(s) accepted but not paid by such drawee bank at maturity".

It means that where a bill of exchange is required it should be drawn on the issuing bank or on "AB" or "CB" if authorised in the letter of credit. A bill of exchange is an order for payment. When it is a sight bill the order to pay is made by the drawee payable on demand but a usance/time bill of exchange orders for payment sometime in future. This is one of the most common methods of giving the drawee/buyer more time to settle the account. A usance/time bill of exchange which meets the terms and conditions of the letter of credit requires the drawee (buyer) to give an undertaking to make payment on the due date and to receive the documents of title to goods in order to collect the goods. A letter of credit is a legal contract between the issuing bank and the seller/beneficiary, and draws the bill on the issuing bank. If documents under a letter of credit meet its requirement, the bank has no alternative but to accept the bill of exchange by signing on the face of the bill with or without adding the word "accepted" thereon. This is known as bank's or banker's acceptance. By adding this statement, the bank acknowledges its legal obligation to pay the face value of the bill of exchange on its maturity date.

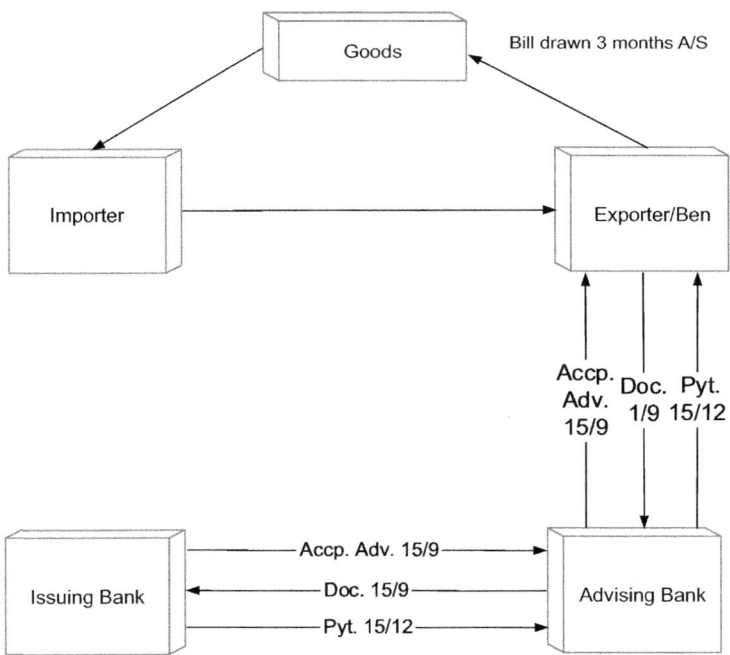

Fig. 8.4 Usance bill on issuing bank: mechanism of settlement

A bill of exchange accepted by a bank is a negotiable instrument, and can be sold or transferred by one party to another merely by endorsement and delivery. Whoever holds the instrument until its maturity actually finances the underlying transaction, whether the holder is a seller or an investor or a bank.

Advantages of Discounting Bankers' Acceptances

A bankers' acceptance can be discounted when the holder sells it. The party which discounts such a bill must ensure that it is a trade bill of exchange and relating to current shipment of goods and that it is correctly drawn. The advantage of discounting such a bill is that (1) bankers' acceptances are considered safe and sound and (2) it is a self-liquidating transaction and the bank will make payment on maturity.

Method of Settlement: Negotiation

Meanings of Negotiation: There are several meanings of the word "negotiation". In general, the term is applied to arranging a contract or discussing the terms and conditions of a contract. The legal meaning of the word, particularly in connection with cheques and bills of exchange, is when such instruments are transferred from one person to another. Negotiation is a means of financing an outward collection or funding the payee of a cheque, bill of exchange or the beneficiary of documents under a letter of credit payable abroad.

We use the term in reference to the specific meaning of the beneficiary of documents under a letter of credit payable abroad. When a bank negotiates an outward collection, it is buying its customer's bills and/or documents drawn on an overseas buyer. It is a convenient method of providing the exporter with working capital. The bank in buying the bill and/or documents will look to the overseas buyer as a source of repayment. In the event of non-payment or delayed payment, the negotiating bank exercises the right of recourse to its customer, the drawer. Therefore, if payment does not arrive within a reasonable time, the negotiating bank will debit its customer's account with the amount advanced plus interest. The cost of negotiation is similar to loan interest when provided by a bank.

When a bank negotiates, it pays its customer straight away and sends the bill and/or documents to the issuing bank.

Under English law the negotiating bank may become a holder in due course of the bill of exchange when it negotiates, and as such it gets a right of action against the drawer in the event of default by the drawee.

Negotiation of a Letter of Credit: The issuing bank usually gives the following undertaking on the letter of credit: "We hereby engage with the drawers and/or bonafide holder that drafts drawn and negotiated in conformity with the terms and conditions of this credit will be duly honoured on presentation and that drafts accepted within the terms of this credit will be duly honoured at maturity".

Negotiation: Sight Bill of Exchange Drawn on Issuing Bank

The following action steps take place:

1. The seller/beneficiary sends the documents evidencing the shipment of the goods to the bank (advising bank/confirming bank) accompanied by a bill/ draft drawn on the issuing bank as specified in the credit (at sight or at a tenor).
2. The bank (AB/NB) examines the documents and, if the documents meet the requirements of a letter of credit, may negotiate, that is, make payment. This bank, if other than the issuing bank, then sends the documents to the issuing bank and claims reimbursement in accordance with the bank's agreed procedures.
3. Negotiation by advising bank is with recourse to the beneficiary and negotiation by confirming bank is without recourse to the beneficiary.

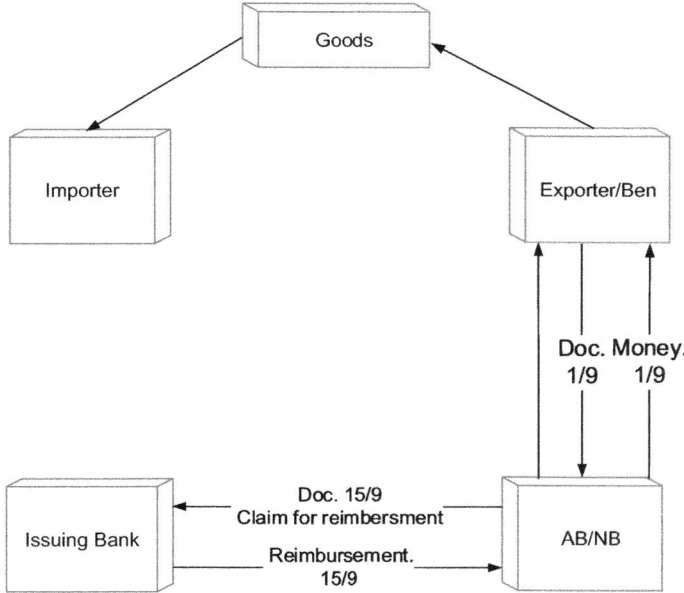

Fig. 8.5 Negotiation sight letter of credit: bill drawn on issuing bank

Negotiation

1. Requires at least three parties;
2. In case of sight negotiation, there may or may not be a bill of exchange;
3. If there is no bill of exchange pure documents drawn under a sight L/C may be negotiated;
4. If there is a bill, it must be a sight bill of exchange;
5. The act of negotiation by a bank, other than the issuing bank, is with recourse;

6. Negotiation by the confirming bank is without recourse.

SITUATION NO. 2
Negotiation under three-month usance L/C bill on issuing bank

Usance Negotiation

1. Requires at least three parties;
2. There must be a bill of exchange;
3. It must be a usance bill of exchange;
4. The act of negotiation by a bank who is not a confirming bank is with recourse;
5. Negotiation by the confirming bank is without recourse to the beneficiary.

Procedure for Advising/Confirming Bank

The seller may sometimes present documents that do not meet letter of credit requirements. In such a case, the bank may act in one of the following ways:

1. Return the documents to the beneficiary (seller) to have them amended for re-submission within the validity of the credit and within the period of time after date of issuance specified in the credit, or applicable under Article number 16 UCP 600);
2. Send the documents for collection;
3. Return the documents to the beneficiary for sending through his own bankers, if the confirming or advising bank is not the beneficiary's bank;

4. If authorised by the beneficiary, cable or send message by SWIFT or write to the issuing bank for authority to pay, accept or negotiate. The bank must provide a full list of irregularities to the issuing bank;
5. Call for an indemnity from the beneficiary or from a bank, as appropriate, that is, pay, accept or negotiate on their undertaking that any payment made will be refunded by the party giving the indemnity, together with interest and all charges, if the issuing bank refuses to provide reimbursement against documents that do not meet the credit requirement;

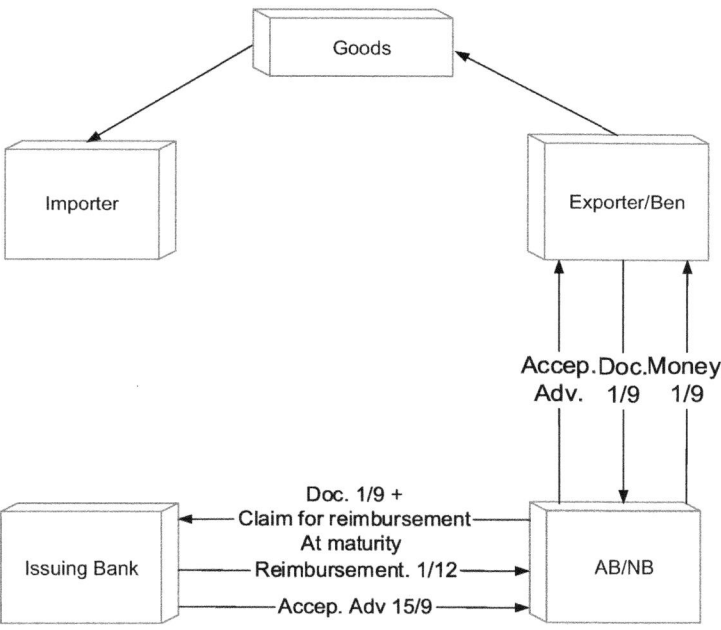

Fig. 8.6   Negotiation: three-month usance L/C bill on issuing bank

6. Based on practical experience, and with the agreement of the beneficiary, pay, accept or negotiate "under reserve", that is, retain the right of recourse against the beneficiary if the issuing bank refuses to provide reimbursement against documents that do not meet the credit requirement.

A suggested format for indemnity when undertaking negotiation under reserve is as following:

Negotiation of Documents under Reserve

(A suggested form of an indemnity bond in case of discrepancies)

The Manager   Date _____

Bank's name: _____

Address: _____

Dear Sir,

Re: _____

In consideration of your *negotiating/accepting/paying on presentation a Bill of Exchange (*delete as appropriate)

Dated _____ for _____ amount in words _____

Drawn under letter of credit No_____ dated _____ Issued by _____
Notwithstanding that the documents tendered therewith fail to conform with the requirements of the said letter of credit by reasons of (state here specifically the irregularities in documents tendered together with the relative precise requirements of the letter of credit)

_____

_____

_____

We undertake to indemnify you from and against all losses or damage, which you may incur or sustain because of the above irregularities in the documents. Provided that any claim upon us hereunder shall be made before

_____ (date).

Yours faithfully

Signature(s) _____

Negotiation of documents under reserve
(A suggested form of an indemnity bond in case discrepancies)

The Manager   Date _____

Bank's name: _____

Address: _____

_____

Dear Sir,

Letter of Credit No. _____issued by _____

In consideration of you paying us the sum of (amount in words and figures) _____

_____

under the above-mentioned credit we hereby indemnify you from all consequences
which may arise notwithstanding the following discrepancies in the documents.

_____

_____

_____

_____

_____

_____

_____   _____
Signed by the beneficiary   Signed by the beneficiary's

                                     bank or third party

Advising/Confirming Bank: Procedural Aspect

The seller may sometimes present documents that do not meet the credit requirements.

In such a case, the bank may act in one of the following ways:

- Return the documents to the beneficiary (seller) to have them amended for re-submission within the validity of the credit and within the period of time after date of issuance of bill of lading specified in the credit;

- Inform the advising/negotiating bank immediately of the irregularities;
- Contact the buyer/applicant and seek his instructions; or
- If the buyer/applicant is not ready to accept the documents, inform the advising/negotiating bank immediately of non-payment or non-acceptance of the documents.

9

Financial Load Variations: Eight Types of Letters of Credit

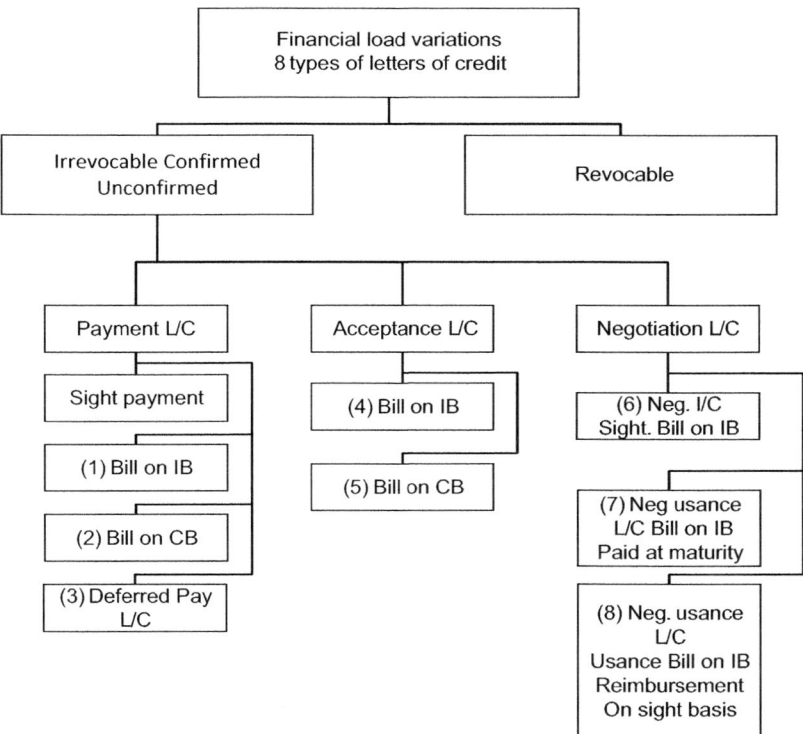

Fig. 9.1 Eight types of letters of credit: financial load variations

© The Author(s) 2019
T. Bhogal, A. Trivedi, *International Trade Finance*, Finance and Capital Markets Series,
https://doi.org/10.1007/978-3-030-24540-5_9

Payment Letter of Credit: Bill Drawn on Issuing Bank

Financial load is for transit time only and borne by the beneficiary

1. The importer applies for a letter of credit to his bank—IB.
2. The IB issues a sight letter of credit with bill on the IB and forwards it to an agent (advising bank [AB]) in the exporter's country with a request to forward it to the beneficiary.
3. The AB forwards a letter of credit to the beneficiary; if satisfied with the terms and conditions the beneficiary makes goods ready, despatches the goods and prepares the documents.
4. The beneficiary forwards the documents to the AB.
5. The AB forwards the documents to the IB.
6. The IB checks the documents and if satisfied debits the importer's account and remits funds to the AB for the credit of the beneficiary's account.
7. The IB forwards the documents to the importer.
8. The AB credits the beneficiary's account and forwards payment advice. Payment by the issuing bank is without recourse.

In this case the beneficiary finances the transaction for the whole period until he receives payment. The financial load is borne by the beneficiary.

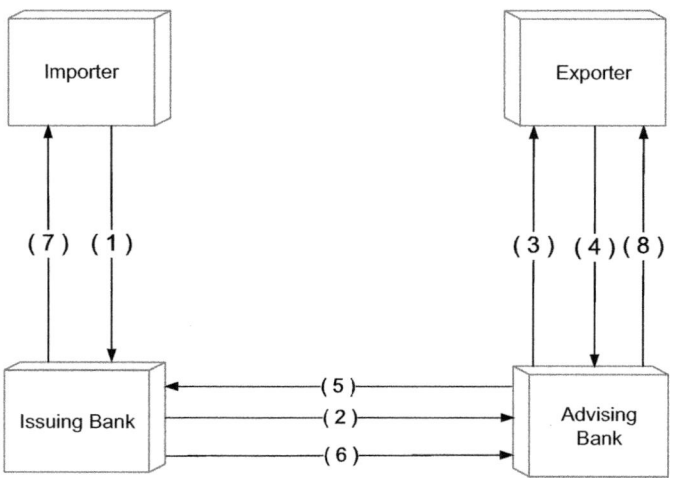

Fig. 9.2   Payment L/C: bill of issuing bank

Payment Letter of Credit: Bill Drawn on Confirming Bank

Financial load is for transit time only and borne by the confirming bank (CB)

1. The importer applies for a letter of credit to his bank—IB.
2. The IB issues a sight letter of credit with a bill on the confirming bank and requests to the AB to confirm the latter and forward it to the beneficiary.
3. The AB confirms the letter (now the AB has become the CB) and forwards the confirmed letter of credit to the beneficiary, and if satisfied with the terms and conditions, the beneficiary makes goods ready, despatches the goods and prepares the documents.
4. The beneficiary forwards the documents to the advising bank (AB/CB).
5. The CB checks the documents and if satisfied makes payment to the beneficiary.
6. The CB forwards the documents to the IB and claims reimbursement from the IB.
7. The IB checks the documents and if satisfied debits the importer's account and remits funds to the CB as reimbursement.
8. The IB forwards the documents to the importer.

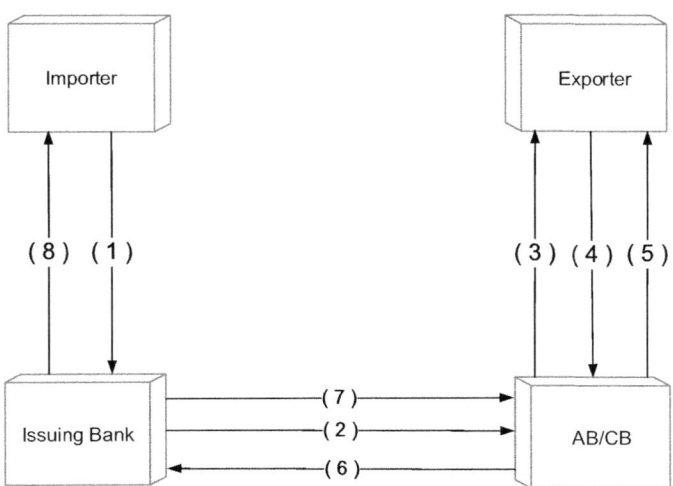

Fig. 9.3   Payment L/C: bill on confirming bank

In this case the CB finances the transaction for the whole period until funds are received from the IB. The financial load is borne by the confirming bank.

Deferred Payment Letter of Credit

Financial load is for transit time plus usance time and borne by the beneficiary.

1. The importer applies for a letter of credit to his bank—IB.
2. The IB issues a deferred payment letter of credit and forwards it to an agent (AB) in the exporter's country with a request to forward it to the beneficiary.
3. The AB forwards a letter of credit to the beneficiary, and if satisfied with the terms and conditions the beneficiary makes goods ready, despatches the goods and prepares the documents.
4. The beneficiary forwards the documents to the AB.
5. The AB forwards the documents to the IB.
6. The IB checks the documents and if satisfied forwards the documents to the importer.
7. The IB acknowledges the receipt of documents to the AB.
8. The AB informs the beneficiary of safe receipt of the document.
9. On the due date the IB debits the importer's account and remits funds to the AB for the credit of the beneficiary's account.
10. The AB credits the beneficiary's account and forwards payment advice.

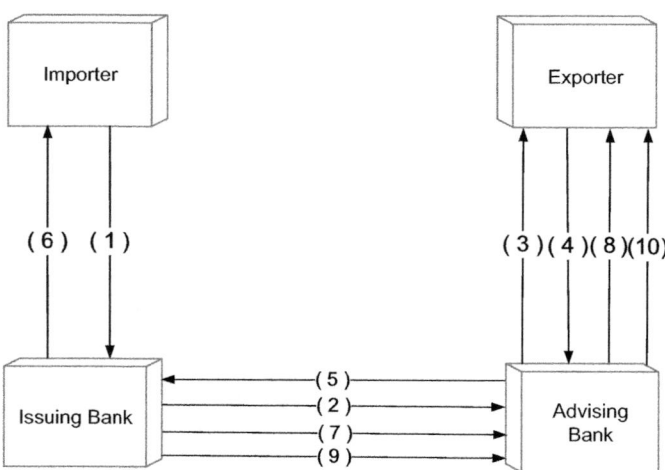

Fig. 9.4   Deferred payment L/C

In this case the beneficiary finances the transaction for the whole period until he receives payment. The financial load is borne by the beneficiary.

Acceptance Letter of Credit: Bill Drawn on Issuing Bank

Financial load is borne by the beneficiary for the whole period.

1. The importer applies for a letter of credit to his bank—IB.
2. The IB issues a usance letter of credit with a bill on the IB and forwards it to an agent AB in the exporter's country with a request to forward it to the beneficiary.
3. The AB forwards a letter of credit to the beneficiary, and if satisfied with the terms and conditions the beneficiary makes goods ready, despatches the goods and prepares the documents.
4. The beneficiary forwards the documents to the AB.
5. The AB checks documents and if satisfied forwards the documents to the IB.
6. The IB checks the documents, and if satisfied accepts the bill of exchange and forwards acceptance advice with maturity date to the AB.
7. The IB forwards the documents to the importer.
8. The AB forwards the acceptance advice with maturity date to the beneficiary.
9. On the due date the IB debits the importer's account and remits funds to the AB for the credit of the beneficiary's account.
10. The AB credits the beneficiary's account and forwards payment advice.

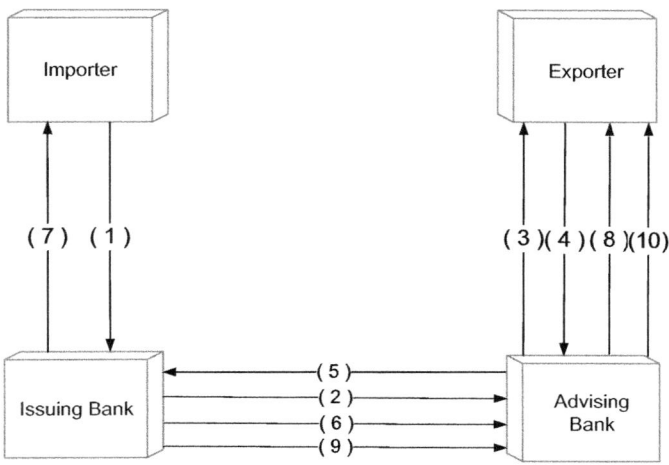

Fig. 9.5 Acceptance L/C: bill on issuing bank

In this case the beneficiary finances the transaction for the whole period until he receives payment. The financial load for the whole period is borne by the beneficiary.

Acceptance Letter of Credit: Bill Drawn on Confirming Bank

Financial load is borne by the beneficiary for the usance time and CB for the transit time period.

1. The importer applies for a letter of credit to his bank—IB.
2. The IB issues a usance letter of credit with a bill on the CB and forwards it to an agent (AB) bank in the exporter's country with a request to allow the bill to be drawn on him (CB) and confirm the letter of credit and forward it to the beneficiary.
3. The AB/CB confirms the letter of credit and forwards it to the beneficiary.
4. The beneficiary, if satisfied with the terms and conditions, makes goods ready, despatches the goods, prepares the documents and forwards the documents to the confirming bank (CB),
5. The CB checks documents and if satisfied accepts the bill and gives the accepted bill, if required, to the beneficiary.
6. The CB forwards the documents to IB with an advice of maturity date.
7. The IB checks documents and if satisfied forwards them to the importer.
8. On the due date the CB credits to the beneficiary's account and claims reimbursement from the IB.
9. On the due date the IB debits the importer's account and remits funds to the CB in reimbursement.

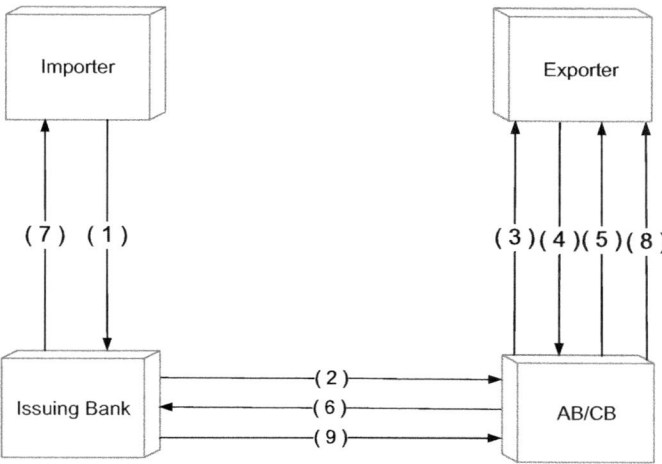

Fig. 9.6 Acceptance L/C: bill on confirming bank

In this case the beneficiary finances the transaction for the usance period and CB for the transit time until CB receives reimbursement. Both beneficiary and confirming bank share the financial load.

Sight Negotiation Letter of Credit: Bill Drawn on Issuing Bank

Financial load is borne by the negotiating bank.

1. The importer applies for a letter of credit to his bank—IB.
2. The IB issues a sight negotiation letter of credit with a bill on the IB and forwards it to an agent (AB) in the exporter's country with a request to forward it to the beneficiary.
3. The AB forwards the letter of credit to the beneficiary, and if satisfied with the terms and conditions the beneficiary makes goods ready, despatches the goods and prepares the documents.
4. The beneficiary forwards the documents to the AB, and requests to AB to negotiate documents, that is, to provide him with funds against the documents until receipt of money from the issuing bank.
5. The AB checks documents, if satisfied with documents and the beneficiary's business and so on. AB agrees to negotiate documents with a condition of recourse that if, negotiating bank (NB) does not receive funds from the

IB the beneficiary will give money back. This negotiation is with recourse as the NB is a third party and the bill is drawn on the IB.

6. The NB forwards the documents to the IB and claims reimbursement.
7. The IB checks the documents and if satisfied debits the importer's account and remits funds to the NB in reimbursement.
8. The IB forwards the documents to the importer.

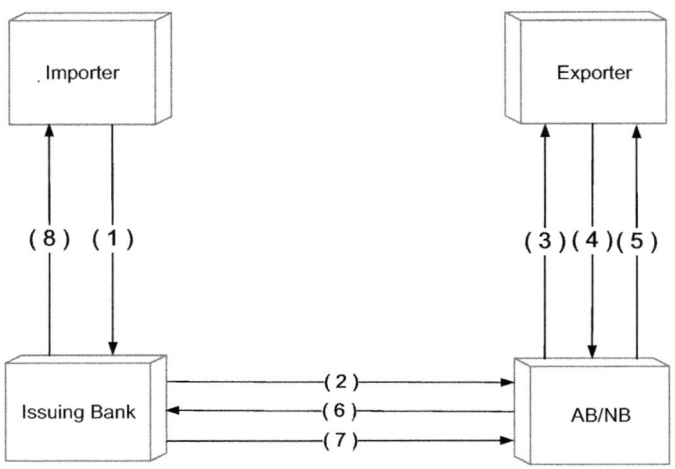

Fig. 9.7   Sight negotiation letter of credit: bill drawn on issuing bank

Usance Negotiation Letter of Credit: Bill Drawn on Issuing Bank Paid at Maturity

Financial load is borne by the negotiating bank.

1. The importer applies for a letter of credit to his bank—IB.
2. The IB issues a usance negotiations letter of credit with Bill on IB and forwards it to his AB in the exporter's country with a request to forward it to the beneficiary and authorising to negotiate documents till maturity of the bill.
3. The AB forwards the letter of credit to the beneficiary, and if satisfied with the terms and conditions the beneficiary makes goods ready, despatches the goods and prepares the documents.
4. The beneficiary forwards the documents to the AB and requests to provide funds until the IB pays against the letter of credit.

5. The AB checks the documents, and if satisfied negotiates the documents and credits the beneficiary's account. This act of negotiation is with recourse to the beneficiary.
6. The NB forwards the documents to the IB informing of having negotiated them under a letter of credit and claims reimbursement at maturity.
7. The IB checks the documents, and if satisfied accepts the bill of exchange and forwards the documents to the importer with an advice of maturity date for payment.
8. On the due date the IB debits the importer's account and remits funds to the negotiating bank.

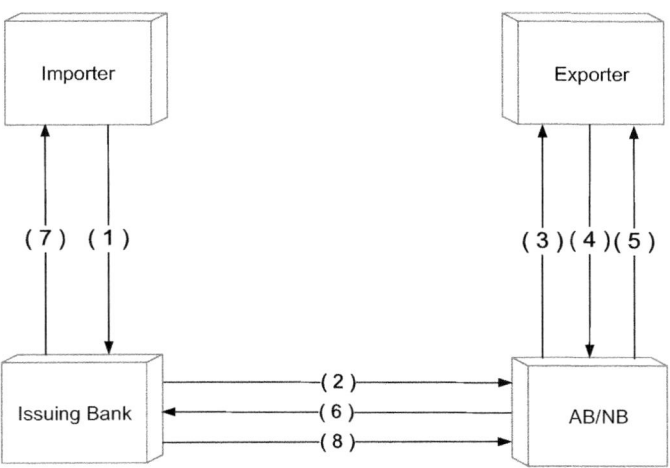

Fig. 9.8 Usance negotiation L/C: bill drawn on issuing bank paid at

In this case the negotiating bank finances the transaction for the whole period until payment is received. The financial load is borne by the negotiating bank.

Usance negotiation letter of credit—bill drawn on issuing bank reimbursement on sight basis.

Financial load is borne by the issuing bank.

1. The importer applies for a letter of credit to his bank—IB.
2. The IB issues a usance negotiation letter of credit with bill drawn on IB and forwards it to the AB authorising the AB to negotiate documents and claim reimbursement immediately.

3. The AB forwards the letter of credit to the beneficiary, and if satisfied with the terms and conditions the beneficiary makes goods ready, despatches the goods and prepares the documents.
4. The beneficiary forwards the documents to the AB and requests to provide funds until the IB pays against a letter of credit.
5. The AB checks the documents and if satisfied negotiates documents and credits the beneficiary's account. AB is now NB, negotiating bank.
6. The NB forwards the documents to IB and claims reimbursement immediately.
7. The IB checks the documents and if satisfied provides reimbursement to the NB by debiting its assets account.
8. The IB forwards the documents to the importer.
9. On the maturity date, the IB debits the importer's account and credits its assets account.

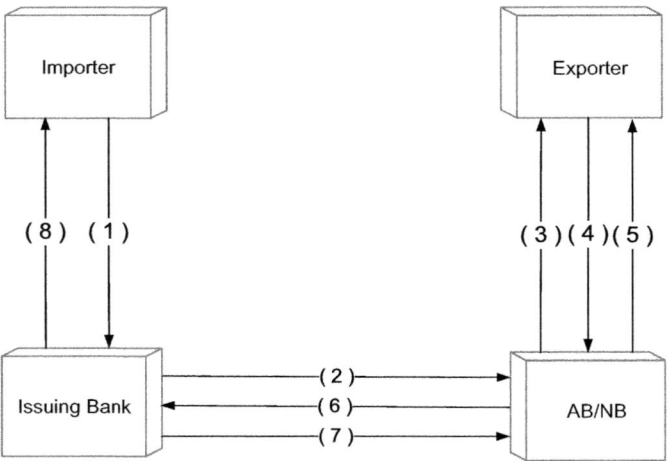

Fig. 9.9 Usance negotiation L/C: bill on issuing bank reimbursement on sight basis

In this case the beneficiary gets finances immediately and the IB finances the transaction for the whole period until it receives payment from the importer. The financial load is borne by the issuing bank.

10

INCOTERMS 2010

Background

INCOTERMS stands for International Commercial Terms for the use of buyers and sellers of goods. When a contract is made between buyer and seller or importer and exporter the terms of sale and purchase for delivery of goods must be clarified to avoid any dispute at a later stage. Very often this is not done in the initial stage and oversight or lack of knowledge of the INCOTERMS on the part of the parties involved can cause difficulty to them and also their bankers.

These terms were established by the International Chamber of Commerce (ICC), after discussions with various interested parties; the value of the INCOTERMS is universally recognised. The utility and practical nature of these terms are clearly established and enable distribution of cost through application of INCOTERMS.

To avoid or minimise disputes and difficulties in trade the ICC introduced these rules in 1933. These rules have been revised periodically, keeping in mind the developments taking place from time to time and the revisions in the systems and procedures to handle international trade. They were revised in 1999 and became effective from 1 January 2000, were revised in 2009 and came into force in 2010.

We understand that new INCOTERMS are being drafted by (Drafting Group) a Committee of Experts the International Chamber of Commerce (ICC) as the body that publishes them since 1930. The new INCOTERMS 2020 are expected to appear in the last quarter of 2019, simultaneously with

© The Author(s) 2019
T. Bhogal, A. Trivedi, *International Trade Finance*, Finance and Capital Markets Series,
https://doi.org/10.1007/978-3-030-24540-5_10

the centenary of International Chamber of Commerce and will enter into force on 1 January 2020.

A contract comes into being when two parties reach an agreement on a transaction. It is fairly universal principle that when one party accepts all the terms offered by the other party a valid contract is established. In principle these two parties are free to decide between themselves how the contract will be fulfilled, what price will be charged, how and when the payment will be effected, who will carry out which functions, who will bear which costs of delivery, who will support which risks and so on.

At times there are governments of countries who have certain regulations restricting international trade, which are required to be observed before entering into such transaction.

Purpose

The purpose is to provide a set of international rules for the interpretation of the most commonly used trade terms in local and foreign trade to:

- avoid misunderstanding the meaning of certain terms, disputes and litigation;
- to adapt the terms to the increasing use of electronic data interchange (EDI);
- accommodate the changes in the use of technology in transportation for example

  - Unitisation of cargo;
  - Use of containers;
  - Multi-modal transport;
  - Roll-on/roll-off traffic with road vehicles;
  - Railway wagons in "short-sea" marine transport.

In every international trade transaction there are certain questions must be asked to the parties concerned. Such questions/assurance need to be satisfied before entering into a sale contract.

1. Who will arrange to pay for the carriage of goods from one point to another?
2. Who will bear the risk if these operations cannot be carried out?
3. Who will bear the risk of loss of or damage to the goods in transit?

Structure of INCOTERMS

For ease of understanding, the terms are grouped in four basically different categories: namely starting with the term whereby the seller only makes the goods available to the buyer at the seller's own premises (the "E"—ex-works), followed by the second group whereby the seller is called upon to deliver the goods to a carrier appointed by the buyer (the "F" terms—FCA, FAS and FOB); continuing with "C" terms where the seller has to contract for the carriage, but without assuming the risk of loss or damage to the goods or additional costs due to events occurring after shipment and dispatch (CFR, CIF, CPT and CIP); and, finally, the "D" terms destination (DAT, DAP and DDP).

The right and obligations of the parties to the contract of sale with respect to the delivery of goods can be explained with the help of INCOTERMS.

INCOTERMS for Any Mode or Modes of Transport

These terms include

a. Ex works (EXW) (at named place of delivery to first carrier)

This term may be used for any Mode or Modes of Transport.
The seller delivers the goods when he places the goods at the disposal of the
    buyer at the seller's named place of delivery, that is, works, factory, ware-
    house, and so on. In this case the seller does not need to the goods on any
    collecting vehicle.

Obligations of the seller:

- To give notice to the buyer that the goods are available for collection at the named place of delivery;
- To provide the goods suitably packed in export quality packaging, unless it is the norm for the goods involved to be delivered unpacked;
- The seller must pay for the costs of checking operations (such as quality, quantity and weight measuring) that are necessary for the delivery of the goods in accordance with the sale agreement;
- Provide the required documents in paper format or an equivalent electronic record or procedure, if agreed between the parties or as customary;
- To provide the buyer at the buyer's request and expense, any assistance in obtaining any export licence or other authorisations required for the export of the goods;

- The seller has no obligations to provide transport of the goods;
- The seller has no obligations to provide insurance to cover the risks of loss or damage to the goods;
- Once the goods have been placed at the disposal of the buyer all responsibilities of the seller come to an end.

Documents provided by the seller:

- The seller provides a commercial invoice or equivalent electronic file to the buyer or
- Any other necessary documents at additional cost to the buyer.

Obligations of the buyer:

- The buyer must provide the seller with appropriate evidence of having taken delivery of the goods.
- The buyer must receive the delivery of the goods and documents from seller's place of business or warehouse as agreed in the sale contract.
- Make payment as agreed.
- Make all arrangements at own costs and expense to transport goods to his own premises.
- It is in the buyer's interests to arrange appropriate insurance to cover the risk of loss or damage to the goods during this journey.
- Obtain relevant export and/or import licences.
- Pay for the export and import duties, if required.
- Complete any customs formalities and payments for the export of the goods.
- The buyer is responsible for the costs of any mandatory pre-shipment inspection, including inspection mandated by the authorities of the country of export.

b. Free carrier (FCA) (at named place)

This term may be used for any Mode or Modes of Transport.
"Free Carrier means the seller delivers the goods to the carrier or another person nominated by the buyer at the seller's premises or another named place.

Obligations of the seller:

- Goods will be suitably packed in export quality packaging, unless it is the norm for the goods involved to be delivered unpacked.

- The seller delivers the goods by his means of transport to the 1st carrier at the place named by the buyer on the agreed date or within the agreed period.
- If the goods were to have been made available at the seller's premises, delivery would not be complete until the goods had been loaded onto the truck/lorry or other means of transport of the carrier named by the buyer.
- Complete export and customs requirements at his own expense.
- Obtain any export licence, if required, at his own expense.
- Make payment of any export duties and taxes.
- The delivery will be completed when the goods have been placed at the disposal of the carrier nominated by the buyer.
- Give the buyer sufficient notice that the goods have been delivered to the named carrier within the agreed time.

Documents provided by the seller:

- Commercial invoice or its equivalent electronic file message;
- Advise delivery of the goods to the named carrier at the place named by the buyer, that is, proof of delivery of goods to the transporter or multimodal transport document.

Obligations of the buyer:

- Receive documents.
- Make payment as agreed.
- Receive goods when delivered.
- Make all arrangements at own costs to transport goods from the place or port of departure.
- Arrange appropriate insurance to cover the loss or damage to the goods from the place of departure.
- Obtain import licence.
- Pay any customs clearance charges and duties.
- Arrange transport of goods to warehouse.

c. Carriage Paid To (CPT) (carriage paid to a named place)

This term may be used for any mode or modes of transport and may also be used where more than one mode of transport is employed.

Obligations of the seller:

- Goods will be suitably packed in export quality packaging, unless it is the norm for the goods involved to be delivered unpacked.
- Goods must be delivered to the carrier on the date or within the agreed period.
- The seller makes arrangement for transportation of the goods and pays freight for the carriage to the named place for the delivery of goods.
- The risk of loss or damage to the goods, as well as any additional costs due to events occurring after the time the goods have been delivered into the custody of the carrier, is transferred from the seller to the buyer.
- "Carrier" means any person who, in a contract of carriage, undertakes to perform or to procure the performance of carriage by rail, road, sea, inland waterway or by a combination of such modes.
- If subsequent carriers are used for the carriage to the agreed destination, the risk passes from the seller to the buyer when the goods have been delivered to the first carrier.
- The CPT term requires the seller to clear the goods for export.
- The seller to obtain export licence, if required.
- The seller clears the goods for export at his own costs and completes other formalities that may be required.
- The seller makes arrangements for insurance to cover risks of loss or damage to the goods.
- The seller must notify the buyer that the goods have delivered to the carrier as agreed.

Documents provided by the seller:

- Commercial invoice
- Transport document freight paid or to pay (as agreed between parties)
- Certificate(s) of quality and quantity, as agreed.

Obligation of the buyer:

- Receive documents.
- Make payment, as agreed.
- Arrange and pay freight of goods, if agreed not to be arranged by the seller.
- Arrange cargo insurance from the point when the goods are delivered into the custody of the first carrier.
- Receive goods.
- Obtain import licence.

- Pay for custom duties and taxes.
- Transportation of goods from the named place to final destination, that is, to the warehouse.

d. Carriage and Insurance Paid (CIP) (named place)

This term may be used for any mode or modes of transport and may also be used where more than one mode of transport is employed.

Obligations of the seller:

- Goods will be suitably packed in export quality packaging, unless it is the norm for the goods involved to be delivered unpacked.
- The seller has the same obligation as under CPT but with the addition that he has to arrange insurance of the goods against the risk of loss or damage to the goods during the carriage and pays the insurance premium.

Documents provided by the seller:

- Commercial invoice;
- Transport document (Clean Bill of Lading) freight paid;
- Cargo insurance policy or certificate, as agreed;
- Quality and quantity certificate(s), if required.

Obligations of the buyer:

- To arrange import licence;
- To clear goods from customs;
- To pay import duties;
- To arrange transportation from the place or port of destination to importer's premises.

e. Delivered at Terminal (DAT) (at named terminal)

This term may be used for any mode or modes of transport. It is not limited to maritime transport. The new changes should be more useful for container traffic.

Obligations of the seller:

- To pack goods in suitably export quality packaging, unless it is the normal practice for the goods involved to be delivered unpacked;
- To notify the buyer in order to allow the buyer to make arrangements to take delivery of the goods;
- To obtain necessary quality and quantity certificate(s), if mandatory for export purposes;
- To obtain export licence at his own risk and expense;
- To clear the goods from customs and pay necessary export duties and charges;
- To arrange carriage of the goods at his own risk and expense to the named terminal;
- The seller fulfils his obligation to deliver when he puts the goods at the disposal of the buyer at the named container port or terminal to take place;
- The goods are unloaded from the arriving means of transportation and placed at the disposal of the buyer at the named terminal;
- The seller has to bear all risks and costs and other charges for delivering the goods at the named terminal or port of destination;
- To provide additional documents, if required by the buyer, at the buyer's risk and additional cost.

Documents provided by seller:

- Commercial invoice;
- Transport document

Obligations of the buyer:

- Receive documents;
- Make payment, as agreed;
- Arrange import licence;
- Receive goods;
- Arrange carriage of the goods to the place of destination;
- Bear the cost of loading and unloading at the destination or his warehouse.

f. Delivered at Place (DAP) (at named place)

This term may be used for any Mode or Modes of Transport. DAP can be used where more than one mode of transport is employed.

DAP means the seller delivers when the seller places the goods at the disposal of the buyer at the named place of destination. The seller bears all risks of loss or damage involved in bringing the goods to the named place.

Obligations of the seller:

- Goods will be suitably packed in export quality packaging, unless it is the norm for the goods involved to be delivered unpacked.
- Under this term the seller fulfils his obligation to deliver when the goods have been delivered at the named place and puts the goods at the disposal of the buyer on the vehicle/container ready for unloading.
- The term DAP may be used for any "Place named by the buyer" including that of the country of exporter. Therefore, it is of vital importance that the place in question must be clearly defined by naming the place and the INCOTERM in the sale contract.

Documents provided by the seller:

- Commercial invoice
- Transport document freight paid up to the named place.

Obligations of the buyer:

- Received document;
- Make payment, as agreed;
- Obtain import licence;
- Receive goods at the place as agreed in the sale contract;
- Arrange cargo insurance and bear the cost of unloading;
- Pay customs, import duties and taxes and so on;
- Pay for re-loading and unloading costs at the place of destination.

g. Delivered Duty Paid (DDP)

This term may be used for any mode or modes of transport and may also be used where more than one mode of transport is employed. This means the seller delivers the goods when the goods have been placed at the disposal of the buyer, cleared for import on arriving ready for unloading at the named place of destination.

Obligations of the seller:

- Goods will be suitably packed in export quality packaging, unless it is the norm for the goods involved to be delivered unpacked.
- To obtain at his own risk and expense export and import licences as required or agreed.
- To obtain at his own risk and expense any mandatory quality or quantity certificates.
- The seller fulfils his obligation to deliver when the goods have been made available at the named palace in the country of importation.
- Deliver the goods by placing them at the disposal of the buyer on arriving means of transportation ready for unloading at the agreed place on the agreed date or within the agreed period.
- Give notice to the buyer to enable him to take delivery of the goods.
- The seller has to bear the risk of loss or damage to the goods and all costs, including export and import duties, taxes and other charges of delivering the goods cleared for importation.
- The EX Works term represents the minimum obligations of the seller.
- DDP represents the maximum obligations of the seller and minimum obligations of the buyer except receiving goods in his warehouse.
- This term should not be used if the seller is unable directly or indirectly to obtain the import licence.
- If the parties wish to exclude from the seller's obligation some of the costs payable upon importation of the goods (such as value added tax (VAT)), this should be made clear by adding words to this effect: "Delivered duty paid, VAT unpaid (…named place of destination)".
- If the parties wish the buyer to bear all risks and costs of import clearance, the DAP term should be used.

Documents provided by the seller:

- Commercial invoice and any other evidence in conformity with the sale contract equivalent electronic record or procedure if agreed between the parties or customary.

Obligations of the buyer:

- Make payment as agreed;
- Receive documents;
- Receive goods.

INCOTERMS for Sea and Inland Waterway Transport Only

These terms include

a. Free Alongside Ship (FAS) (named port of shipment)

This term is to be used for Sea and Inland Waterway Transport only.

Obligations of the seller:

- Goods will be suitably packed in export quality packaging, unless it is the norm for the goods involved to be delivered unpacked.
- Obtain at his own risk and expense export licence.
- Deliver the goods alongside the vessel on the quay or in lighters at the named port of shipment.
- If the goods are in containers, it is for the seller to hand the goods over to the carrier at a terminal and not alongside the vessel. In such case the term FAS should not be used but instead use the more appropriate term FCA.
- The seller bears the cost of transportation of the goods from his warehouse or factory to the port of shipment for loading on the ship.
- Give sufficient notice to the buyer that the goods have been delivered alongside the vessel.
- Goods must be delivered on the agreed date or within the time agreed.

Documents provided by the seller:

- Commercial invoice;
- Clean Bill of lading "Received for shipment".

Obligations of the buyer:

- The buyer has to bear all costs loading, unloading, freight charges.
- The buyer has to arrange insurance to cover risk of loss or damage to the goods from the moment the goods have been placed on the quay alongside the vessel.
- To clear the goods for export, where applicable, and pay duties and charges.
- To clear the goods at the port of destination and pay duties and taxes.

Note: The FAS term requires the buyer to clear the goods for export. This term should not be used when the importer cannot carry out directly or indirectly the export formalities. This term can only be used for sea or inland waterway transport only.

b. Free On Board (F.O.B) (named port of shipment)

This term may be used for Sea and Inland Waterway Transport only.

Obligations of the seller:

- To pack the goods in suitably export quality packaging, unless it is the norm for the goods involved to be delivered unpacked;
- To deliver when the goods have passed over the ship's rail at the named port of shipment;
- To clear the goods for export;
- To obtain export licence at his own costs;
- To pay export duties and taxes;
- To pay cost of loading goods on the vessel;
- To give sufficient notice to the buyer that the goods have been shipped on the agreed date or within the time agreed.

Documents provided by the seller:

- Commercial invoice;
- Clean Bill of Lading "On Board" Freight to pay;
- Certificates of quality and quantity, if agreed.

Obligation of the buyer:

- Receive documents;
- Make payment for the goods, as agreed;
- Receive goods;
- Arrange and pay to cover the risk of loss of or damage to the goods from the point the goods are loaded on the vessel;
- Arrange for payment of freight, unloading costs and other duties, taxes and so on at the port of destination;
- Clear the goods from the port of destination.

c. Cost and Freight (CFR) (named port of destination)

This term may be used for Sea and Inland Waterway Transport only.

Obligations of the seller:

- Goods will be suitably packed in export quality packaging, unless it is the norm for the goods involved to be delivered unpacked.
- The seller fulfils his obligation when he has delivered the good on board the ship.
- The seller must pay the costs of freight necessary to take the goods to the named port of destination.
- The seller DOES NOT cover the risk of loss or damage to the goods, as well as any additional costs due to events occurring after the time the goods have been delivered on board the vessel. This risk is transferred from the seller to the buyer when the goods have passed the ship's rail in the port of shipment.
- The seller is required to clear the goods for export.
- The seller is required to pay for export licence.
- The seller is required to pay for export duties and taxes.
- This term can only be used for sea and inland waterway transport. When the ship's rail serves no practical purpose, such as in the case of roll-on/roll-off or container traffic, the CPT term is more appropriate to use.

Documents provided by the seller:

- Commercial invoice;
- Clean "On Board" Bill of Lading "Freight paid";
- Quality and Quantity Certificate(s), if agreed.

Obligations of the buyer:

- To receive documents;
- To make payment, as agreed;
- To arrange and pay for the insurance of the goods;
- To pay unloading costs;
- To arrange and pay for import licence and import duties, taxes;
- To clear the goods from the port of destination;
- To arrange and pay for transportation of goods from port of destination to the buyer's premises including unloading costs.

d. Cost, Insurance and Freight (CIF) (named port of destination)

This term may be used for Sea and Inland Waterway Transport only

Obligations of the seller:

- To pack the goods in suitably export quality packaging, unless it is the norm for the goods involved to be delivered unpacked.
- The seller has the same obligation as under CFR but
- The seller's additional obligation is to procure marine insurance against the buyer's risk of loss or damage to the goods during the carriage.
- The seller contracts for insurance and pays the insurance premium.
- The CIF term requires the seller to clear the goods for export.

Documents provided by the seller:

- Commercial invoice;
- Quality and Quantity Certificates, if required;
- Marine insurance policy;
- Clean Bill of Lading "On Board" freight paid.

Obligations of the buyer:

- To receive documents;
- To make payment for the goods, as agreed;
- To receive goods;
- Arrange import licence;
- Pay import duties and taxes;
- To clear goods through customs;
- To arrange and pay transportation costs from port of destination to importer's premises.

11

Documents in Foreign Trade

Genesis and their Significance

A letter of credit is an undertaking between the issuing bank and the beneficiary to pay, accept bill(s) of exchange and make payment on maturity provided the beneficiary fulfils the requirement under a credit. The applicant requests the bank to issue a letter of credit to ensure that he receives the right quality and quantity of goods from the supplier. Banks do not deal in goods but only with documents. The issuing bank requires the beneficiary to present the documents evidencing the quality and quantity of the goods dispatched by him to meet the requirement of a letter of credit. Therefore, both the applicant and the issuing bank should be clear about the type of documents required and the significance of each document.

Extreme care must be taken in listing documents under a letter of credit transaction. The applicant must give precise instructions to the issuing bank. Some specific documents are a requirement when dealing with particular countries, and import or export licences may be required. There are articles of the UCP 600, which refer to different types of documents. It is important that the documents required under a letter of credit mechanism satisfy the requirements under UCP 600.

Banks require each document in original unless more copies are asked for under the credit. Under article 21(b)(c)(d) of UCP 600 banks accept as original(s) document(s) produced by reprographic, automated or computerised systems, and carbon copies, provided these are marked original and signed.

The applicant should specifically indicate the document(s) required and by whom these documents should be issued, and with required details or contents

© The Author(s) 2019
T. Bhogal, A. Trivedi, *International Trade Finance*, Finance and Capital Markets Series,
https://doi.org/10.1007/978-3-030-24540-5_11

thereof. Otherwise banks will accept them as presented, provided they are in compliance with the terms and conditions of a letter of credit and are not issued by the beneficiary himself.

The details of most common documents are given hereunder.

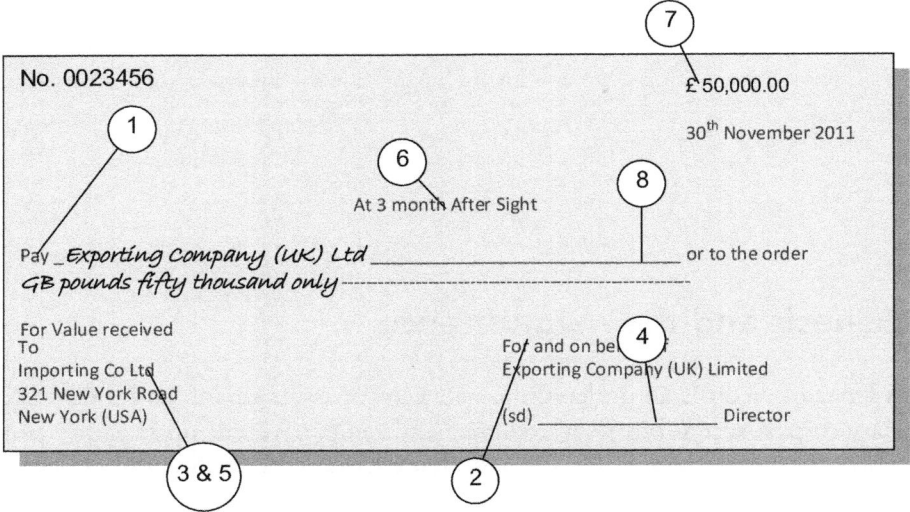

Fig. 11.1 Specimen of bill of exchange

Bill of Exchange

The requirements of a bill of exchange are:

1. Be written in ink or printed to prevent alteration;
2. Drawn by the seller/beneficiary;
3. Drawn on the drawee (IB in case of L/C);
4. Must be signed by the drawer/beneficiary;
5. Requiring the person to whom it is addressed, drawee (on signature becomes the acceptor), to pay;
6. On demand or at a fixed or determinable future time;
7. A sum certain in money;
8. To the payee, a specified person or to his order.

For ease of reference the phrases are numbered to correspond to the parts of the bill of exchange shown above. All of the information above must be shown on every bill of exchange.

A documentary letter of credit will stipulate when payment is to be made and the bill of exchange must be drawn accordingly. In the diagram, the bill of exchange calls for payment three months after sight (this is known as a tenor bill). If a bill of exchange is drawn at sight, that is, without writing a period, it is called a "sight" bill, which requires immediate payment by the drawee on presentation of the bill of exchange.

The bill of exchange must be worded to conform exactly to the terms of the credit and the sum specified must not exceed the amount of the credit. In addition, the capacity of all signatories must be stated if the forms "for", "per" or "pro" are used.

Unless a documentary letter of credit stipulates that bills of exchange are required in duplicate, a single (sola) bill of exchange will be acceptable. Bill of exchange forms may be purchased from printers or stationers but bills of exchange may also be drawn on a company's notepaper or even a blank sheet of paper.

When a bill of exchange is being presented for payment it needs to be properly endorsed by the payee, if required.

Invoice

A commercial invoice must be issued by the beneficiary of a letter of credit addressed to the applicant/importer of the goods. An invoice gives details of the goods, which are the basis of the transaction between the exporter and the importer. It is usually completed on the exporter's own headed invoice form, and several copies are normally required for use by Customs and Excise authorities overseas (UCP 600 Article 18(a)).

The invoice must carry a description of the goods, stating prices and terms exactly as specified in the credit, as well as shipping marks. The following details are usually required and the inclusion of other information, for example export and/or import licence numbers, may also be necessary, if required under a letter of credit. Letter of credit usually requires three or more copies of the invoice.

1. Beneficiary's name and address (usually exporter/seller);
2. Accreditor's name and address (usually importer/buyer);
3. Place and date of issue;
4. Shipment terms;
5. Marks and numbers on packages;
6. Number and type of packages;

7. Description of the goods;
8. Cost of freight and insurance (if specifically requested);
9. The quantity of goods;
10. Total amount payable;
11. Signature of the exporter, if required under L/C.

Pro-Forma Invoice

This is a price quotation by the seller/exporter to a potential buyer/importer. This document gives the details of goods and other terms and conditions of sale of the goods. The pro-forma invoice can serve various purposes for the buyer/importer, that is, to apply for import licence, and can be used to tender for an export contract and so on. If the buyer/importer accepts the quotation, he will place a firm order and it will be considered as a "sale contract". A commercial invoice will be sent later.

Bill of Lading

DEFINITION: A bill of lading is a memorandum of the contract of carriage of goods signed by or on behalf of the master of a ship, certifying that goods have been received on board in good order for transportation and delivery as specified in the document.

It is a receipt given by the shipping company upon shipment of the goods and a document of title to the goods, enabling the consignee to transfer the title by endorsement and delivery. As such, it will be required by the importer to clear the goods at the port of destination. It is a quasi-negotiable document because unlike a bill of exchange, the transferee takes it subject to equities. (The transferee will not have better title than the transferor.)

In the US, the Bill of Lading Act 1916 makes a bill of lading a fully negotiable instrument if issued in the country.

A documentary letter of credit will specify what type of bill of lading is required. It will also indicate what additional information must be shown on the bill of lading.

A bill of lading normally embodies the following:

1. The name of the shipping company;
2. The name of the shipper (usually the exporter);

3. The name and address of the importer (consignee) or ORDER;
4. The name and address of the notify party (the person to be notified on arrival of the shipment, usually the importer);
5. The name of the carrying vessel;
6. The names of the ports of shipment and discharge;
7. The shipping marks and numbers identifying the goods;
8. A brief description of the goods (possibly including weights and dimensions);
9. The number of packages;
10. Whether freight is payable or has been paid;
11. The number of originals in the set;
12. The signature of the ship's master or his agent;
13. The date on which the goods were received for shipment and/or loaded on the vessel (this must not be later than the shipment date indicated in the credit);
14. The signature of the exporter (or his agent) and his designation if applicable.

Bills of lading are usually made out and signed in sets of two or three original copies known as negotiable copies, any one of which can give title to the goods. The number of copies in a set is shown on each copy. There may also be non-negotiable (unsigned) copies, which are not documents of title and are normally used for record purposes. The credit will indicate how the various copies of the bill of lading are to be distributed.

The reverse of the bill of lading bears the terms and conditions of the contract of carriage. The clauses on most bills of lading will be similar in effect if not in wording. A bill of lading should be "clean", that is, contain no superimposed clause recording a defective condition of the goods or their packing.

The goods can be consigned to ORDER, which means the importer can authorise someone to collect the goods on his behalf. In this case, the exporter will endorse on the reverse of the bill of lading. If the importer (consignee) is named, the goods will only be released to him, unless the importer transfers his rights by endorsement. (The bill of lading must, however, provide for this.)

Types of Bills of Lading

A "Shipped" or "Shipped on Board" bill of lading indicates that the goods have been received on board ship and will bear a clause to that effect.

A "Received for Shipment" bill of lading merely signifies that the ship owner has the goods in his custody but they have not yet been placed on board the vessel. It can be marked "Shipped on Board" (or similar) by the shipping company once the goods have been received on the vessel. This is known as "on board" notation and should be dated and signed or initialled by the shipping company.

Through Bill of Lading: If ocean transport forms only part of the complete journey and overland transport has to be used as well, a "Through" bill of lading can be issued to cover all stages of the journey.

Clean Bill of Lading: A clean bill of lading is one which bears no superimposed clause or a notation that expressly indicates the defective condition of the goods or the packaging. The bill of lading indicates that the carrier has received the goods in apparent good order and condition.

Claused/Foul or Dirty/Unclean Bill of Lading: This is a bill of lading which contains a superimposed clause expressly declaring that the goods or packaging is defective. In this case the ship owners can refuse to accept liability to deliver the goods in good order and condition. This type of bill of lading is not acceptable to banks.

"Transhipment" Bill of Lading: This is issued if the goods have to be off-loaded and re-loaded on to a second ship because there is no vessel available to complete the full journey to the port of destination. The transhipment port will be shown on the bill of lading.

Container Bill of Lading: Containers play an important role in international business and "Container" bills of lading may be issued to cover goods from port to port or from inland point of departure to inland point of destination. It indicates that the goods are carried in a container as one cargo.

Stale Bill of Lading: If the original bill of lading reaches the consignee after the arrival of the vessel at the destination, it is known as a "stale bill of lading". The consignee is not able to get the goods cleared from the port within the time allowed by the port authorities. In such cases the consignee has to obtain a bond, known as "Shipping Guarantee", from his bank to get delivery of the goods from the port authorities.

Charter Party Bill of Lading: A charter party bill of lading is by a charter party who has hired a ship/vessel or full or part of the space in the ship/vessel for his use. The charter party bills of lading are issued subject to the terms and conditions as agreed by the hirer and the ship owners. The charter party bills of lading are not acceptable to banks unless authorised under a letter of credit, because the ship owner may refuse to deliver the goods if the charter party does not pay hire charges.

House Bill of Lading: This is issued by cargo consolidators who collect cargo from various shippers and give it to the shipping company in their own name. By combining the shipment from various parties the consolidators are able to obtain bulk discount, which is better than the rates an individual shipper has to pay.

The shipping company issues one master bill of lading on the basis of cargo and the consolidator issues their own house bill of lading. The master bill of lading is sent to the cargo consolidator(s) and to their agents at the port of discharge to take the delivery of the entire cargo. The consignee holding the house bill of lading takes the delivery of the goods from the agent on presentation of the document.

Short Bill of Lading: This is also known as "Short Form of Bill of Lading". It is a bill of lading which does not bear the full details of the terms and conditions of carriage of goods that are printed on a full bill of lading.

Air Waybill

An air waybill is a receipt for goods for despatch by air. It takes the place of the bill of lading but is not a document of title, and the importer can take possession of the goods without it. Air waybills (or "air consignment notes" as they are also known) are issued in a minimum of three and frequently in sets of ten or more.

The credit may ask for certain specific information or instructions to be shown in the air waybill but the following details are those normally given.

- The names and addresses of the exporter, importer and carrier (airline);
- The names of the airports of departure and destination together with details of any special route;
- The date of the flight;
- The declared value for customs purposes;
- The number of packages with marks, weights, quantity and dimensions;
- The freight charge per unit of weight/volume;
- A description of the goods;
- Whether freight charge has been prepaid or will be paid at destination;
- The signature of the exporter (or his agent);
- The place and date of issue;
- The signature of the issuing carrier (or his agent).

The air waybill should also bear the carrier's stamp indicating the flight number and departure date on which the goods were sent.

Certificate of Origin

This is a signed declaration stating the country of origin of the goods. This certificate may be required for various purposes, that is, by the customs and excise authority of certain countries for the purpose of assessing import duty. In some cases this certificate may be incorporated into the commercial invoice. Generally it has to be authenticated by a Chamber of Commerce of the exporter's country or as required by the letter of credit. A certificate of origin is a signed statement providing evidence of the origin of the goods. It is issued in a mandatory form and manner in most countries, although prepared by the exporter or his agent. It is usually certified by an independent official organisation, for example a Chamber of Commerce, and contains details of shipment to which it relates:

- Origin of the goods;
- The signature and seal or stamp of the certifying body;
- If the credit calls for a "certificate of origin" without giving further details, banks will accept the document tendered even if issued by the beneficiary (seller), provided it is not inconsistent with the other documents.

Certificate of Inspection

A certificate of inspection is issued by an approved inspecting organisation after inspection or examination of the goods. It is used to ensure that the goods to be shipped are of the required standard and quality. Terms such as "first class", "well known", "qualified" and "independent" should not be used to describe the issuer. If used, the banks will accept the relative documents as presented.

Banks will accept such documents as presented where the credit does not stipulate by whom such documents are to be issued and their wording or data content.

Packing List

A packing list gives the details of the goods, that is, item and number in a package. It is often required by the customs authorities to facilitate spot checks or thorough investigation. It does not necessarily give details of the cost or price of the goods.

Post Parcel/Courier Receipt

A post parcel receipt is issued by the post office for goods sent by parcel post—it acts both as a receipt and as proof of despatch. It is not a document of title. Goods sent by post should be consigned to the party specified in the documentary credit.

A courier receipt is an acknowledgement issued by the courier company for goods received for despatch by courier. It acts both as a receipt and as proof of despatch. It is not a document of title. Goods sent by courier should be consigned to the party specified in the documentary credit.

Forwarding Agent's Receipt

A forwarding agent arranges the transport of the goods and will issue a receipt stating that he has taken charge of the goods for delivery to the importer. The forwarder is often the agent of the importer and exporters should ensure that the details on the receipt are exactly as required by the credit before relinquishing control of the goods.

Rail, Road Consignment Notes/Truck and Carrier Receipt

These are issued by the rail authorities or road haulage companies and are receipts for the goods accepted for consignment. They are not documents of title, and the goods are released to the importer on application, provided the importer has proof of identification. They should show the name of the importer and the date of despatch, bear the stamp of the issuing authorities and be marked "Freight Paid" where appropriate.

Consular Invoice

This type of document is sometimes required by certain countries of the world for customs purposes. It is a specially printed document that can be obtained from embassies or consulates. It is completed by the exporter and usually authenticated by the consulate of the importer's country.

Veterinary Certificate/Health Certificate

This may be called for when livestock/domestic animals/agricultural products are being exported. A veterinary certificate or a health certificate must be signed by the approved Health Authority of the exporter's country.

Non-Negotiable Sea Waybill (UCP Article 21)

The use of this document is increasing in European, Scandinavian, North American and certain Far Eastern Trade areas. Under this article, banks will, unless otherwise stipulated in the credit, accept a document, however named, which appears on its face to cover all the terms and conditions of carriage relating to the goods in question and fulfils the normal requirement of documents under a credit and negotiable sea waybill.

Multimodal Transport Document (UCP Article 19)

It should be clearly understood by the parties to the credit that this covers a traditional ocean bill of lading and is one that allows for the contract of carriage from the place of receipt of goods to the place of delivery by more than one mode of transport. The document however named must appear to:

- Indicate the name of the carrier and be signed by:
  - The carrier or a named agent for or on behalf of the carrier or
  - The master or a named agent for or on behalf of the master

Any signature by the carrier, master or agent must be identified as that of the carrier, master or agent.

The information in the document must match in accordance with the letter of credit.

Combined Transport Document

Nowadays, with the widespread use of containerised transport, goods are transported from a place of "taking in charge" of the cargo (container) to a place of "delivery" in the same container, but on different modes of transport, that is, by lorry to a sea port and the container will be loaded on a ship. It will be shipped to a port of destination, unloaded, transferred to another lorry, and then by road, to a place of delivery.

The goods (container), although carried by two or more modes of transport, are shipped under a single contract of carriage of goods. A single bill of lading is issued and it is known as "Combined Transport Document" (CTD).

FIATA Bill of Lading

FIATA (International Federation of Freight Forwarders Association): Documents are issued under licence only to members of FIATA or affiliated organisations, for example the Institute of Freight Forwarders Limited. The exporter receives the forwarder's receipt in exchange for the goods. The FIATA bill of lading is a combined transport document, which is issued by a member of the Institute of Freight Forwarders in the UK. The FIATA bill of lading is approved by the ICC and is acceptable to banks. A FIATA Combined Transport Bill of Lading serves as evidence that a freight forwarder is acting as a principal, that is, accepting carrier responsibility for performance of the entire contract of carriage and responsibility for loss or damage.

Other Documents

If a credit calls for an attestation or certification of weight in the case of transport other than by sea, banks will accept a weight stamp or declaration of weight which appears to have been superimposed on the transport document by the carrier or his agent, unless the credit specifically stipulates that the attestation or certification of weight must be by means of a separate document.

Note

If a person signs a document (e.g. a bill of exchange) on behalf of a company or another party, his signature must be preceded by one of the following forms: "for and behalf of", "pp" or "per pro". If the first of the three forms is used, the designation or official position of the signatory must be shown against the signature. The forms "pp" or "per pro" do not require further justification.

12

Negotiation of Documents

Meanings of Negotiation

1. There are several meanings of the word "negotiation". The general term is applied to arranging a contract or discussing the terms and conditions of a contract. The legal connotation of the word "negotiation" refers particularly in connection to cheques and bills of exchange when transferred from one person to another. Negotiation is a means of financing an outward collection or funding the payee of a cheque, bill of exchange or the beneficiary of documents under a letter of credit payable abroad.

2. We refer to the meaning of the beneficiary of documents under a letter of credit payable abroad. When a bank negotiates an outward collection it is buying its customer's bills and/or documents drawn on an overseas buyer. It is a convenient method of providing the exporter with working capital. The bank in buying the bill and/or documents will look to the overseas buyer as a source of repayment. In the event of non-payment or delayed payment, the negotiating bank exercises the right of recourse to its customer, the drawer. Therefore, if payment does not arrive within a reasonable time, the negotiating bank will debit its customer's account with the amount advanced plus interest. The cost of negotiation is similar to loan interest when provided by a bank.

3. When a bank negotiates, it pays its customer/the beneficiary straight away and sends the bill and/or documents to the issuing bank.

4. Under English law the negotiating bank may become a holder in due course of the bill of exchange when it negotiates, and as such is given a right of action against the drawer in the event of default by the drawee. Should

© The Author(s) 2019
T. Bhogal, A. Trivedi, *International Trade Finance*, Finance and Capital Markets Series,
https://doi.org/10.1007/978-3-030-24540-5_12

instruction be given for the bill not to be protested, this right is lost; as a result negotiating banks rely for reimbursement, when a bill is unpaid, on the specific right of recourse signed by their customer. The currency of the bill/or documents, be it in GB pound or US dollars, makes no difference.

Role of Advising and Confirming Banks

The seller may sometimes present documents that do not meet the letter of credit requirements. In such a case, the bank may act in one of the following ways:

1. Return the documents to the beneficiary (seller) to have them amended for re-submission within the validity of the credit and within the period of time after date of issuance specified in the credit.
2. Send the documents for collection. Or
3. Return the documents to the beneficiary for sending through his own bankers, if the confirming or advising bank is not the beneficiary's bank. Or
4. If authorised by the beneficiary, cable or send message by SWIFT or write to the issuing bank for authority to pay, accept or negotiate. The bank must provide a full list of irregularities to the issuing bank. Or
5. Call for an indemnity from the beneficiary or from a bank, as appropriate, that is, to pay, accept or negotiate on their undertaking that any payment made will be refunded by the party giving the indemnity, together with interest and all charges, if the issuing bank refuses to provide reimbursement against documents that do not meet the credit requirements.
6. Based on practical experience, and with the agreement of the beneficiary, pay, accept or negotiate "under reserve", that is, retain the right of recourse against the beneficiary if the issuing bank refuses to provide reimbursement against documents that do not meet the credit requirements.

Role of Issuing Bank

In case of discrepancies in documents the following options are available to the issuing bank:

- Check all documents carefully.
- Make a list of all irregularities.
- Contact the buyer/applicant and seek his instructions immediately.

- If the buyer/applicant is not ready to accept the documents, inform the advising/negotiating bank immediately of non-payment or non-acceptance of the documents with details of irregularities within five banking days following the day of presentation/receipt of documents (UCP 600 Article 14 (b)).

Negotiation of Documents Under Reserve

FORM OF AN INDEMNITY FOR DISCREPANCIES

The Manager   Date: _____

Bank's name _____

Address _____

_____

Dear Sir,

Letter of Credit No. _____ issued by _____

In consideration of your paying us the sum of _____ *(amount in words and figures)* _____ under the above-mentioned credit we hereby indemnify you from all consequences which may arise notwithstanding the following discrepancies in the documents.

1. _____

2. _____

3. _____

4. _____

5. _____

6. _____

7. _____

8. _____

9. _____

10. _____

_____   _____
Signed by the beneficiary   Signed by the beneficiary's
                                                   bank or third party

Letter of Credit: Processing Cost (Indicatives)

Table 12.1 Letter of credit: inactive processing cost

Activity	Scale of charges	Amount
Issuing of letter	Sight or Usance L/C 0.4% for three months or part thereof. Minimum £50 or US$80. Usance charges 0.1% per month	
Postage/telex or SWIFT charges	£20/US$35. Courier charges UK/Europe £10/US$20 other countries	
Advising bank's commission	By mail £15 brief telex/SWIFT £30. Full telex/SWIFT £50	
Advise of due date etc. postage/ courier	Telex £20/US$35	
Handling charges	£20/US$35 per month or part thereof if bill not accepted within 30 days of intimation	
Amendment fee	£40/US$65 per amendment. Plus 0.3% for three months or part thereof 0.5% up to 90 days, thereafter 0.1% per month or part hereof	
Payment charge	0.2% per payment minimum £40/US$65	
Advising L/C	£40/US$65	
Pre-advising L/C	£40/US$65	
Discrepancy fee	£40/US$65 plus £10/US$20 postage/telephone	
Confirmation charges L/C	0.3% for three months minimum £50/US$80, thereafter 0.1% per month or part thereof One per mile per month confirmation commission	
Payment commission	2% minimum £40/US$65 per payment plus telex/ cable charges £20/US$35	
Transfer of L/C	0.4% of amount min.£50/US$80	
Any other out of pocket expenses		
Total		

13

Factoring and Forfaiting

Factoring: Genesis

Factoring represents the sale of outstanding receivables related to export of goods by the exporter to overseas buyers. The seller of the receivables thus transfers the risk of default on contractual obligations arising from non-payment by the buyer to a third party. The seller of the receivables is paid discounted value of the receivables, arising either from a letter of credit, guarantee or bill. Factoring is possible with recourse or without recourse. The advantages enjoyed by an exporter due to such financing are immediate payment after export. The exporter can enjoy financial benefit, in the case of without recourse, at no risks arising from the deal after factoring.

Factoring and Cash Flow

Factoring is the selling of invoices by a seller to a third party called a factor. Factors may be independent or subsidiaries of major banks and financial institutions. The factor processes invoices and allows the seller to withdraw money against the amount owed under the invoices. It is used by businesses to improve their cash flow and also to reduce administration and overhead costs. Another method used to finance the exporters is called invoice discounting. This way the factor allows the business to withdraw money against the

© The Author(s) 2019
T. Bhogal, A. Trivedi, *International Trade Finance*, Finance and Capital Markets Series,
https://doi.org/10.1007/978-3-030-24540-5_13

invoices. The business maintains control over the administration of the sales ledger. Both of the procedures are used by businesses to improve their cash flow. It helps the business to boost cash flow or release money for expansion or other purposes. Factoring is commonly used by companies selling goods on a wholesale basis to businesses on a credit basis. It is not normally available to retailers or to cash traders.

After signing the agreement, the factor will agree to advance up to an agreed percentage of approved invoices or up to a certain credit limit. All sales are required to go through the factor.

Factoring and Legal Implications

Most factors require notice of a certain period to end the service, though some have notice periods of a long time of up to for example a year or so which could be expensive. The debtor should understand the terms and conditions of the contract before signing the agreement. Factoring is a complex, long-term agreement that could have a major effect on the business development. It is advisable to the debtor to seek an independent legal opinion from a solicitor on the legal and financial implications of factoring.

Factoring Mechanism

1. Seller raises an invoice on buyer, with instructions to pay the factor directly, and sends it to the customer.
2. Seller sends a copy of the invoice to the factor.
3. The factor pays an agreed percentage of the invoice amount to the seller.
4. The factor operates credit control procedures including maintaining ledger, correspondence and telephoning the buyer, if necessary. The factor sends a statement of account to the buyer on behalf of the seller.
5. The buyer makes payment of the full amount of the invoice to the factor as per agreed terms.

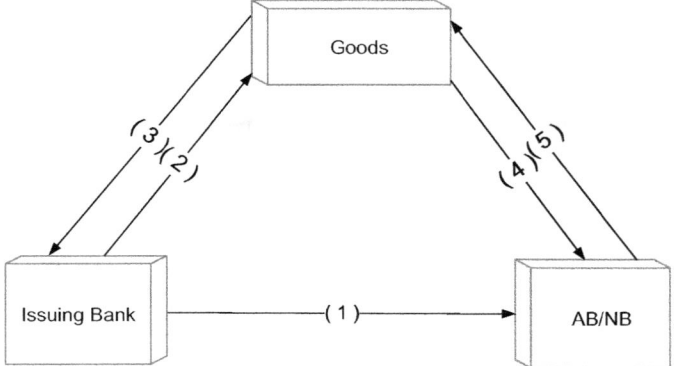

Fig. 13.1   Factoring: mechanism

When an invoice is not paid on the due date the liability will depend on the type of agreement, for example whether it is with recourse or without recourse to the seller.

Advantages of Factoring

- The factor provides a quick boost to cash flow within a short time.
- It is a competitive business and competitively priced.
- It can be a cost-effective way of outsourcing sales ledger while freeing up owner's time to manage the business.
- It assists smoother cash flow and financial planning.
- Businesses may be given useful information about the credit standing of the customers (buyers) if they pay on time.
- The buyers can negotiate better terms with suppliers.
- Factors can provide an excellent strategic as well as financial resource when planning business growth.
- Businesses will be protected from bad debts if they choose without recourse factoring.
- Cash is released to the seller by the factor as soon as invoices are received by the factor.

Disadvantages of Factoring

- It may be more expensive than a bank overdraft/loan.
- It may reduce the scope for borrowing from the bank because book debts will not be available as security.
- Factors may/would like to vet the customers (buyers) before a business sells goods.
- A business may find it difficult to end factoring at short notice as it will have to pay off any money the factor has advanced on invoices if the customers have not paid them yet.
- It may take a long time to settle in the case of a dispute.

Invoice Discounting

Invoice discounting is an alternative way of drawing money against invoices. A business retains control over the administration of the sales ledger. It provides a cost-effective way for profitable businesses to improve their cash flow. It is only available to businesses that sell products or services on credit to other businesses.

The invoice discounter will first do a credit check on the business, its systems and also a credit check of its customers. It may then agree to advance a certain percentage of the total amount of outstanding sales ledger.

The business will pay a monthly fee to the invoice discounter and also interest on the net amount advanced. This is in addition to advances received or money repaid.

Each month, more money is advanced by the discounter or repaid by the business. This will depend on whether the total amount owing has gone up or down.

If the invoice discounter agrees to advance a certain percentage (say 80%) of the total owing and the total of outstanding invoices is steadily changing, then so will the amount the business will receive. If the outstanding debt drops month on month, the business must repay a proportionate amount (say 80%) of the fall in debt. If the debt rises month on month, the business will receive a similar amount of the increased amount.

Advantages to Exporter

- The seller collects the debts and does the credit control.
- The customers do not usually know about the invoice discounting, although it is sometimes disclosed.
- Annual turnover must usually be at least £500,000, although increasingly, smaller businesses will be accepted. Generally, discounters will review the credit history and profit track record of the business. They will have stringent requirements regarding the quality of sales ledger systems and procedures.
- The invoice discounter will check regularly to see that business procedures are effective.
- A business can choose between recourse and without recourse facilities, determining who is responsible for recovering the amount of unpaid invoices.

Export Factoring

Some factoring companies offer a facility for the financing of international sales. They will typically work with a partner abroad who will be responsible for the collection of payment in the country to which the exports are made by the seller. The services of a local agent will prevent any problems that could arise because of differences in laws, customs and language.

In terms of credit limits and process, there is no material difference between local and international factoring and invoice discounting. Some factors will offer the exporter the choice of being paid in GB Pounds or in another currency. The exporter should carefully evaluate which is to his advantage. If the importer customer insists on being invoiced in their country's currency, investing in protection against currency fluctuations needs to be considered. Factors may approve a lower level of prepayment for export invoices than in local sales.

Export Factoring: Sales Criteria

- An annual turnover of at least £100,000; this may include domestic sales.
- Companies based in the European Union (EU) can still factor debts owed from other EU countries if sales within that country are relatively small.
- Outside the EU higher sales to a single country will be required. For the USA annual sales of £500,000 will typically be necessary.

Most companies, assuming that all factoring companies are the same, take the simplest route signing up with the subsidiary of their clearing bank without first establishing whether or not there are more suitable options available but unlike most other financial facilities, factoring and to a lesser extent invoice discounting, is the provision of finance geared to a service and that service element is not only highly important but equally highly variable from one factoring company to another. In general terms, factors owned by the big banks do not rank well in the service stakes with one even outsourcing its credit control function to India.

Selecting the right factoring company is important as some factors offer poor services and that is why the cheapest quote may work out much more expensive in practice, plus details of the hidden extra costs that some factors may add.

Amongst the factors we find major British banks, subsidiaries of major banks and financial institutions, independent financial institutions and factoring brokers.

Forfaiting: Genesis

The word "forfait" is a French word meaning surrendering rights, which is of fundamental importance in forfaiting. Forfaiting is the purchase of a series of credit instruments such as bills of exchange, promissory notes, drafts drawn under usance (time), letters of credit or other freely negotiable instruments on a "non-recourse" basis (non-recourse means that there is no comeback on the exporter if the importer does not pay). The forfaiter deducts interest (in the form of a discount), at an agreed rate for the full credit period covered by the negotiable instruments. The debt instruments are drawn by the exporter (seller), accepted by the importer (buyer), and will bear an aval or unconditional guarantee normally issued by the importer's bank. In exchange for the payment, the forfaiter then takes over responsibility for claiming the debt from the importer. The forfaiter either holds the instruments until full maturity (as an investment), or sells them to another investor on a without recourse basis. The holder of the bills/notes then presents each receivable to the bank at which they are payable, as and when they fall due.

Fixed Rate Export Finance

A proven method of providing fixed rate export finance for international trade transactions, in recent years, forfaiting has assumed an important role for exporters who wish to receive cash instead of deferred payments, especially from countries where protection against credit, economic and political risks has become more difficult. Typically the importer's obligations are evidenced by accepted bills of exchange or promissory notes which a bank avals or guarantees by way of a "per aval" endorsement on the instrument. The bills of exchange or promissory notes when endorsed as such are known as avalised bills/notes. Equally the receivable may take the form of term bills of exchange drawn under documentary letters of credit.

Forfaiting: Capital Goods Sale

Forfaiting is often applied where the exporter is selling capital goods, and having to offer export finance for a longer period such as up to five or more years. The forfaiter will then quote a price being a discount rate to be applied to the paper, calculated on the underlying cost of funds, that is (LIBOR) plus a margin. It is usually possible to have a fixed price quoted for shipment taking place up to six months forward, and the exporter is thus able to lock into his profit from the outset.

Forfaiting: Secondary Markets

There is an active secondary market for avalised export finance papers in London. Forfaiting companies can offer a wide range of trade-related services including various forms of buyers' credits, forfaiting and arranging bank-to-bank loans, loans to financial organisations as well as providing insurance for trade related business through confirming letters of credit and letters of guarantee. Significant export financing and insurance facilities support exports to the emerging markets. Export-credit financing and insurance facilities are provided in co-operation with the Export Credit Guarantee Department in the UK. There are similar agencies in other countries.

Forfaiting is used for international trade transactions. Normally, a forfaiting house would not expect to handle transactions worth less than $100,000. Forfaiting is at a fixed rate and is short- or medium-term (one to five years) finance, but forfaiters have become very flexible about the terms they will accept. Some forfaiting houses will accept paper with tenors up to ten years; and in other cases for shorter periods down to 180 days. The market for forfaiting generally ranges between one and ten years, depending upon various risks in respect of the country, the importer financed and the guarantor's financial standing.

Payments will normally be made semi-annually in arrears, but most for-faiters may accommodate payments which are made quarterly, semi-annually, annually or on a bullet basis. These can include capital and interest repayment holidays.

Table 13.1 Difference between factoring and forfaiting

Factoring	Forfaiting
Factoring is suitable for financing the export of consumer goods	Forfaiting is used for financing capital goods
Credit terms between 90 to 180 days	Credit terms for medium and long term

Risks in Export Finance

Political risk: Extraordinary state measures or political incidents like war, revolution, invasion or civil unrest can lead to losses for the exporter.

Currency risk: One of the most important risks in forfaiting is that of payment in a currency other than the exporter's local currency. Floating exchange rates can have the effect of changing the contract value by a considerable amount when converted into the exporter's own currency, and can lead to a loss for the eventual holder of claim.

Commercial risk: This risk concerns the inability or unwillingness of the obligator or guarantor to pay, and applies to all forms of credit as well as forfaiting. The danger is that commitment may not be honoured and necessitates in each case an evaluation of the creditworthiness of the guaranteeing bank. The commercial risk of default by state entities falls into the category of political risks.

Transfer of funds risk: This risk lies with the inability or unwillingness of states or other official bodies to effect payment in the currency agreed upon including the risk of moratorium.

Advantages to the Exporter

- Relieves the balance sheet of contingent liabilities;
- Improves liquidity;
- No interest rate risk;
- No risk of inflation in the exchange rate;
- No risk of changes in the status of the debtor;
- No credit administration and collection problems and related risks and costs.

Disadvantages to the Exporter

- High cost of financing.

Requirements of a Forfaiter

- Name of the buyer, his nationality;
- Nature of the goods to be sold;
- Date of delivery of goods;
- Value and currency of the contract;
- Date and duration of the contract;
- Credit period and number and timing of payments (including any interest rate agreed with the buyer).

Documents Required by the Forfaiter

- Evidence of debt to be used (bills of exchange, promissory notes or letters of credit), and the identity of the guarantor or name of the availing bank;
- Date of delivery of the documents;
- Import export licences, if required;
- Exchange control permission to transfer funds, if required;
- Copy of supply contract, or of its payment terms;
- Copy of signed commercial invoice;
- Copies of all shipping documents;
- Letter of assignment and notification to the guarantor;
- Letter of guarantee, or aval.

The letter of guarantee must be irrevocable and assignable. The forfaiter would like to have all this information, indications or quotations immediately.

Where a letter of credit to cover the debt under a supplier's credit is used, it may be a deferred payment letter of credit that specifies one or a series of more usance (time) bills of exchange, which the bank will accept (guarantee) upon presentation of the usual documents required by the letter of credit. The letter of credit must be subject to the Uniform Customs and Practice for Documentary Credits of the International Chamber of Commerce, Paris (Revision 2007 ICC Publication No. 600 (UCP)).

Charges would depend on the level of interest rates relevant to the currency of the underlying contract at the time of the forfaiter's commitment, and on the forfaiter's assessment of the credit risks and other risks related to the importing country and to the avalising (or guaranteeing) bank. Interest cost is made up of:

- A charge for the money received by the seller;
- Forfaiter's refinancing costs;
- Charge for covering the political, commercial and transfer risks attached to the avalisor/guarantor;
- Commitment fee.

Forfaiting Procedures in Practice

The exporter approaches a forfaiter who confirms that he is willing to quote on a prospective deal, covering the export in "x" number of months' time bearing the aval of ABC Bank PLC.

If the transaction is worth $10 M, the forfaiter will calculate the amount of the bills/notes, so that after discounting the exporter will receive $10 M, and will quote a discount rate of "y" %. The forfaiter will also charge for some days grace, if applicable, and a fee for committing him or herself to the deal, worth "Z" % per annum computed only on the actual number of days from the date of commitment and discounting. The forfaiter will stipulate an expiry date for his commitment (i.e. when the paper should be in his hands).

This period will allow the exporter to ship his goods and get his bills of exchange avalised and to present them for discounting. The exporter gets immediate cash on presentation of relevant documents, and the importer is then liable for the cost of the contract and receives credit for number of years at "y" % interest.

Many exporters prefer to work with forfait brokers because they deal with a large number of Forfait Houses. They can assure the exporter of competitive rates on a timely and cost-effective basis. Such brokers typically charge a nominal (1%) fee to arrange the commitment. This is a one-time fee on the principal amount and frequently is added to the selling price by the exporter. The broker frequently consults with the exporter to structure the transaction to fit the forfait market.

Mechanism of a Forfaiting Transaction

1. Commercial contract between importer and exporter;
2. Delivery of goods by the exporter to the importer;
3. Delivery of bill of exchange from importer to the avalising bank;
4. Delivery of avalised bill of exchange by avalising bank to the exporter;
5. Forfaiting contract between exporter and the forfaiter;
6. Delivery of bill of exchange by exporter to the forfaiter;
7. Cash payment by forfaiter to the exporter;
8. Presentation of the avalised bill of exchange to the avalising bank on maturity;
9. Payment made by the avalising bank to the forfaiter.

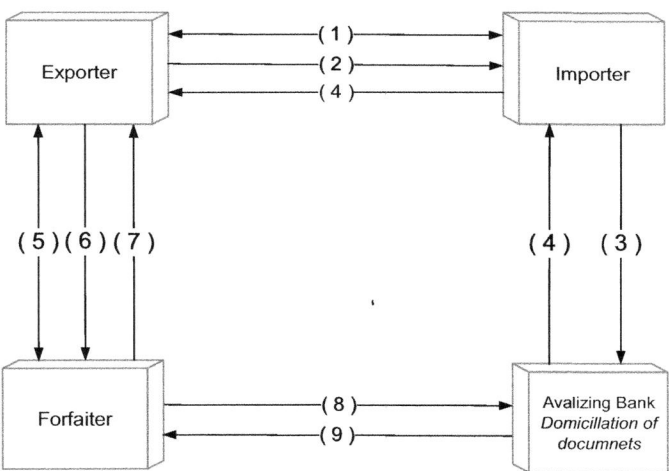

Fig. 13.2   Forfaiting transaction: mechanism

14

Electronic Documents (eUCP)

Background to eUCP (Uniform Custom and Practice) 600: The emergence of electronic commerce in the international trade system has completely transformed the way the business community does business with its overseas counterparts. This has created the need for a new set of rules and procedures governing global trade operations including entering into sale contracts, trade payment and handling of goods and documents. This has given rise to a new agency being introduced into the international trade mechanism, that of a reliable and trusted third party to do the important work of authentication and safe keeping of messages and their integrity, storage and retrieval; give instructions to various service providers; and trigger release of goods and payment.

Development of Electronic Model: An acceptable electronic commerce model was evolved with the initiative of Bolero and other organisations. It will take care of electronic presentation of trade documents and with the passage of time the paper-based presentation of documents would vanish under a documentary credits system.

Banks have to be aware of the requirement of the rules, which can take care of presentations whether paper-based, electronic or both paper-based and electronic. The ICC started giving thought as to whether a revision of the then UCP 500 or some other mechanism could take care of the evolving system. A Task Force was constituted by the ICC Banking Commission at its meeting on 24 May 2000 on the future of the Commission on Banking Technique and Practice with a main focus on electronic trade. The Task Force identified that there was a need to develop a bridge between the UCP and the processing of the electronic equivalent of a paperless documentary credit

© The Author(s) 2019
T. Bhogal, A. Trivedi, *International Trade Finance*, Finance and Capital Markets Series,
https://doi.org/10.1007/978-3-030-24540-5_14

system. It is important to note that UCP has been extremely successful over many years of its history in providing self-regulation for the letter of credit trading system. It is time, however, to update the rules to accommodate the changes in developing technology.

Setting up of Working Group: A Working Group was set up, comprising experts from the UCP, electronic trade, legal and related industries such as transport, who after a very hard work of over a year and a half prepared a set of rules as a supplement to UCP. These rules are not a revision of UCP 600. The UCP 600 will continue to be the rules for paper-based documentary letters of credit. The eUCP is a supplement to the UCP 600 to provide necessary guidance for presentation of the electronic equivalents of paper documents under documentary letters of credits. Development of eUCP: The eUCP provides definitions to allow current UCP terminology to accommodate electronic presentation and the necessary rules to allow the UCP and the eUCP to work together. It has been written to allow for presentation completely electronically or for a mixture of paper documents and electronic presentation. Although the practice is evolving, providing exclusively for electronic presentation is not entirely realistic at this stage, nor will it promote the transition to total electronic presentation. It should be noted that the eUCP does not address any issues relating to the issuance or advice of letters of credits electronically. The current practice of issuing, advising and amendment of letters of credit is done electronically, through the SWIFT system. Many Articles of the UCP are not impacted by the electronic presentation of the equivalent of paper documents and do not require any changes to accommodate it. UCP 600 and eUCP together are good enough to allow for developing practice in this area of trade. The eUCP is specific to UCP 600.

It is important to note that the eUCP has been drafted to be independent of specific technologies and developing electronic commerce systems. They do not address or define the specific technologies or systems necessary to facilitate electronic presentation. The technologies are evolving and the eUCP leave the parties free to agree on the technology or the format for example, e-mail or one of the various document processing programs to be used in the transmission of electronic messages. It is the responsibility of the parties concerned to decide it.

Synopsis of eUCP Articles: All the Articles of eUCP are consistent with the UCP except as they relate specifically to electronic presentations. Where necessary, changes have been made in the eUCP to address the differences between presentations in paper and electronic form. With a view to avoiding confusion between the Articles of the UCP and eUCP, the eUCP Articles have an "e" preceding each Article number.

Just as is the case with UCP 600, it will be necessary to specifically incorporate the eUCP if the parties wish them to apply for credits allowing for the presentation of electronic documents (or a mixture of paper and electronic presentation). Since the eUCP supplement incorporates the UCP 600 in any credit subject to it, it is not necessary to incorporate both in the same credit.

Among the key issues of electronic presentation addressed by eUCP include:

- The format in which electronic records are to be presented;
- The consequences if a bank is open but its system is unable to receive an electronic record;
- How notice of refusal of an electronic record is to be handled;
- How original documents are to be defined in the electronic world;
- What happens when an electronic record is corrupted by a virus or other defect.

UCP 500 has now been revised and the new publication is known as "2007 Revision ICC publication No. 600 (UCP)". It will be effective from July 2007

Supplement to the Uniform Customs and Practice for Documentary Credits (2007 Revision ICC Publication No. 600 (UCP)) for Electronic Presentation

Article e1	Outlines the scope of the eUCP including its applicability and incorporation in a credit. Just as UCP, eUCP will apply only if it is specifically incorporated in the credit calling for presentation of electronic records alone or in combination with paper documents; that it shall apply as a supplement to the UCP; and that unless a specific version is indicated, the version effective on the date the credit is issued, or amended will apply.
Article e2	Defines the relationship of the eUCP to the UCP. As per this Article, a credit subject to the eUCP shall also be subject to the UCP without express incorporation of the UCP; that eUCP shall prevail if they would produce a result different from that of the UCP; and if eUCP allows the beneficiary to choose presentation and he chooses paper presentation or eUCP permits paper presentation only, the UCP alone shall apply.
Article e3	Gives definition of terms that appear on its face (to apply to the examination of data content), document (to include an electronic record), place for presentation (to mean an electronic address), sign and the like (to include an electronic signature), superimposed notation or stamped (means data content whose supplementary character is apparent in an electronic record) in

relation to electronic presentation. This Article further defines electronic record (to mean data created, generated, sent, communicated, received or stored by electronic means that is capable of being authenticated as to the apparent identity of a sender and the apparent source of the data contained in it, and that it has remained complete and unaltered, and is capable of being examined for compliance with the terms and conditions of the eUCP credit.), electronic signature (to mean a data process attached to or logically associated with an electronic record and executed or adopted by a person in order to identify that person and to indicate that person's authentication of the electronic record), format (the data organisation in which the electronic record is expressed or to which it refers), paper document (a document in a traditional paper form) and received (the time when an electronic record enters the information capable of being accepted by that system. An acknowledgement of receipt does not imply acceptance or refusal of the electronic record) again in its application to UCP.

Article e4   Enjoins the eUCP credit to specify the formats in which electronic records are to be presented. If not specified, any format will do.

Article e5   Deals with the presentation. According to this Article, "an eUCP must state a place for presentation for the electronic records, if to be presented and also state a place for presentation of the paper documents, if both to be presented". It adds that electronic records may be presented separately from paper documents. If electronic record/s is part of the presentation, it is the responsibility of the beneficiary to provide a notice to the bank concerned as to when the presentation is complete. This notice may be an electronic record or paper document. If the necessary notice is not received, the presentation will deemed not to have been made. Each paper document presentation under eUCP credit must identify the credit under which it is presented, failure to do so will render presentation as not received. If the system of the bank to which presentation is to be made is unable to receive the electronic record on the expiry date and so on despite being open, it will be deemed to be closed and the date for presentation will set extended.

Article e6   Is another important Article, which deals with the examination of documents (or records in the case of electronic presentation).

According to this Article, if an electronic record contains a hyperlink to an external system or a presentation indicates that it may be examined by reference to an external system, then the relevant hyperlink or external system will be the electronic record to be examined. It will be a discrepancy if the indicated system fails to provide access to the required electronic record at the time of examination. The forwarding of electronic records by the nominated bank will signify its having checked the apparent authenticity of the electronic record. It will, however, not be a basis for refusal if the bank concerned is unable to examine an electronic record in format required by the eUCP credit, or in the form presented if no format is stipulated.

Article e7   It covers the Notice of Refusal. The time period, according to this Article, commences on the banking day after receiving the notice of completeness. If this time period gets extended, the time for the examination of documents commences on the first following banking day on which the bank is able to receive the notice of completeness. It is added that the bank shall return any paper documents not previously returned to the presenter, if the concerned bank does not receive instructions from the party to which notice of refusal is given within 30 calendar days from the date of the notice. It may dispose of the electronic records in any manner deemed appropriate without any responsibility.

Article e8   It stipulates that any requirement for presentation of one or more originals or copies of an electronic record is satisfied by the presentation of one electronic record.

Article e9   The date on which an electronic record appears to have been sent by the issuer is deemed to be the date of issuance of that record, as per Article e9. If no other date is apparent, the date of receipt will be deemed to be the date it was sent.

Article e10   Except for transport document, there is no other Article in eUCP covering documents. Article e10 states that if an electronic record does not indicate a date of shipment or despatch, the date of issuance of the electronic record will be the date. If, however, the electronic record bears a notation evidencing the date of shipment, that notation date will be the date of shipment or despatch. A notation showing additional data content need not be separately signed or otherwise authenticated.

Article e11   It deals with the corruption of an electronic record after presentation. As per this Article, the bank receiving an electronic record, which appears to have been corrupted may inform the presenter and may request for its re-presentation. If the bank concerned does not request re-presentation, the time for examination is suspended and resumes when the presenter makes re-presentation and that if the nominated bank is not the confirming bank it must provide the issuing bank and any confirming bank with notice of the request for re-presentation and also of the suspension. If the said electronic record is not re-presented within thirty (30) calendar days, the bank may treat the electronic record as not presented; and any deadlines are not extended.

Article e12   It is a disclaimer of liability clause for presentation of electronic records. It puts no liability on the bank, by checking the apparent authenticity of an electronic record, for the identity of the sender, source of the information, or its complete and unaltered character other than that which is apparent in the electronic record received by the use of commercially acceptable data process for the receipt, authentication and identification of electronic records. (Source: ICC)

15

Scrutiny of Documents: Procedures

Documentary Credits: Documentary credits are classic instruments for financing purchasing of foreign goods and foreign equipment. They may provide assistance to the issuing bank to grant financial facility to the importer. They may also provide assistance to the advising/confirming bank to grant financial facility to the exporter.

Scrutiny of Documents: A documentary letter of credit is a legal contract between the issuing bank and the beneficiary. The issuing bank undertakes to honour its commitment to pay, accept bill of exchange and pay on maturity provided the beneficiary presents the documents in accordance with the terms and conditions mentioned in the credit.

It must be remembered that banks deal with documents and not in goods. Therefore, it is very important to ensure the quality and quantity of the goods be satisfied by presenting appropriate documents in this respect. The beneficiary is the party to supply the goods under a letter of credit and provide the appropriate documents to the issuing bank. If the documents presented do not satisfy the terms and conditions of the credit, the issuing bank cannot honour its commitment.

As a letter of credit is issued at the request and on behalf of the buyer/importer in favour of the beneficiary, the issuing bank is a middleman to facilitate completion of sale and purchase of the goods. There is a separate contract between the applicant and the issuing bank that he (the applicant) will honour his commitment provided the issuing bank also fulfils the requirements mentioned in the application for a letter of credit, which stipulates the documents.

Therefore the buyers and sellers have certain responsibilities in respect of documents required under a letter of credit.

© The Author(s) 2019
T. Bhogal, A. Trivedi, *International Trade Finance*, Finance and Capital Markets Series,
https://doi.org/10.1007/978-3-030-24540-5_15

Buyer's Responsibilities

The buyer must give clear and precise instructions to the issuing bank, without excessive detail. The issuing bank cannot guess what the buyer wants and cannot check complicated and technical specifications. The documents called for under the credit should be with the agreement of sale contract. The buyer should not ask for the documents that the seller cannot or may not be able to provide, or set out conditions that the seller cannot meet.

Seller's Responsibilities

When a letter of credit is received by the seller/beneficiary he should immediately study the terms and conditions of the credit and ensure that these are in accordance with the sale contract between him and the buyer. If there is a need to make changes to the terms of the credit he must make such a request in writing without delay. Banks are not concerned with such contracts between them.

At the time of presentation of the documents the seller should present the required documents exactly with the same terms and conditions as called for by a letter of credit. The documents should be presented as soon as possible within the validity period specified in the credit.

The seller must remember that if the documents do not meet the terms and conditions of a letter of credit, the issuing bank will have no obligation to honour its commitment but will refuse to accept the documents.

Responsibilities of Other Parties (Banks)

Advising/Confirming bank: It is very important for all other parties involved in a letter of credit to understand what documents are required and the terms and conditions that need to be fulfilled. There are three main parties involved in a letter of credit, that is, the applicant, the issuing bank and the seller. For the purpose of convenience in the process a fourth party is known as the advising bank/confirming and/or negotiating bank.

The advising/confirming bank: When documents are presented by the seller the advising and/or confirming bank need to check all the documents to ensure these are correct and satisfy the terms and conditions of the letter of credit. If they do not satisfy them, then the procedure mentioned under the section on "Negotiation of Documents" should be followed.

The Issuing Bank

When documents are received from the seller/advising/confirming bank, the issuing bank must check all the documents to ensure these are correct and satisfy the terms and conditions of a letter of credit. If they do not satisfy them it must immediately inform the party seller/advising/confirming bank from where it received them that the documents do not meet the terms and conditions of a credit and it refuses to accept them.

It should also contact and inform the applicant of the irregularities and seek his mandate if he is willing to accept those documents.

Scrutiny of Documents: In order to ascertain the conformity of documents with the terms of a letter of credit it is necessary to carry out the following checks on various documents relating to letter of credit.

Letter of Credit

- It is irrevocable.
- The signature on the letter of credit must be verified.
- All amendments must be attached to a letter of credit.
- Documents are submitted within the validity of a letter of credit.
- All the required documents are received.
- All documents should be presented/submitted by the original beneficiary unless it is a transferable letter of credit. In that event, documents would be accepted from a second beneficiary in accordance with the transferred letter of credit.
- If the documents evidence partial shipment it should not be accepted unless it is permitted by a letter of credit.
- If a forward foreign exchange contract is required it should be booked.

Bill of Exchange

- It must be drawn in accordance with the terms of a letter of credit.
- It must be correctly dated.
- It must be signed by the drawer/beneficiary specified in a letter of credit.
- It must be drawn on the issuing bank.
- The currency of the drawing must be the same as of the letter of credit.
- The amount in words and figures must agree.

- Its value must be exactly the same as on the invoices, unless otherwise permitted by a letter of credit.
- It must be drawn at sight or usance as required and in accordance with the terms of a letter of credit.
- It must be drawn for a usance period from or after sight or from or after the "On Board" bill of lading date as per a letter of credit terms.
- Letter of credit reference number and date must appear on the bill of exchange as per letter of credit terms.
- Alteration to the instrument, if any, must be signed by the authorised signature.
- There must not be any irrelevant clauses mentioned.
- Stamp duty of the proper value must be affixed (wherever stamp duty is applicable). It is not applicable in the UK.

Commercial Invoice

- It must be addressed to the buyer—unless a letter of credit stipulates otherwise. In that case it has to be addressed to the party stipulated.
- The value must not be in excess of that available under a letter of credit.
- The description of the goods on the commercial invoice must correspond exactly as given in a letter of credit.
- It must show import licence number, pro-forma invoice or other numbers, if required by a letter of credit.
- It must not evidence shipment of additional goods such as advertising samples, which are not required by a letter of credit.
- The price basis must not differ from any pro-forma invoice attached to a letter of credit or terms stated on a letter of credit.
- The calculations must agree with those in other documents and there must be no computational errors.
- There must be no extra charges or commission shown which are not permitted under a letter of credit.
- Invoice must show the beneficiary's name as per a letter of credit terms.
- The invoices must be certified, signed, legalised, if required under a letter of credit.
- Shipping marks, weight, number of packages/cases must agree with those shown on the bill of lading and other documents.
- Packing details must agree with other documents and must also be as required by a letter of credit.

- The correct number of copies of invoices must be submitted.
- If a letter of credit requires a combined certificate of value and origin, the certificate of origin section must be complete and signed.
- If a letter of credit requires that the transport documents evidence the amount of the freight paid, or that in some form the insurance premium is specified, the invoices must show such amounts exactly.
- The quantity of goods shown must be consistent with any part shipment clause in a letter of credit.

Insurance Document

- It must evidence coverage of risks exactly as stipulated in a letter of credit.
- It must be issued/signed by an insurance company or underwriter or an agent on behalf of an insurance company or underwriter.
- It should not be a broker's certificate or cover note, unless it is specifically authorised in the letter of credit.
- It must not be dated later than the date of shipment, despatch or taking in charge. If it is, it must include "warehouse to warehouse" clause or "lost or not lost" clause.
- It must be issued in the currency of a letter of credit or as otherwise stipulated.
- It must be issued in a transferable form or endorsed to the order of a specified party if so required by a letter of credit.
- There must not be any unauthenticated alterations.
- It must show marks, numbers, weights, quantities and a description of the goods in accordance with the bill of lading and other documents.
- It must indicate the method of carriage of the goods, the port of loading, despatch, or taking in charge, name of the carrying vessel and port of discharge or place of delivery and so on.
- It must state a named place where claims are payable (usually at the place of issuing bank) (if this is required by a letter of credit).
- When the transport document shows trans-shipment of goods, the insurance document must cover the trans-shipment.
- If the goods are being shipped in containers or if a letter of credit's terms permit shipment on deck, the insurance document must cover "Loaded on Deck" shipments.
- The document must be presented in original. Copies are accepted only if allowed in a letter of credit.

Bill of Lading

- It must be issued and signed by a named carrier or on behalf of the named carrier by his agent.
- It must indicate that the goods have been "loaded" or "shipped on board" a named vessel.
- The bill of lading must not be issued by a freight forwarder, unless it indicates that the freight forwarder is acting as the actual carrier or as an agent for a named carrier.
- The documents presented must comprise a full set of originals and, if required, a set number of non-negotiable copies.
- If a letter of credit's terms require that the goods be consigned to the "order" of a nominated party it must not be otherwise consigned or endorsed by the seller.
- The date shown as being the "On-Board" date when goods were placed on the vessel must not be later than the latest date of shipment.
- If a "Received for Shipment" bill of lading is presented, it is acceptable if it bears an "On-Board" notation and date, duly initialled by the carrier or his agent, if required by a letter of credit.
- The bill of lading must not indicate any detrimental clauses as to the defective conditions of goods and/or packing.
- The shipping marks or numbers must agree with those shown on other documents.
- There must not be any alterations, which have not been authenticated by the carrier or his agent.
- It must not show that any other goods have been shipped in addition to those required.
- It must not show that the vessels' name and/or the port of loading and/or port of discharge are "intended".
- It must not show that the goods have been loaded "On Deck" unless specifically authorised.
- It must not omit any required notify parties.
- It must be marked "Freight Paid" if the shipping terms are C&F or CIF.
- It must show the amount of the freight charge, if so required by a letter of credit.
- It must not bear a clause covering part container loaded stating that the goods will be released only when all original copies of bill of lading are presented by the holders.
- The bill of lading must have been presented within the period allowed under a credit or otherwise within 21 days from its date.

- If it is a charter party/short form bill of lading it must be allowed as per letter of credit terms.
- The vessel must not be on the banned list.

Air Waybill and Air Consignment Note

(Unless the letter of credit specifies otherwise)

- The air waybill must be issued and signed by a named carrier or signed on behalf of a named carrier by his agent.
- If it is a "House air waybill" it must be signed for and on behalf of a named carrier.
- The correct copy, which has been signed by the carrier or on behalf of a named carrier or by his agent, must be submitted.
- The "Freight Collected" and "Freight Prepaid" columns must be completed.
- The goods must be consigned as required under the letter of credit.
- The required notify parties must be shown.
- The despatch of goods must be made from and to the specified places.
- The despatch date must not be later than the latest shipment date.
- Trans-shipment must be effected only if the letter of credit allows.

Parcel Post/Courier Receipts

- They must show despatch of goods from a post office/courier in the nominated place.
- The date stamp must indicate that despatch was made within the specified period.
- If the amount of postage paid is required to be shown, it must be stated on the receipt.
- The consignee as per a letter of credit's terms must be shown on the receipt.

Other Transport Documents

- It must show, on its face, that it has been issued by a named carrier and signed by the carrier or on his behalf by this agent.
- If it is issued in more than one original, a full set must be presented.
- There must be non-negotiable copies, if required by a letter of credit's terms.

- It must state that the goods have been despatched loaded, shipped on board or taken in charge as required by the letter of credit.
- If shipment is by sea, that it must not be subject to a charter party.
- There must be no detrimental clause indicating defective goods or packing.
- The marks and numbers and description of goods must not differ from the other documents presented.
- Alterations, if any, in transport documents must be signed by the carrier or by the agent of the named carrier.
- It must not show shipment of goods in addition to those required by a letter of credit's terms.
- It must evidence notify party(ies) if required by a letter of credit.
- It must not show "loaded on deck" if shipment is by sea, unless specified in a letter of credit.
- It must be marked "Freight Paid" if shipment dispatch terms are C&F, CIF, DCP or CIP.
- If required by a letter of credit the document must show the freight charges.
- In case of combined transport document, the cross-border certificate should be attached, wherever required.

Certificate of Origin

- The details must conform to other documents presented.
- It must indicate as the consignee, the applicant for a letter of credit.
- It must be issued by a Chamber of Commerce or other specified organisation.
- Any alterations must be authenticated.
- Marks, number, weight, and so on must agree with those shown on other documents.

Packing List

- It must show the contents of each individual package.
- It must show marks, case numbers, weights and so on; these should not differ from the other documents.

Weight List/Note

- It must show both net and gross weights.
- It must quote a weight, which does not differ from that stated on other documents.
- It must not show details, which differ from other documents.
- It must state individual weights of the package.
- It must show weights, which add up to the stated total.
- It can be specifically identified with the other documents.

Other Documents

In addition to the documents mentioned above, which are by far the most common, there are several other documents that are called for from time to time. Certain countries, particularly those in the Middle East, require certified invoices or certificates of origin confirming that the goods have been produced in a particular country. UK-produced goods may have certificates of origin issued by local Chambers of Commerce who are authorised by the Department of Trade and Industry to make such declarations. These include:

- Inspection Certificates;
- Health Certificates, for example Fumigation, Sanitary and Veterinary;
- Customs Invoices;
- Pro-forma Invoices;
- Legalised Invoices;
- Consular Invoices.

1. The documents required must be stated in a letter of credit and the name of the organisation to issue such documents and the information should match with the requirement.
2. Documents can be specifically identified with the other documents under the letter of credit.
3. Documents describe the goods generally in accordance with a letter of credit description.

16

Common Irregularities in Documents

Compliance of Terms

It is essential that documents called for in a documentary letter of credit comply correctly and are in accordance with the terms of the credit. However, mistakes do occur and these cause extra work for the exporter and the bank(s) involved. This extra work causes delay in receiving payment from the importer/bank, and may involve extra cost for the exporter. The irregularities/discrepancies can be avoided by paying due attention.

Documentary Credit

- Does not comply strictly with the terms of sale contract;
- Has expired;
- Late presentation of documents;
- Difficult documents asked for under L/C.

Bill of Exchange

- Drawn incorrectly or for a sum different from the amount of a credit;
- Capacity of signatories not stated, if required;
- Drawn in different currency;
- Tenor of the bill does not match with L/C;
- Bill of exchange not endorsed or incorrectly endorsed;
- Bill does not bear the notation "Drawn under L/C No.—Issued by—Bank".

© The Author(s) 2019
T. Bhogal, A. Trivedi, *International Trade Finance*, Finance and Capital Markets Series,
https://doi.org/10.1007/978-3-030-24540-5_16

Invoice

- Amount exceeds that of a letter of credit;
- Amount differs from that of the bill of exchange;
- Prices of goods different from those indicated in a letter of credit;
- Description of goods differs from that in a letter of credit;
- Price and shipment terms ("FOB", "CIF", "C&F", etc.) not mentioned/ incorrect;
- Extra charges included are not specified in a letter of credit;
- Is not certified, legalised or signed as required by a letter of credit;
- Does not contain declaration required under a letter of credit;
- Importer's name differs from that mentioned in a letter of credit;
- Is not issued by the exporter;
- Order or L/C. Number not stated, when required under letter of credit.

Bill of Lading

- Not presented in full set when requested;
- Alterations not authenticated by an official of the shipping company or its agent;
- Is not "clean", that is, carries remarks that the condition and packing of the merchandise is defective;
- Is not marked "on board" when so required;
- "On board" notation not signed or initialled by the carrier or agent as required under L/C;
- "On board" notation not dated;
- Is not endorsed by the exporter when drawn to "order";
- Is not marked "freight paid" as stipulated in the credit (under C&F, CIF contracts);
- Is made out "to order" when the credit stipulated "direct to consignee" (importer) (and vice versa);
- Is dated later than the latest shipment date specified in the L/C;
- Is not presented within the period specified in the letter of credit;
- Included details of merchandise other than that specified in a credit;
- Rate at which freight is calculated and the total amount not shown when credit requires these details. The following are acceptable only if expressly permitted in a credit:

– Shipment "on deck", that is, the goods are not stored in the hold;
– Shipment from a port or to a destination other than that stipulated;

• Presentation of types of bills of lading not specifically authorised in a credit, for example Charter Party bill of lading and so on.

Marine Insurance

• Amount of cover is insufficient;
• Does not include risks mentioned in a credit;
• Is not issued in the currency of a credit;
• Is not endorsed by the insured and/or signed by the insurers;
• Certificate or policy bears a date later than the date of shipment/despatch, except where a warehouse to warehouse clause is indicated;
• Incorrect description of goods;
• Alterations are not authenticated;
• It is not in transferable form when required;
• Carrying vessel's name not recorded;
• Does not cover transhipment when bills of lading indicate it will take place.

Note

When a policy is called for under a credit, a certificate is not acceptable. However, a policy is acceptable when a certificate is called for. Broker's cover notes are not acceptable unless specifically permitted in a credit.

Remember

When these and any other documents are required by a credit they should comply with the stipulated terms and conditions of a credit and be

• Properly signed and
• Have all alterations duly authenticated.

17

Bank Guarantees and International Bonds

Guarantees and international bonds are two separate subjects. A guarantee is usually an undertaking given by a person/guarantor as security for a credit facility offered by a creditor/bank to a borrower. An international bond is an undertaking given by a bank or issuer at the request of its customer (contractor/supplier) in favour of a project owner or beneficiary/buyer in another country.

Guarantees as Security

Definition: A guarantee is defined in section 4 Statute of Frauds 1677 as a "written promise by one person to be responsible for the debt, default or miscarriage of another person incurred to a third party".

From this simple definition it is evident that for a guarantee to be legally enforceable certain conditions must be present.

(a) The guarantee must be in writing. Thus, any oral promise expressed to be by way of a guarantee is legally unenforceable. However, if the oral promise is by way of an indemnity, then such promises are legally enforceable.

  1. "A" gives guarantee to the creditor (C).
  2. "C" gives money to the borrower (B).
  3. The creditor claims repayment from the borrower (B).
  4. If repayment does not come from the borrower (B), the creditor claims from the guarantor (A).

© The Author(s) 2019
T. Bhogal, A. Trivedi, *International Trade Finance*, Finance and Capital Markets Series,
https://doi.org/10.1007/978-3-030-24540-5_17

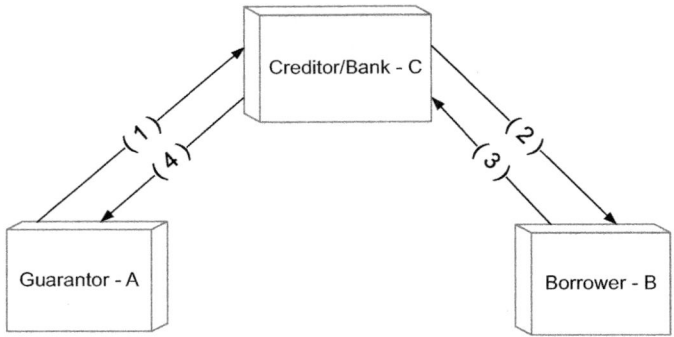

Fig. 17.1 Guarantee as security—mechanism

(b) There are three parties to a contract of guarantee.

1. The person who gives the written promise is known as the guarantor.
2. The person whose responsibilities are being secured is known as the debtor or more often is described as the principal debtor or the borrowing customer.
3. The third party who is known as the creditor in actual fact is the bank.

(c) By another part of section 4, a guarantee is unenforceable unless signed by the guarantor(s) or his agent. Thus no one can be held liable on the guarantee unless they have actually signed the written document. This simple statement needs to be extended with regard to joint and several guarantees, that is, promises by more than one person to sign the same guarantee. For, under English law, until all guarantors have signed the form of a guarantee, it is unenforceable even against those who have signed it.

(d) There is no provision within the definition for the signing to be witnessed. Thus, when a banker witnesses the signing of such forms, it is not out of legal compulsion. There are two reasons as follows:

1. It avoids contentions that the form contains a forgery of a guarantor's signature.
2. It avoids claims that no one took the trouble to explain the contents of the document.

(e) A bank guarantee does not have to be in any set style. The only provision is that it must be in writing. However, banks today require guarantors to sign a very complex and lengthy document, which contains a lot of legal jargon. This is intended to give the bank the maximum possible protection against a whole range of contingencies, while at the same time it deprives the guarantors of many rights, some of which would be available through common law.

Distinction Between Guarantees and Indemnities

By signing a bank guarantee, a guarantor promises to be collaterally answerable for the debt (default or miscarriage) which the principal debtor owes to the bank. So if the principal debtor who is primarily liable does not repay the bank debt, the guarantor, who is secondarily liable, will have to.

1. "A" gives guarantee to the creditor (C).
2. "C" gives money to the borrower (B).
3. The creditor claims repayment from the borrower (B).
4. If repayment does not come from the borrower (B), the creditor claims from the guarantor (A) who will have to pay to the creditor.

This should be compared with an indemnity, where there are only two parties to a contract of indemnity, and the person giving the indemnity (the indemnifier) assumes primary liability. Thus, the indemnifier undertakes to pay the debt to the bank (creditor) (rather than paying only if the principal debtor cannot or will not pay).

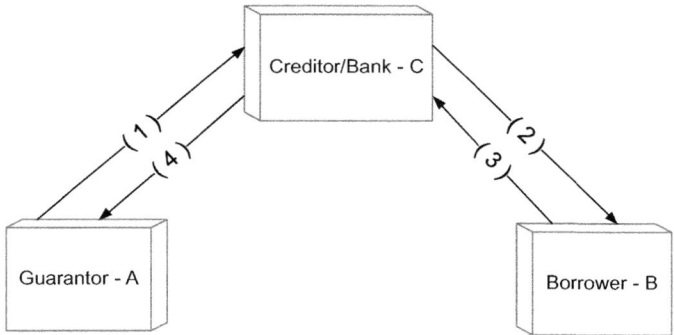

Fig. 17.2 Distinction between guarantee and indemnity

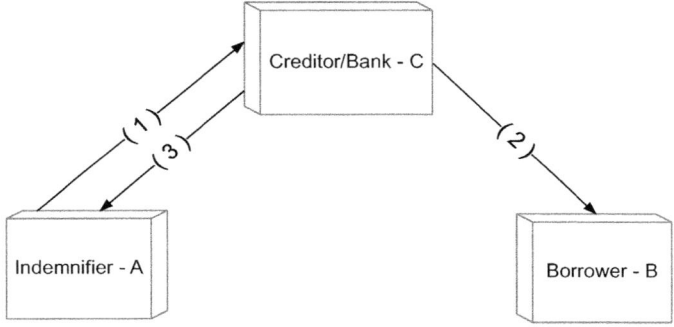

Fig. 17.3 Distinction between guarantee and indemnity

1. "A" requests the creditor to lend money to "B" and indemnifies the creditor (C).
2. "C" gives money to the borrower (B).
3. The creditor claims repayment from the borrower (A).

This latter situation can be of considerable benefit to a banker particularly where the guarantee has been taken as security for a principal debtor who is not legally liable for a debt he has created—say because the principal debtor is a minor, or the guarantee is securing an advance which is ultra vires a company—even though in the latter case s.9 European Communities Act 1972 may be available as protection. In the past, when bankers have tried to enforce their security, they have been unsuccessful, and the classic legal case on the matter is Coutts & Co. V. Browne-Lecky (1947).

Banks overcome this general problem today by including a special clause known as an indemnity clause in their form of a guarantee. This clause converts the guarantee into an indemnity. Thus, if a bank had given an advance to a borrower that was secured by an indemnity, the bank could recover from the indemnifier even though recovery would not be possible from the debtor customer. The reason for this is that the indemnifier has assumed primary liability.

Advantages of Guarantees as Security

The guarantees are easy to take, for it is not necessary to carry out an investigation of title or registration—even when given by a company. But remember if supported, then depending upon the nature of the supporting security, all the usual formalities regarding registration and so on will be necessary for the latter.

The various clauses contained within a bank guarantee give the bank the maximum possible protection and powers.

With the exception of an unlimited guarantee, the guarantor's maximum liability is fixed to the amount quoted on the form.

With the exception of a specific guarantee all the principal debtor's liabilities are secured, both current and in the future.

Provided the guarantor remains financially sound (a point determined by status enquiry), the guarantee has a stable value.

Where supporting security has been taken, which itself is stable in value, then the security is a very strong one.

If the guarantor defaults on his promise, it is a simple matter to pursue recovery through the courts.

Because the guarantees are third-party securities, they can be ignored when claiming against the principal debtor for recovery. This is particularly useful if the principal debtor has had a receiving order presented against him as a proof can be submitted ignoring any payment made or promised from the guarantor.

Where the principal debtor has no assets to offer as security this is always given by a third party which may be the only alternative offered to the banker. If a guarantee is offered by someone of good financial standing then the bank will usually be happy to accept it.

Bankers often request directors of limited companies to give guarantees to secure the liabilities of their companies. This action will ensure that they have a greater incentive for the business to succeed particularly if they have been required to support the guarantee.

Disadvantages of a Guarantee as Security for a Credit Facility

If the guarantee is not supported by tangible security having a stable value, then the worth of the guarantee is dependent on the financial stability of the guarantor. In situations where the guarantee has been given by director in favour of his company, then the downfall of the latter may lead to the downfall of the former for both are dependent on each other.

Although a guarantee contains many legal clauses, a guarantor may still be able to avoid liability on technical reasons. It is often considered that the giving of a guarantee is a formality—and that the liability is not a real one. This of course is not true. If the bank finds it necessary to call upon the guarantor for repayment, bad feeling often results, particularly where the guarantor is a customer of the bank. If the guarantor will not pay, then legal action may be necessary—which may be time-consuming and expensive.

Procedures for Taking as Security

Establish the financial standing of the guarantor(s). If the guarantor is already a customer of the bank/branch, then the bank will be fully aware of his financial standing. However, if the guarantor is a customer of another branch or bank, then it will be necessary to carry out a status enquiry. If a joint and several guarantee is being taken, an enquiry for the full amount is made on all the guarantors, but the joint and several liabilities aspect of the guarantee must be mentioned.

Review the general considerations: It is essential that an intending guarantor must obtain independent legal advice. After this, the advising solicitor should add the attestation clause and act as a witness as regards the signing of the document.

Use the bank's standard guarantee form or a guarantee to be enforceable (as established earlier it must be a written document). Although the wording has not been provided for by statute, each bank has developed its own form, which affords it the best possible protection. Thus, a bank will not be prepared to accept any form of a guarantee which is not its own. Where a guarantor suggests alterations, additions or deletions, then reference will have to be made to the bank's legal advisor.

Place where the guarantee should be signed: A banker would prefer it if all guarantees given in favour of his customers were signed at his bank/branch in his presence. This is not always possible and so various alternatives must be considered.

(a) At one of the bank's branches (which is near to the guarantor's home or place of business);
(b) At a branch of another bank. This procedure is used when the guarantor's bank does not have a branch in the locality of the guarantor(s) home or place of business;
(c) At a solicitor's office, if independent legal advice has been sought. Wherever it is signed, then, it is essential for the signature to be witnessed. The witness normally prints his name, address and occupation and, then adds his signature as confirmation. If the guarantor's signature is not known then the guarantee form must be sent to his bankers so that they can confirm its authenticity.

A bank must never send a guarantee form direct to a guarantor however unique the circumstances of the request might be. Although there is no legal justification for declining such a request, a guarantor should be told that it is not possible to meet this request. The guarantor should, however, be told that the guarantee can be made available for his signature at a convenient branch or bank. There are three main reasons for acting this way:

1. It minimises the risk of a forged signature being placed on the form and the consequences of such a problem.
2. It minimises the risk of a guarantor claiming non est factum. But as we have seen, pleas under this heading are very unlikely to succeed today because the banks ask the solicitors to confirm the identity of the person signing the document.
3. It reduces the likelihood of a successful claim that there was no opportunity for the guarantor either to ask questions or to have the nature of the guarantee liability explained.

Joint and several guarantees: The bank must ensure that when there is more than one guarantor, all must sign, otherwise, the security is unenforceable. Furthermore, if the terms have been agreed, one guarantor cannot vary anything unless all other guarantors agree. A banker would be expected to specify the names of the principal debtor(s) and guarantor(s) correctly.

After the guarantee form has been completed and signed, each of the guarantor(s) should be provided with a copy. A receipt should be obtained from each guarantor. A diary card should be completed as a reminder to carry out an annual status enquiry on each guarantor. Where a subsequent enquiry shows deterioration in the guarantor's financial standing the matter should be discussed with both the principal debtor and the guarantor.

A diary card should also be completed as a reminder to advise the guarantor of his liability at reasonable intervals and obtain an acknowledgement from him. This is for convenience purposes and is not a procedure required by law, nor does it have any relevance to the six- or twelve-year status barred time unit.

Precautions

Where the guarantee is being taken as additional security, then the other procedures have to be considered. If the guarantor had already given the bank a guarantee in favour of the same principal debtor, then a separate memorandum is usually taken or a clause added to indicate that the security is in addition to, and not in replacement of, the earlier one.

If the arrangement was to cancel one guarantee as soon as a new one was completed then a memorandum or clause similar to the one mentioned above would not be needed. Clearly no competent banker would cancel the old guarantee until the new one had been taken, even though a customer may try to indicate that this was the agreement between him and the banker.

If another security, irrespective of whether it is direct or indirect, is held, then it is not necessary to tell the guarantor of its existence or the earlier mortgagors that further security is lodged. For contracts of guarantee are not contracts uberrimae fidei.

International Bonds/Bank Guarantees

Introduction

Over recent years, the demand from overseas buyers for bonds to support contractual obligations entered into by UK exporters has increased substantially.

As a result of the increase in demand, coupled with an overall increase in the average size of contracts and recent litigation, the subject of foreign bonds and guarantees has gained greater attention in international trading.

Many exporters will be aware that Bid Bonds and Performance Guarantees are one of the basic ingredients of doing business overseas and that liability under the bond/guarantee will remain during the life of the bank contract and beyond.

A bank guarantee/bond is usually no more than a written undertaking to a foreign beneficiary that the bank will pay him a sum of money against the production of a document or documents, or when demanded upon the occurrence of a specified failure.

A bond or guarantee is often an indication of the financial standing of a supplier or contractor and his ability to fulfil a contract.

The bank puts its name and its reputation behind the promise to pay and will protect that reputation by paying a claim if, and only if, the claim meets the requirements set out in the guarantee.

Parties

There are mostly three parties involved in the provision of a guarantee/bond.

The Seller—is to perform the work covered by the bond (also known as the supplier or contractor, principal or exporter);

The Buyer—to whom the bond is issued (also known as the customer, client, employer or beneficiary);

The Guarantor—bank, surety or insurance company who issues the guarantee/bond on provision of a written Counter Indemnity from the seller.

Bank's Role

It is often forgotten that important duties are owed by a bank issuing a guarantee to both the beneficiary and to its customer and that their interests must accordingly be balanced. The bank's role is restricted to that of ensuring that a claim is paid only if it complies with the literal terms of the guarantee issued, and it therefore does not wish to be put in a position of having to adjudicate the relative merits of the parties to the underlying contract.

When issuing guarantees, banks should not be concerned with the terms of the contract. The only reference to the contract which should appear in the guarantee is a reference sufficient to identify and connect the guarantee with the underlying transaction and such would normally appear in either the heading or in a preamble.

A guarantee/bond should be a stand-alone document, payable either on simple demand or against documents called for in the guarantee.

The neutral position of a bank between buyer and seller only holds after the guarantee has been issued. Beforehand the seller is the bank's customer and is entitled to as much advice and assistance as the bank is able to provide. All too often banks do not receive the opportunity of providing that help, for the first information they receive of an impending contract is frequently an urgent request to arrange the delivery of a tender bond in some distant corner of the world, in time for the opening of tenders at 9 o'clock the following morning.

Format of Bank Guarantees/Bonds

Over the years banks have accumulated a considerable volume of data on guarantee requirements, acceptable formats, local costs and so on, and are happy to share that data with customers whose own experience may well be more limited.

Advantages

Some countries nominally require all guarantees from abroad to be issued through a local bank. A determined exporter and a willing buyer can arrange for a direct guarantee to be given.

The advantages of a direct guarantee to the exporter are substantial:

(a) It is cheaper because it cuts out the correspondent bank's charges.
(b) It can be made subject to English law.
(c) Most important is the fact that the local bank is in charge of the operation of the guarantee and not the foreign bank.

If a claim materialises, local banks are in a better position to assess the validity of the claim than is the case when the guarantee is a correspondent bank's guarantee and if the correspondent has paid, a local bank must respond without question to this demand.

Categories of Bank Guarantees/Bonds

Guarantees fall into two broad categories—on demand and conditional.

1. An on-demand guarantee/bond, once given, can be called at the sole discretion of the buyer as the nature of the document is such that claims must be met without being contested.
2. The unconditional nature of these guarantees/bonds makes it difficult—if not impossible—for the exporter to interfere with the bank's obligation to pay.
3. Conditional guarantees/bonds, that is, those specifying documentary evidence, give maximum protection to the exporter if claims made under the bond are required to be substantiated through the production of specified documents, for example certificate of an award by an independent arbitrator.

A contentious matter for many exporters is the question of expiry dates and in some countries the provisions of local law and practice permit claims to be submitted beyond the nominal expiry date of the guarantee—this prevails in Algeria for example.

Provisions such as these, which are generally applicable to guarantees issued by local banks, may well apply to guarantees issued by the bank direct to an overseas buyer. It is also important that both the exporter and his bank reach agreement on the wording format of a guarantee and if there is a strong possibility that guarantees are going to play an important role in gaining an overseas contract, an early approach to the bank would create the opportunity to provide helpful information on bonding in the country concerned. In particular, it would enable the bank to establish whether its direct guarantee is likely to be acceptable and—if necessary—to provide standard guarantee text. These may not always be acceptable to the buyer, but at least they can provide the exporter with a useful basis from which to begin negotiations.

Types of Bank Guarantees/International Bonds

During the last century overseas buyers of capital goods and large projects have increasingly demanded that suppliers and contractors provide them with a guarantee or bond covering them against non-performance. A bank issuing such bonds is liable to reimburse in full for the amount of the bond to the bondholder.

The main types of guarantees or bonds which banks are requested to issue on behalf of contractors or suppliers for large overseas projects are as follows:

Bid Bonds or Tender Bonds

Exporters who tender for foreign contracts often find that the conditions of tender require a bank guarantee to be established for a percentage. Usually one to 5% of the value of the contract, to assure the buyer that the accompanying bid is a serious offer. This is known as a bid/tender Bond.

It is demanded by the buyer to protect the buyer if the seller refuses to accept or enter into a contract after the bid has been awarded to him. In the event that the seller refuses or fails to open a performance bond as required by the buyer, the buyer can call the bid bond and recover the losses suffered by him in re-inviting the tender.

This is issued in support of a customer's tender sometimes in lieu of a cash deposit. It is to confirm the genuineness of the tender so that, in the event of the failure of the contractor to enter into any contract granted in accordance with the terms of the tender, a sum (usually about 5%, but sometimes as low as one or as high as 10%, of the total contract price) may be claimed by the company or organisation in whose favour it has been issued. Callings under such a bond are normally payable on demand. Such a guarantee usually takes the form of a request to a bank abroad to issue the bond against the British (or home) bank's indemnity. Like all types of guarantees given by banks, a counter indemnity is taken from the customer.

Mechanics of Bid Bond

1. Invitation for Bid. The project owner/promoter sends a tender to bid on a project to a contractor. The tender requires a bid bond and permits the bid bond to be in the form of a standby letter of credit.
2. The contractor applies to his bank for the issuance of a bid bond.
3. The contractor's bank (issuing bank) issues a bid bond and forwards it to the contractor.
4. The contractor forwards his bid together with the bid bond to the project owner.
5. The project owner accepts the contractor's bid and sends a contract to the contractor.
6. If the contractor fails to sign the contract or fails to obtain and forward to the project owner a performance bond, the project owner will demand payment under a bid bond.
7. When the contractor has signed the contract and obtained a performance bond, or whatever else the contract may require, the project owner will return the bid bond to the contractor to be cancelled.
8. The issuing bank informs the contractor of his action. The matter is closed from the bank's point of view. However, in the case of a dispute between the two parties, it has to be resolved through a legal court in accordance with the conditions of the document.

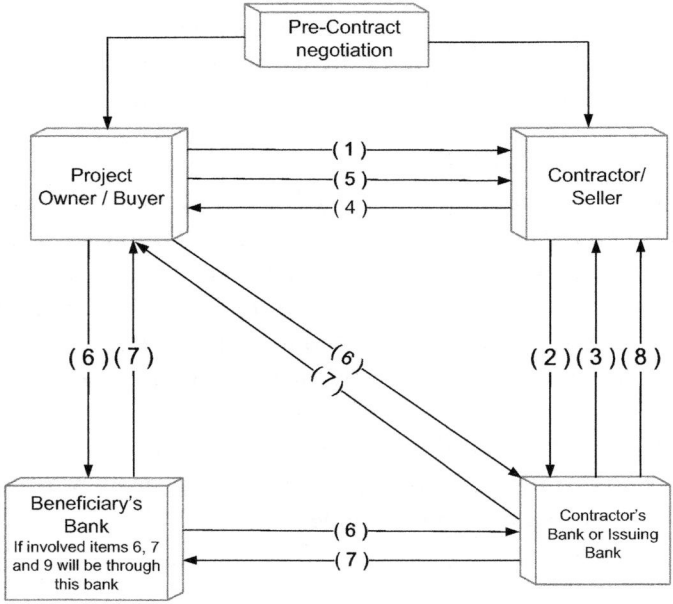

Fig. 17.4 Bid bond—mechanism

From XYZ Bank PLC

To Name and address of beneficiary

Messrs ABC & Co. Limited (supplier) submitted on their bid for the supply of _____
under your bid invitation No _____ dated _____According to your tender
conditions a bid bond has to be provided.

At the request of Messrs _____*(supplier)*___, we, __*XYZ Bank of Address*___Postcode
____, hereby irrevocably undertake to pay to you on first demand, irrespective of the
validity and the legal effects of such bid and waiving all rights of objection and defence
arising therefrom, any amount up to _____*(currency/maximum amount) (full amount in
words)*___ upon receipt of your duly signed request for payment stating that Messrs ABC
& Co. Limited:

- have withdrawn their offer before its expiry date without your consent or

- have failed to sign the contract awarded to them in the terms of their offer or

- have failed to open the performance bond foreseen in the tender upon signature
  of the contract.

The total amount of this guarantee will be reduced by any payment effected hereunder.

For the purpose of identification, your request for payment in writing has to be presented
through the intermediary of a first rate bank confirming that the signatures thereon are
legally binding upon you.

Your claim is also acceptable if transmitted to us in full by encoded telex/SWIFT through a
first rate bank confirming that your original claim has been sent to us by registered mail
and that the signatures thereon are legally binding upon you.

Your claim will be considered as having been made once we are in possession of your
written request for payment or the encoded telex/SWIFT to this effect.

Our guarantee is valid until _____*(date in words)* and expires in full and automatically if
your claim has not been made on or before that date, regardless of such date being a
banking day or not.

This guarantee is governed by English Laws of the United Kingdom and the place of
jurisdiction is London.

_____   _____

Authorised Signature   Authorised Signature

Date: _____

Specimen of bid bond/guarantees

Performance Bond

If the exporter is subsequently awarded a contract, he is usually required to arrange a performance bond for perhaps 5% or 10% of the value of the contract, which remains in force until the contract is completed. It guarantees satisfactory performance of the seller's obligations under the contract.

It is usual for the tender bond to be released shortly after the issue of the performance bond.

The issue of these bonds provides buyers with an indication of the financial standing of the tendering party. It is also intended to act as a safeguard should the contract not be carried out in a satisfactory manner.

This is given in support of a customer's obligation to fulfil a contractual commitment. When issued by a bank it usually provides for payment to the beneficiary of about 10% of the contract value in the event of the undertaking not being fulfilled. It may be payable on demand, but payment is often related to the production of evidence showing non-fulfilment.

A performance bond is usually issued after the tender guarantee is cancelled, although the tender guarantee may be extended to become a performance bond.

This guarantee is usually 10 to 20% of the contract value and is provided by the seller for the money given to him by the "buyer" in advance to finance initial stages of the contract.

Date: _____

From: XYZ Bank PLC

You have concluded on _____ a contract No _____ with Messrs _____ ABC & Co. _____ for the delivery of _____ at a total price of _____ As security for the due performance of the delivery, a guarantee by a bank shall be furnished.

At the request of Messrs _____ ABC & Co. Limited, we, XYZ Bank PLC, of _____Postcode _____, hereby irrevocably undertake to pay to you on first demand, irrespective of the validity and the legal effects of the above-mentioned contract and waiving all rights of objection and defence arising from said contract, any amount up to ___(currency and maximum amount in words) upon receipt of your signed request for payment stating that Messrs ------ABC & Co. Limited ------have failed to deliver the ordered merchandise or have not delivered such merchandise as specified in the above mentioned contract and that as a consequence you have suffered a loss equalling the amount requested under this performance bond.

The total amount of this guarantee will be reduced by any payment effected hereunder.

For the purpose of identification, your request for payment in writing has to be presented through the intermediary of a first rate bank confirming that the signatures thereon are legally binding upon you.

Your claim is also acceptable if transmitted to us in full by encoded telex/SWIFT through a first rate bank confirming that your original claim has been sent to us by registered mail and that the signatures thereon are legally binding upon you.

Your claim will be considered as having been made once we are in possession of your written request for payment or the encoded telex/SWIFT to this effect.

Our guarantee is valid until _____ (date in words) and expires in full and automatically if your claim has not been made on or before that date, regardless of such date being a banking day or not.

This guarantee is governed by English Laws of the United Kingdom and place of jurisdiction is London (UK)

Authorised Signature   Authorised Signature

_____   _____

Advance or progress payment bonds

Specimen of a performance bond/guarantee

Retention or Maintenance Bonds

By providing such a bond a seller can obtain 100% of payment, instead of a portion being withheld by the buyer to cover possible future maintenance obligations.

Banking Facility

The above-mentioned guarantees can be conditional or unconditional, open ended, or providing an expiry date or method by which they can expire or be cancelled.

Other Types of Bonds

Bonds or guarantees may also be required to cover completion of a project, purchase of equipment, transportation of crude oil or bulk commodities and retention monies and so on.

Where the provision of bonds and guarantees is a feature of a contract, the exporters/importers are advised to seek the advice of the local branch of their bank.

Precautions

Sellers and issuing banks should resist issuing unconditional guarantees. Banks should advise their customers of the consequences and dangers of providing such guarantees.

However, in view of big projects and supply contracts, exporters, often for fear of losing a contract, submit too easily to erroneous bonding conditions without first trying to negotiate more satisfactory terms.

This is a variation on a performance bond which guarantees the refund, in the event of certain terms and conditions not being completed (e.g. if goods are not shipped or a contract complied with), of amounts paid by the purchaser in advance to the contractor; it is therefore issued in favour of the buyer. It can provide for an increase as further amounts are paid to the contractor, or for a reduction as various portions of the contract are fulfilled.

Most contracts provide for a period during which the contractor or supplier is responsible for the maintenance and effectiveness of the completed project. The bond guarantees financial support to the buyer for the warranty period. It is often issued to obtain the release of funds on completion of the contract, which under the terms and conditions of the contract would not otherwise be paid over until the warranty period had expired.

Note: All these bonds are normally payable on the demand of the claimant. Banks are not able to act as arbitrators in deciding whether or not the contractor has fulfilled his obligations. Any claims made will be paid in full and it is then for the parties to refer the matter to an arbitrator or take the matter up in court.

International Bonds/Guarantees: Precautions

- The name and address of the guarantor (bank) should be clearly written.
- Names and addresses of the other parties involved should also be stated.
- The tender to which a tender guarantee relates and the contract to which any other guarantee relates should be clearly identified in the guarantee. The reference number (if any) and date should also be mentioned. This is important as the guarantee may not be valid for any other, or an amended tender or contract.
- The guarantee should indicate the maximum liability of the guarantor. Care should be taken if the contract price is variable, or expressed in amounts involving different currencies, or by using a percentage figure if an amount and currency of the guarantee. The amount or the percentage figure of a guarantee should be realistic and avoid over-protection, since the cost of such over-protection may be reflected in the contract price.
- In the case of an Advance Payment Bond, it may well be appropriate to specify in the guarantee pro rate reduction in the guarantee amount as part re-payments are made by the principal. Performance bonds may also be treated in a similar way, that is, by specific provision for pro rate reduction in the guarantee amount to match partial performance.

Time for Payment

- When a claim has been presented, duly supported by the appropriate documentation, payment is to be effected by the bank without any delay other than that necessary for the bank to check the documentation and satisfy itself that requirements stipulated in the guarantee have been met. No particular time for paying a claim under a tender guarantee can be defined.
- In the case of a performance or repayment bond the procedure for checking the documentation, for example where an arbitral award may have to be translated, may take some time. It is advisable to specify in the guarantee a maximum period for the checking of documents.

Arbitration Clause

- All guarantees may provide for an arbitration clause in the case of disputes. If the parties prefer to delete the provision on arbitration, disputes will then be settled by the courts at the guarantor's (main) place of business or, at the option of the beneficiary, at the competent court covering jurisdiction where the guarantee was issued

Documentation

- It is obviously desirable that these details should as far as possible be clearly defined in the guarantee. Considerations to be taken into account may, however, differ according to the type of guarantee and the problem.

Expiry Date

- The expiry date is a matter of primary importance for all parties concerned. If, after the expiry date, the bank has not received any claim, its liability to the beneficiary comes to an end. It is therefore advisable for such date and the place to receive the claim to be specified in the bond itself.

Return of Guarantee Document

- When a guarantee has ceased to be valid in accordance with its terms and conditions it should be returned to the bank without delay.

Issuing Bank Guarantees: Action Steps

All customers who wish the bank to issue a guarantee on their behalf are required to make a request in writing to the bank giving all the details to be given in the Letter of Guarantee to be issued. On receipt of the request the following steps are to be followed:

1. Establish the time limit within which the guarantee has to be issued and presented to the beneficiary.
2. Check the mandate and the signature(s).
3. Check the contents/clauses in the letter as to whether they are acceptable.

4. Refer to legal department for any clarification, if required.
5. Check the balance of the account.
6. Check for existing facilities granted by the bank.
7. If the customer (applicant) is a company, follow points 8–10.
8. Check memorandum and articles of association.
9. Obtain necessary resolution of the Board of Directors.
10. Check quorum requirements for validity of the resolution.
11. Obtain (necessary) counter indemnity, where required.
12. Prepare credit report and/or facility application to seek approval required of the competent authority.
13. Check details of the security to be offered by the customer.
14. Prepare credit line security to credit control department.
15. Submit draft to manager for approval and signature.
16. Prepare draft for the guarantee to be issued and submit to a credit control department for perusal and return.
17. Show/discuss the draft with the customer.
18. Obtain customer's signature on the draft.
19. Mark lien on the balance, if required.
20. Recover percentage of the facility as margin.

   (a) DEBIT Customer's account.
   (b) CREDIT Margin on guarantees' account.

21. Record the details on Liabilities Register.

   (a) DEBIT Customer Liabilities—Guarantees.
   (b) CREDIT Bankers Liabilities—Guarantees.

22. Obtain authorised signatures on the Letter of Guarantee.
23. Obtain authorised signatures on the respective vouchers.
24. Recover commission and charges in respect of the guarantee issued (at appropriate rate according to the bank's schedule of charges for each three-month period).
25. Post guarantee form to the principal.
26. Record a separate file and attach negotiation sheet.
27. Record expiry date on the negotiation sheet.
28. Diarise the expiry date.
29. Post vouchers on the terminal on the same day under the respective value date.
30. Amend all the records, if extension is requested.
31. Diarise to recover commission or charges periodically.

32. In the event of no reply being received from the customer, the facility will be withdrawn on the expiry date and entries on Liabilities Register will be reversed.
33. Advise the principal of withdrawal of bank facility.
34. Advise the customer accordingly.

International Bonds and Bank Guarantees: Specimens

To:

XYZ Bank PLC   From: ABC Bank PLC

Address

At the request of _____ *of* _____ -
(hereinafter referred to as suppliers) we _____ Bank PLC, hereby issue
our letter of guarantee in your favour up to an amount of GB Pounds _____
(GB Pounds: _____only).

This guarantee is issued in consideration of suppliers, supplying
_____

To _____ on behalf of Messrs. _____ of _____ under
letter of credit no. _____ *dated* _____, opened by XYZ Bank of -
_____ branch _____ in favour of _____

This letter of guarantee is irrevocable on our part and we, hereby undertake to
pay upon your first simple demand in writing that Messrs. _____ have
advised to you that defective parts of _____ equipment and accessories
supplied to _____ were not fitted and replaced by _____ and
that they failed to do so within _____ months and 15 days from the date of
acceptance of merchandise as detailed in credit no._____ issued by
_____, date of which to be advised to us by yourselves.

For and on behalf of:

ABC BANK PLC.

Signatures _____   _____

Performance bond (amend wording as required)

To:

Bank _____ Dated: _____

Address

Test _____GB Pounds 0,000,000/=

RE: Our guarantee No: L/G _____

We

_____ *XYZ Bank PLC of* _____Postcode_____, Hereby issue our
letter of guarantee No L/G _____ in your favour for a maximum amount, not
exceeding GB Pounds 0,000,000/= (GB Pounds: XXXXXXXXXXX only) inclusive of any
interest and charges in consideration of your allowing banking facility to Mr/Messrs

_____

Any claims under this guarantee will be met on your first demand provided they are:

1)   Made in writing, by letter, or authenticated telex, cable stating that Mr/Messrs-----
     ----------------has failed to meet his/their obligations towards you in respect of the
     banking facilities extended to him/them by yourselves and

2)   Lodged so as to reach us during the validity of the guarantee.

Banking facility guarantee specimen (amend wording as required)

To:

Bank's Name   Dated: 27-07-200X

Address Jeddah Saudi Arabia.

Test _____ on S. Riyals 4,000.00

RE: Our letter of guarantee No: L/G _____

You are requested to issue your own letter of guarantee in the standard form acceptable to Saudi government and government agencies.

1) Favour _____ Ministry of Agriculture of Government of Saudi Arabia
2) Principal _____ M/S Together & Co. Limited – Istanbul, Turkey, on behalf of T & Z Ltd. Jeddah, Saudi Arabia
3) Amount _____ S.R. 4,000,000.00 (Saudi Riyals: Four millions only)
4) Type of bond _____ advance payment, being 10% of the contract amount of S.R. 40,000,000.00 (Saudi Riyals: forty million only) for the project contract No. XXXXXX dated 1st January 200X
5) Starting from _____ .and validity_____ months from the
6) Date of expiry date of_____ receipt of advance payment of S.R. 4,000,000/= (Saudi Riyals: four million only) by you for our account
7) This guarantee will only become operative subject to the strict compliance of the following terms and conditions:
   a) Upon receipt of 100% advance payment of S.R. 4,000,000/= (Saudi Riyals: four million only) into and to the order of the XYZ Bank PLC Saudi Riyal A/C No. XYZ 12345678 held with you, receipt and crediting of which to be confirmed to us by your tested telex or swift advice.
   b) An irrevocable undertaking from the beneficiary to you, stating in writing that any payments by them to M/S Together & Co. Limited, Jeddah, Saudi Arabia, under the contract No. XXXXXX dated 1st January 200X for a total amount of S.R. 40,000,000/= (Saudi Riyals: forty million only) shall be paid to you only.
   c) That on receipt of proceeds, referred to in clause (b), above you will credit the entire proceeds of S.R. 40,000,000/= (Saudi Riyals: forty million only) into and to the order of XYZ Bank PLC account No. XYZ 12345678 held with you for account: M/S Together & Co. Limited, Istanbul, Turkey.

In consideration of your issuing the above-mentioned letter of guarantee, we, XYZ Bank PLC, of 300 commercial street, London E1 3AD, hereby absolutely irrevocably and unconditionally guarantee, under our counter guarantee No. 000000 to pay to you on your first demand by letter, telex or cable any amount upto Saudi Riyals 4,000,000/= (Saudi Riyals: four million only) as and when required to be paid by you to the above-mentioned beneficiary plus your charges and expenses as determined by you and to indemnify you against any loss or damage whatsoever resulting from issuing your guarantee, notwithstanding any objection and deficance by a third party arising from said obligation

The validity of this guarantee extended to _____(allow ten days after validity of our guarantee to allow for processing) by which date all demand under this guarantee should be received by us. Any payment made hereunder shall be made free and clear of and without deduction for any present of future withholding or

Other taxes, duties, imports etc, of whatsoever nature and any whomsoever imposed. We hereby confirm that foreign exchange control and all other necessary approvals for the issuance of this counter guarantee have been obtained and are in full force and effect.

Our counter guarantee is subject to the laws and regulations of the Kingdom of Saudi Arabia.

Signature_____   Signature_____

Advance payment guarantee specimen (amend wording as required)

From: M/S _____ Of _____

To: XYZ Bank PLC   Date _____

Address

Abu Dhabi

Test _____ *On GB Pounds* _____

Ref our guarantee number L/G_____

At the request of _____ bank, _____ branch London and on
behalf of their clients M/S _____ we _____ bank PLC, of _____,
hereby request you to kindly issue a guarantee for USD _____ *(GB Pounds:* _____ -
only) in favour of M/S _____ *Co. of* _____ as per following text:

Quote

Messrs. M/S _____.

Address _____

At the request of M/S _____ of _____, we _____ bank PLC of
_____ guarantee to you for a sum of GB P_____ (GB Pounds:
_____ only).

This guarantee is in respect of replacement and fitting of defective parts of
_____ being supplied in accordance with our LC No. Lon _____ dated
_____

This guarantee will remain valid for a period of _____ months from the date of acceptance
of merchandise to _____ and in case M/S _____ or their nominee
fail to replace the defective parts of the _____, the beneficiary of the guarantee is
authorised to claim the amount of the guarantee along with the letter from _____
stating that despite their notification to M/S _____ of _____, or their
nominee the defective parts of the _____ were not replaced.

Any claim made under this letter of guarantee must be presented at our office within the validity
period, after which no claims will be entertained hereunder and our liability will cease to exist.
Before any claim is made notification must be given to us _____ M/S _____

Unquote

1. Please treat this telex as an operative instrument and send us two copies of the guarantee
   issued by you for our record.
2. Please claim your charges in GB Pounds.
3. On the expiry of the above guarantee our liability thereunder will cease to exist.

In consideration of your issuing this guarantee we undertake to hold you harmless against any claim which may arise by reasons of your so doing provided that the amount does not exceed GB Pounds _____ (United States Dollars _____ only). Please quote our reference No _____ in all communication relating to this guarantee.

Authorised Signature   Authorised Signature

_____   _____

18

SWIFT and Letters of Credit

Introduction

SWIFT is a global member-owned cooperative, headquartered in Belgium. SWIFT's international governance and oversight reinforces the neutral, global character of its cooperative structure. SWIFT's global office network ensures an active presence in all the major financial centres.

SWIFT is the world's leading provider of standard, uniform and secure financial messaging services. The co-operative provide their users with a platform for messaging, standards for communicating and also offer products and services to facilitate access and integration; identification, analysis and regulatory compliance.

SWIFT's messaging platform, products and services connect more than 11,000 banking and securities organisations, market infrastructure and corporate customers that basically include banks, broker-dealers and investment managers. The broader SWIFT community also encompasses corporate as well as market infrastructure in payments, securities, treasury and trade in more than 200 countries and territories. Whilst SWIFT does not hold funds or manage accounts on behalf of customers, they enable the global community of users to communicate securely, exchanging standardised financial messages in a reliable way, thereby facilitating global and local financial flows, and supporting trade and commerce all around the world.

As a trusted provider, SWIFT relentlessly pursues operational excellence and continually seeks ways to lower costs, reduce risks and eliminate operational inefficiencies. SWIFT products and services support the user community's access and integration, business intelligence, reference data and financial crime compliance needs.

© The Author(s) 2019
T. Bhogal, A. Trivedi, *International Trade Finance*, Finance and Capital Markets Series,
https://doi.org/10.1007/978-3-030-24540-5_18

Definitions

"SWIFT" means Society for Worldwide Interbank Financial Telecommunication. **"SWIFTStandards"** means any message-based standard or component thereof, developed by or for SWIFT, including the related business model, messages, message flows and documentation, whether in draft or final form.

"IP Rights" means all copyright, proprietary know-how, patent rights (including patent applications) or other intellectual or industrial property rights.

License

SWIFT hereby grants the user a world-wide, royalty-free, non-exclusive license to use or promote SWIFT Standards (i) for information transmission purposes in or outside the context of SWIFT messaging services and/or (ii) to develop software, products or services which support transmission of information in accordance with SWIFT Standards.

Limitations

User may not directly or indirectly sell SWIFTStandards. User may not modify SWIFTStandards while maintaining "SWIFTStandards" as a reference for the modified standard. This License Agreement does not grant user a license to use any of SWIFT's trademarks, except the trademark "SWIFTStandards" for the use as defined and embodied by the SWIFT Agreement concluded for the purpose.

Sub-licensing

User may grant sub-licenses on a royalty free basis only and provided that any such sub-license remains within the scope of the user's rights under the License Agreement.

Ownership of SWIFTStandards

All IP Rights, worldwide ownership of and rights, title and interest in and to SWIFTStandards, and all copies and portions thereof, are and shall remain exclusively in SWIFT and its licensors.

Termination

The license will terminate immediately without notice when users fail to comply with any material provision of the License Agreement.

Disclosure of IP Rights

During the thirty (30) days period immediately following the date that SWIFTStandards are provided to the user, user may disclose that the publication of, use of or compliance with SWIFTStandards as presented, in whole or in part, would infringe any of user's IP Rights. Upon timely disclosure and considering the non-commercial nature of SWIFTStandards, user agree to license any such IP Right to SWIFT (including the right to grant sub-licenses) on royalty-free or otherwise reasonable and non-discriminatory terms and solely for the purpose of developing, implementing, promoting and using SWIFTStandards.

Non-enforcement of IP Rights

Any non-disclosure of user's IP Rights pursuant to Section 7 of the License Agreement shall be considered as a final and irrevocable waiver to assert or enforce any such IP Right that user may own or control, against SWIFT or any other third party that may use SWIFTStandards, if the allegedly infringing activity is caused solely by the use of SWIFTStandards in accordance with this License Agreement.

Disclaimer

SWIFTStandards are provided "as is". SWIFT makes no express or implied representations, including but not limited to, warranties of merchantability or fitness for any particular purpose nor any warranty that the use of SWIFTStandards will not infringe any third party IP Rights.

Limitation of Liability

Since SWIFTStandards result from industry consultation and are adopted by consensus amongst relevant industry participants, SWIFT will not be liable for any direct, indirect, special or consequential damages arising out of any use of SWIFTStandards even if SWIFT is expressly advised of the possibility of such damages.

Choice of Law: Arbitration

The License Agreement shall be governed by the Belgian law.

Any dispute concerning the License Agreement that cannot be amicably resolved, shall be finally settled under the Rules of Conciliation and Arbitration of the International Chamber of Commerce (ICC) by three arbitrators appointed in accordance with the rules. The arbitration proceedings shall take place in Brussels, Belgium and shall be conducted in the English language.

SWIFT UCP 600 Usage Guidelines

Exceptional Update to Achieve Alignment

Published on 12 January 2007

During its 24–25 October 2006 meeting, the ICC Commission on Banking Technique and Practice approved new UCP 600 rules for documentary credits. These rules were made effective on 1 July 2007. With the purpose to remain aligned with the new UCP 600 from this date onward, the "SWIFT UCP 600 Guidelines" provide guidance to banks on how to use today's category 7 standards in compliance with UCP 600.

Traditionally, SWIFT groups all its MT standards changes in one annual standards release, usually in October or November. In 2007, this will be on 27 October. In other words, the 1 July 2007 effective date of the UCP 600 did not coincide with the implementation date of SWIFT's Standards Release 2007.

This means that the only way to let the ICC and SWIFT "live" dates coincide and to publish how the UCP 600 affects category 7 standards was by issuing "SWIFT UCP 600 Guidelines" that financial institutions could start using as soon as the UCP 600 rules went 'live'. All guidelines are based on the use of narrative text in existing fields. The arrangement ensured a seamless transition to the new rules.

The November 2006 SWIFT release caters for the UCP 600 using today's existing category 7 messages. A new mandatory field 40E Applicable Rules contains codes to indicate adherence to specific rules. Other changes as described below were implemented in October 2007.

James Wills, the then Head of Trade Services Standards Development at SWIFT, noted, "The difference in dates for UCP 600 (1 July 2007) and the annual SWIFT Standards Release (November 2006 and October 2007) had provided something of a challenge. However, SWIFT did work with the industry to develop this approach to managing the issue, so that the community was and is able to work successfully with the dates and guidelines."

The SWIFT UCP 600 Guidelines were duly reflected in the official Standards Release 2007 documentation (Standards Release Guide and User Handbook) of 27 October 2007. ICC Task force members are working on revision of UCP 600 that is already due. Following a comprehensive consultation with the experts a decision would be circulated by 2020 by the ICC.

Changes That Financial Institutions Could Use from 1 July 2007

Date and Place for Presentation of Documents Under a Credit

(a) Field 31D "Date and Place of Expiry" of the MT 700, 705, 710, 720 and 740
The definition of this field should be interpreted as follows: "This field specifies the latest date for presentation under the documentary credit and the place where documents may be presented." This guideline does not change the usage of this field.
(b) Field 41a "Available With… By…" of the MT 700, 705, 710 and 720
The definition of this field should be interpreted as follows: "This field identifies the bank with which the documentary credit is available (the place for presentation) and an indication of how the credit is available." This guideline does not change the usage of this field.

Expiry Dates in Reimbursement Authorizations (or Amendments Thereof)

(a) Field 31D "Date and Place of Expiry" of the MT 740 the following usage rule should be added: "This field should not be used to specify the latest date for presentation of a reimbursement claim or an expiry date for the reimbursement authorization."
(b) Field 72 "Sender to Receiver Information" of the MT 740 The following usage rule should be added: "Any latest date for a reimbursement claim or an expiry date for the reimbursement authorization should be indicated in this field and not in field 31D.
(c) Field 31E "New Date of Expiry" of the MT 747
The following usage rule should be added: "This field should not be used to specify a new latest date for presentation of a reimbursement claim or a new expiry date for the reimbursement authorization."

(d) Field 72 "Sender to Receiver Information" of the MT 747
The following usage rule should be added: "Any new latest date for a reimbursement claim or a new expiry date for the reimbursement authorization should be indicated in this field and not in field 31E."

Details About the Disposal of Documents in a Notice of Refusal

Any details regarding the disposal of documents for which the two existing code words "HOLD" and "RETURN" in field 77B "Disposal of Documents" of the MT 734 Notice of Refusal cannot be used, must reflect the content of article 16.c of UCP 600 as follows:

(a) The code word "NOTIFY" to signify that "The issuing bank is holding the documents until it receives a waiver from the applicant and agrees to accept it, or receives further instructions from the presenter prior to agreeing to accept a waiver."
(b) The code word "PREVINST" to signify that "The bank is acting in accordance with instructions previously received from the presenter."

Because the contents (including code words) of field 77B "Disposal of Documents" of the MT 734 are not centrally validated (i.e. checked) by SWIFTNet, users may start using the above codes as of 1 July 2007 (live date of UCP 600). Alternatively, field 77B may contain a narrative text, reflecting the content of article 16.c of UCP 600.
Please refer to the usage guidelines section of field 77B of the MT 734 for further details.
(Source: SWIFT)
SWIFT provide means of communications among the financial institutions who are members of the SWIFT.
The financial institutions can:

- Send and receive messages to themselves;
- Send and receive messages within a "Close Group".

The Policy of SWIFT is:

- To overview the SWIFT system;
- Service Description;
- The SWIFT system description;
- Responsibility and liability.

SWIFT Administration:

- Issue and activation of login tables;
- Authenticator keys;
- Pricing structure;
- Security procedures.

SWIFT Operations:

- Functional overview of the network;
- System description: addressing, access, applications, message referencing;
- Test and training;
- System messages and reports;
- User response to network faults.

SWIFT TRAINING/INTERNATIONAL SEMINARS

SWIFT also brings the financial community together—at global, regional and local levels—to shape market practice, define standards and debate issues of mutual interest or concern; SIBOS is one of the important opportunity and attract the global user community in big number; as per past experience of the authors.

SIBOS (Swift International Banking Operations Seminar) is an annual banking and financial conference organized by the Society for Worldwide Interbank Financial Telecommunication (SWIFT) in various cities around the world. It has been held most frequently in cities in Europe, viz. Amsterdam, Copenhagen, Berlin and Helsinki; Boston in North America and Sydney in Australia. In recent years, SIBOS was held more frequently in Asia, Oceania, and other regions. Future plans (2018—Sydney, 2019—London (UK), 2020—Boston, 2021—Singapore) are of interest to the user fraternity/ participants in view of political and financial developments impacting logistics and other infrastructural issues are of concern for those who work in financial markets around the world. Such delegates participate as exhibitors and attendees and discuss issues relevant to the financial industry. In retrospect topics at the 2009 event in Hong Kong—"integrated risk management, innovation, and assorted related issues" were well received. Pertinent issues like "Cyber technologies—a challenge for regulators and supervisors", "Cyber security—threats to business and state bodies" and "Cyber resilience and the financial sector—how to reach an EU policy that balances security, innovation and regulation" Eurosystem and EBA CLEARING respectively, Artificial Intelligence and its impact on Financial System and so on; in view of current political and financial scenario particularly with reference to BREXIT and post—BREXIT status.

SWIFT ADDRESS/ HEADER:

- Name of the bank (four characters, i.e. BARB for Bank of Baroda);
- Name of the country (two characters, i.e. GB for Great Britain);
- Location of the main server of the member bank (two characters, i.e. two Ls for second location in London);
- Branch address (three characters XXX).

Messages Types (MT)

MT 0XX Series	Messages sent by SWIFT regarding:
	• Network architecture;
	• System architecture;
	• Communication concepts;
	• Protocols;
	• Message and address standards;
	• General text and field rules.
MT 103 Series	Customer fund transfers from one customer to another in another bank;
MT 200 Series	Financial Institutions fund transfers (MT 202) from one bank to another bank (institutional funds);
MT 300 Series	Treasury/Foreign Exchange Transactions, Confirmations and so on (unauthenticated messages);
MT 400 Series	Collections/Cash Advices; Foreign Bills for Collection, Foreign Bills Purchased, Acknowledgements/payment advices;
MT 500 Series	Securities Dealing;
MT 600 Series	Precious Metal Dealing;
MT 700 Series	Documentary Credits/Guarantees;
MT 800 Series	Travellers Cheques;
MT 900 Series	Cash Management (Unauthenticated messages).

When the two zeros (00) (unit and tens) are replaced in the any of the above series of MT then messages indicate:

99 Free Format (i.e. MT 199) relating to customer fund transfer;

92 Request for cancellation (i.e. MT 192) relating to customer fund transfer cancellation request;

95 Query (i.e. MT 195) it is a query relating to customer fund transfer;

96 Answer or Reply (i.e. MT 196) It is a reply relating to customer fund transfer.

M	50	Applicant. (Name & address																		
M	59	Beneficiary. (a/c no. if known																		
M	32B	Currency Code, Amt																		
#	39a	%age of DC amt. tolerance																		
#	39B	Max. DC Amt. Specificati on. Max. 4 lines																		
#	39c	Additional amt covered																		
M	41a	Available with/By	By Payment / Acceptance / Negotiation																	
#	42c	Drafts At /Drawn on	D	R	A	F	T		A	T										
#	42a	Drawee	D	R	A	W	N		O	N										
#	42 m	Mixed Payment detail																		
#	42P	Deferred payment details																		
#	43P	Partial Shipments:	*ALLOWED / FORBIDDEN																	
#	43T	Transhipm ent:	*PERMITTED / PROHIBITED																	
#	44E	Port of Loading on board/Airp ort of Departure																		
#	44F	Port of Discharge/ Airport of Destination																		
#	44c	Latest date of shipment																		
#	44 D	Shipment period																		

(continued)

(continued)

#	45A	Description of goods/serv ices																				
#	46A	Documents required																				
#	47A	Additional conditions																				
#	71B	Charges																				
#	48	Period of presentation																				
M	49	Confirmation instructions																				
#	53a	Reimbursi ng Bank																				
#	78a	Instructions to paying/ accepting/ negotiating bank																				
#	57a	Advise through Bank																				
#	72	Sender to Receiver information																				

# = Optional M = Mandatory * = Delete whichever not required				
Authorised Signature	Prepared by:	Taped by	Checked by:	Sent by:

Issuing Documentary Letter of Credit Using SWIFT MT (Page 701)

Title Page Guide to message Text Standards 5		Volume 2	Section 3		
Subject Issue of a Documentary Credit					
BKIDGBLAXXX Issue of a Documentary Credit (701) Please note that the boxes are compulsory and must be completed					
Message Addressing Details	PRIORITY: SEND TO: FROM: Telegraph Serial No	K = Normal U = Urgent D = deferred			DATE
m d d				y y m	
MESSAGE TEXT	TO: _____ OR SWIFT Address CBID CODE FROM				
M/#	Field Tag No.	Issue of a Documentary Credit			
M	27	Sequence of Total:			
M	20	DC No.			
#	45	GOODS: (maximum 20 lines)			
#	46	DOCUMENTS REQUIRED: (maximum 20 lines)			
#	47	ADDITIONAL CONDITIONS: (maximum 20 lines)			
		Col.:			
#= Optional M= Mandatory					
Authorised Signature		Prepared by:	Taped by:	Checked by:	Sent by:

Pre-advice of a Documentary Letter of Credit MT 705

Title				
Guide to message Text Standards				
Subject				
Pre-Advice of a Documentary Credit				
BKIDGBLAXXX				
Pre-advice of a Documentary Credit MT 705				
Please note that the boxes are compulsory and must be completed				
Message Addressing Details	Priority:	K=Normal U=Urgent D=Deferred		
	Send to:			
	From:			
	Telegraphic Serial No		Date	
			y y m m d d	
Messa ge	To:_____ or			
Text	SWIFT address CBID CODE			
M /#	Fie ld Ta g No.	Pre-Advice of a Documentary Credit		
M	40 a	Form of Documentary Credit	Irrevocable / Revocable / Transferable	
M	20	Documentary Credit No.		
M	31 D	Expiry Date & Place		
			y y m m d d	
M	50	Applicant Name and address)		
M	59	Beneficiary: (a/c No. if known should be quoted on first line)		
M	32 B	Currency Code, Amount		
#	39 A	%age Credit Amount Tolerance		
#	39 B	Maximum Credit Amount. Specification		
#	39 C	Additional amount covered		
#	41 a	Available with / By		
			Payment / Acceptance / Negotiation	
#	44 a	Loading on board/Taking in charge at/from/Shipment Details:		

(*continued*)

(continued)

#	44 B	For transportation to																															
#	44 C	Latest date of shipment																																
#	44 D	Shipment period																																
#	45 A	Description of Goods and / or services:																																
#	57 A	Advise through bank																																
#	79	Narrative																																
#	72	Sender to receiver information																																

#=Optional M=Mandatory

Advice of a Third Bank's Documentary Letter of Credit MT 711

Title																					
Guide to message Text Standards																					
Subject																					
Advice of a Third Bank's Documentary Credit																					
Bank Name																					
Pre-advice of a Documentary Credit																					
Please note that the boxes are compulsory and must be completed																					
Message Addressing Details	Priority: Send to:		K = Normal U = Urgent D=Deferred																		
	From:																				
	Telegraph Serial No.							Date													
															y		y				
m m d d																					
Message Text	Continuation of DC No.																				
M	27	Sequence of total																			
		Number of a message Total No. of Messages																			
M	20	Sender's Reference number																			
M	21	Documentary Credit No.																			
#	45A	Description of goods and/or services																			
#	46A	Documents Required																			

(continued)

(continued)

#	47A	Additional Conditions																					
			#49G SPECIAL PAYMENT CONDITION FOR BENEFICIARY																				
			#49H SPECIAL PAYMENT CONDITIONS FOR RECEIVING BANK																				
			#=Optional M = Mandatory																				
Authorised Signature						Prepared by:			Taped by:		Checked by:			Sent by:								

Documentary Credit Amendment Page 1 (707A)

Title		Volume	Section
Page			
Guide to message Text Standards		2	5
2			

Subject	
Documentary Credit Amendment	

H K B G	
MT 707 Amendment to a Documentary Credit	

Please note that the boxes are compulsory and must be completed

Message Addressing Details	PRIORITY: SEND TO:	K = Normal U = Urgent D=Deferred
	FROM:	
	Telegraph Serial No.	DATE

y m m d d
y

Message Text	To _____or	
	SWIFT Address CBID CODE FROM	

M /#	Field Tag No.	DOCUMENTARY CREDIT AMENDMENT						
M	20	OUR REF:						
M	21	YOUR REF:						
M	23	ISSUING BK'S REF:						
#	52A	ISSUING BANK						
#	31C	DATE OF ISSUE	y	y	m	m	d	d
M	30	Date of Amendment:	y	y	m	m	d	d
#	59	Beneficiary: (a/c No. ,if known should be quoted on 1st line)						
#	31E	New Expiry Date:	y	y	m	m	d	d
#	32B	Increase of DC Amt:						
#	33B	Decrease of DC Amt:						

(continued)

(continued)

#	34	New DC Amt:																								
#	39	Amt. Specification:																								
#	44	SHIPMENT DETAILS																								
M = Mandatory		# = Optional							(Continued on page 2)																	

Documentary Credit Amendment Page 2 (707B)

Title Page			Volume	Section
Guide to message Text Standards 3			2	5
Subject				
Documentary Credit Amendment				
H K B G				
MT 707 Amendment to a Documentary Credit				
Please note that the boxes are compulsory and must be completed				

Message Addressing Details	PRIORITY:	K = Normal U = Urgent D=Deferred		
	SEND TO:			
	FROM:			
	Telegraph Serial No.		Date	

m m d d   y y

Message Text	Continuation of DC No.	

#	7 9	Other Documents:

#	7 2	Bank to Bank information

Authorised Signature	Prepared by:	Taped by:	Checked by:	Sent by:

Transfer of a Documentary Credit MT 720

Title																			
Guide to message Text Standards																			
Subject																			
Transfer of a Documentary Credit																			
Name of Bank																			
Transfer of a Documentary Credit																			
Please note that the boxes are compulsory and must be completed																			

Message Addressing Details:	PRIORITY: SEND TO:	K = Normal U = Urgent D=Deferred																	
	FROM:																		
	Telegraph Serial No.					DATE													
												d	d						
m m y y																			

| MESSAGE TEXT | To _____ or SWIFT Address CBID Code From: | | | | | | | | | | | | | | | | | | |

M	Field /#	Tag No.	Transfer of a Documentary Credit																
M	27		Sequence of total:																
M	40B		FORM OF DC	IRREVOCABLE/REVOCABLE TRANSFERABLE ADDING / WITHOUT OUR CONFORMATION															
M	20		Transferring Bank's Reference:																
M	21		Documentary Credit No:																
#	23		PRE-ADVICE: Ready	P	R	E	A	D	V					y	y	m	m	d	d
M	31c		DATE OF ISSUE	y	y	m	m	d	d										
M	31D		DATE & PLACE: OF EXPIRY	y	y	m	m	d	d										
M	52a		Issuing Bank of the original documentary Credit																
M	50		First Beneficiary																
M	59		Second Beneficiary																

(continued)

(continued)

M	32B	Currency Code, Amount															
#	39A	%age Credit Amount Tolerance															
#	39B	Maximum Credit Amount															
#	39C	Additional Amounts covered															
M	41a	Available with/By:															
		BY PAYMENT/ACCEPTANCE/NEGOTIATION															
#	42C	Drafts at															
#	42a	Drawee															
#	42M	Mixed Payment Details															
#	42P	Negotiation/ Deferred Payment Details															
#	43P	Partial Shipment															
#	43T	Transhipment															
#	44A	Loading on Board/Dispatch/Taking in Charge at/from ----															
#	44B	Place of final destination/For Transportation to --															
#	44C	Latest date of Shipment															
#	44D	Shipment period															
#	45A	Description of goods and/or services															
#	46A	Documents required															
#	47A	Additional conditions															
#	71D	Charges															
#	48	Period for Presentation															
M	49	Confirmation Instructions															

(continued)

(continued)

#	78	Instructions to the paying/Accep ting/Negotiati ng Bank																			
#	57a	Second Advising Bank.																				
#	72Z	Sender to receiver information																				
Authorised Signature					Prepared by:		Taped by:		Checked by:			Sent by:										

SWIFT Format of a Letter of Credit

S.W.I.F.T Format of a Letter of Credit

TO SWIFT

40A	FORM OF DOCUMENTARY CREDIT	IRREVOCABLE
20:	DOCUMENTARY CREDIT NO:	XXXXXXX
31C	DATE OF ISSUE	YY-MM-DD
31D:	DATE & PLACE OF EXPIRY	YY-MM-DD, LONDON
51A:	APPLICANT BANK	BANK ID
50:	APPLICANT ADDRESS CODE	FULL NAME AND INCLUDING POST
59:	BENEFICIARY ADDRESS CODE	FULL NAME AND INCLUDING POST
32B:	CURRENCY CODE AND AMOUNT	USD XXX,XXX.XX
41A:	AVAILABLE WITH	ADVISING BANK BY NEGOTIATION
42C:	DRAFTS AT	SIGHT
42A:	DRAWEE	BANK ID NAME OF BANK, LONDON
43P:	PARTIAL SHIPMENT	ALLOWED IN FULL CONTAINER LOAD ONLY
43T:	TRANSHIPMENT	ALLOWED
44A:	ON BOARD/DISP/TAKING CHARGE AT/F: Country	Name of port &
44B:	FOR TRANSPORTATION TO Country	Name of port &
44C:	LATEST DATE OF SHIPMENT	YY-MM-DD

(*continued*)

(continued)

45A: DESCRIPTION OF GOODS AND/OR SERVICES

FULL DETAILS AND SPECIFICATIONS AS PER
BENEFICIARY'S PROFORMA INVOICE NO:XXXXXXXX DATED
XXXX-XX-XX.

46A: DOCUMENTS REQUIRED

47A: ADDITIONAL CONDITIONS
79.   UCPDC 600

19

ICC DOCDEX Rules

Genesis

The International Chamber of Commerce initiated a system giving expert opinion in matters of disputes in the international trade, which have increased over the years. The increasing number of discrepancies in documents and resultant disputes between the parties involved in documentary credits necessitated evolution of a system for dispute resolution. The amount of commercial crime as ICC has put the value of Frauds at over multi-million US Dollars per day but it may be an underestimation. DOCDEX Rules Prescribed by International Chamber of Commerce (ICC):

ICC DOCDEX

It is a dispute resolution procedure specifically designed for the world of trade finance, whereby a panel of three independent and impartial experts render a decision on a dispute arising out of a trade finance instrument, undertaking or agreement. Document-based procedure offers an attractive alternative to costly and protracted litigation.

DOCDEX is administered exclusively by the ICC International Centre for resolution, in accordance with the ICC DOCDEX Rules set out for the purpose, which came into force on 1 May 2015.

Source: International Chamber of Commerce, Paris www.iccdocdex.org.

© The Author(s) 2019
T. Bhogal, A. Trivedi, *International Trade Finance*, Finance and Capital Markets Series,
https://doi.org/10.1007/978-3-030-24540-5_19

Background

Since 1997, the ICC DOCDEX Rules have provided a trusted dispute resolution system for documentary credits incorporating ICC banking rules. In 2002, the Rules were extended to guarantees and collections also incorporating ICC banking rules. The 2015 revision further extends their scope to a wider range of trade finance instruments, including transactions or aspects of transactions not covered by existing ICC banking rules, such as trade loans, syndications, negotiable instruments, risk purchase agreements, conflicts of priority and fraud in letters of credit. This change enabled disputants previously left outside the ambit of DOCDEX.

DOCDEX comprises 12 Articles embodying (1) Definitions, (2) Scope, (3) Claim, (4) Answer, (5) Supplementary Information and Additional Documents, (6) Filing and Finality of Submissions, (7) Appointment of Experts, (8) The Proceedings, (9) The Decision, (10) Costs, (11) Notifications or Communications; Time Limits, (12) General. There is an appendix covering Fees and Costs to the main document available in web reference http://www.iccdocdex.org/ which is subject to change without notice by the ICC, as per the disclaimer clause mentioned in the document.

Speed: A Hallmark

Speed has always been a hallmark of the DOCDEX process: decisions are reached within thirty days of the experts receiving the file. A new and original feature of the 2015 revision is the requirement that filings be made in electronic form using standard templates downloadable from the ICC website. This change helps to streamline case administration and further accelerate the proceedings. As a joint product of the ICC Banking Commission and ICC Dispute Resolution Services, DOCDEX capitalises on ICC's expertise and experience in both fields. While retaining the traditional features of DOCDEX, the 2015 Rules are attuned to best professional practices and include safeguards to ensure the competence, independence, impartiality and availability of experts, quality assurance through the scrutiny of decisions, confidentiality, cost transparency and procedural efficiency.

Scope

A dispute arising from any trade finance related instrument, agreement or undertaking can be referred to DOCDEX—there is no requirement that the relevant agreement incorporate any ICC trade finance rules. The removal of this requirement has also expanded the type of dispute that can be referred to DOCDEX. For example, the old rules did not permit disputes which were not covered by the relevant ICC trade finance rules (such as disputes concerning the governing law of the relevant instrument).

Administration

DOCDEX filings are now primarily to be made in electronic form, with the DOCDEX rules providing that standard online forms are to be used to file claims and answers. This will streamline case administration and accelerate proceedings. The ICC expects that parties will receive a decision within two months of submitting a dispute to DOCDEX.

DOCDEX: Transparency and Independence

The DOCDEX rules strengthen transparency and independence by way of two key improvements to the old rules.

A. The ICC will now publish anonymised copies of every DOCDEX decision. This will establish a body of precedents, which will:

- allow the Centre to more thoroughly monitor the quality of experts' decisions;
- provide certainty as to how issues will be decided by DOCDEX experts; and
- identify areas of the ICC's trade finance rules which are frequently in dispute and may need improvement.

B. The old rules provided that appointed experts declare their independence from the parties to a dispute. The DOCDEX rules go much further in strengthening the requirement for independence and quality, by:

- stipulating that those experts cannot act/have acted in any other capacity in respect of the dispute;
- requiring prospective experts to make a statement declaring their availability, impartiality and independence at the outset of the dispute;
- empowering the chair of the ICC's Banking Commission to remove poorly performing experts from the DOCDEX panel; and
- expressly allowing the ICC's banking Technical Advisor to scrutinise the substance of decisions (not just the form of the decisions, as was the case under the old rules).

Speed Vs. Quality: Decision-Making

The quality of the decision-making is not prejudiced by the speed of the procedure. The DOCDEX rules are expressly stated to be unsuitable for disputes requiring oral or expert evidence, and are not intended as a substitute for litigation or arbitration. The procedure is only suitable for certain types of disputes which, by their nature, can be dealt with relatively quickly. The experts are also limited in what documents they can review to reach decisions—they can only consider the claim, any answer and international practice.

DOCDEX Rules: Benefits

(a) DOCDEX has a number of advantages. Perhaps the most obvious is its speed: the panel of experts must provide a draft decision within 30 days of receipt of the documents relating to a dispute. That time can only be extended in "exceptional" circumstances. The Centre expects that parties will receive decisions within 60 days of submitting a dispute.

(b) DOCDEX has other advantages. Its costs are fixed and, depending on the amount in dispute, the total cost of the process is capped at US$5000 or US$10,000 (with an absolute maximum of US$15,000). Not only are these costs much lower than in litigation or arbitration, but the parties also have certainty at the outset as to the costs of the procedure.

(c) The procedure is non-adversarial and, like other forms of alternative dispute resolution, this generally helps to maintain business relationships with trading partners (especially compared with litigation or arbitration). This is especially important in a trade context, where repeat transactions with counterparties are the norm.

(d) The procedure is also flexible. The experts are not bound by strict rules of evidence and are expressly empowered to consider international practice when making decisions.

(e) As (anonymised) DOCDEX decisions are published, there is a body of precedents for the appointed experts to consider. The Centre also scrutinises draft awards to ensure consistency and quality. Both measures are prescribed to promote certainty of outcome.

(f) Also, as the parties do not know the identity of the experts and because the experts can have no other involvement in the dispute, the procedure safeguards transparency and the independence of the experts.

DOCDEX and the Trade Finance Lawyers

Trade finance lawyers should be aware of the new DOCDEX rules, and in particular their wider scope, so that they can advise their clients in appropriate circumstances to consider using DOCDEX as a means of dispute resolution.

DOCDEX: When Trade Finance (TF) Documents Are Subject to General ICC Rules

There is no "opt-in" to DOCDEX—trade finance documents governed by ICC Rules do not contain DOCDEX "dispute resolution" clauses. The DOCDEX rules should only be chosen after a dispute has arisen, because certain types of disputes (for example, those requiring oral or expert evidence) cannot be referred to DOCDEX. Accordingly, parties should not include a DOCDEX dispute resolution clause in their trade finance agreements, nor should they otherwise agree to use DOCDEX before a dispute has arisen.

DOCDEX: Implications on Trade Finance Documentation

There is no material implication for trade finance documentation. However, parties should not choose DOCDEX in their trade finance agreements. There is no need to refer to DOCDEX in any contractual documents, as the parties choose DOCDEX by completing the relevant forms and sending the same to the centre for consideration and to seek resolution to dispute.

For more information about the DOCDEX system, reader needs to refer the web site at **www.iccdocdex.org**, or contact in the following addresses:

ICC International Centre for Expertise
38, Cours Albert 1er
75008 Paris, France
Tel.: +33 1 49 53 30 53
Fax: +33 1 49 53 29 29
E-mail: docdex@iccwbo.org

www.iccwbo.org
www.iccbooks.com
ICC Publication No. 811
ISBN-10: 92-842-1325-8
ISBN-13: 978-92-842-1325-2
International Centre for Expertise
38, Cours Albert 1er, 75008 Paris, France
Telephone +33 1 49 53 30 53 Fax +33 1 49 53 29 29
www.iccdocdex.org E-mail docdex@iccwbo.org
International Chamber of Commerce
(Source: International Chamber of Commerce, Paris)

20

UK Export Finance

Background

The term "ECGD" stands for Export Credit Guarantee Department. It is a separate department of the British Government. It was set up in 1919 to help British exporters to export goods to other countries. Like any other country, the UK also needs foreign exchange but there are more risks in exporting overseas than selling in the local market. The manufacturers and services providers are not willing to take such risks in selling their products and services overseas. The ECGD encourages the exporters to export more of their products and services by providing insurance against the commercial and political risks of not being paid by overseas buyers after goods were exported. A section of ECGD dealing with exporters trading on short terms of credit basis (i.e. up to two years) was sold to Atradius (formerly NCM Credit Insurance Limited) in 1991.

ECGD derives its powers from the 1991 Export and Investment Guarantees Act and report to the Secretary of State for Trade and Industry who provides Parliament with a report on its activities and trading operations on an annual basis.

Equivalent Organisations in the World

- France: COFACE
- Germany: Euler Hermes
- USA: Export–Import Bank of the United States
- Italy: Servizi Assicurativi del Commercio Estero
- China: Exim Bank of China
- India: Exim Bank/ECGC

T. Bhogal, A. Trivedi, *International Trade Finance*, Finance and Capital Markets Series, https://doi.org/10.1007/978-3-030-24540-5_20

Break Even Basis: ECGD operated on a break-even basis, by charging exporters premium at levels to match the risks of non-payment. The premium rates charged depend on various considerations and assessing the risks of each contract individually, that is, the nature of the project, its duration and the type of risks to be covered, buyer or borrower and country risks. This means under their Active Portfolio Management (APM) ECGD assessed risks systematically. The charge or premium fee therefore varied from case to case. Some reserves are built up from the revenue earned from the premiums to pay for claims, if overseas buyers/borrowers default on payments.

No Finance by the ECGD

The Export Credits Guarantee Department did not provide finance itself for exports, but it stayed duly involved in indirect export finance. It also played a vital role by safeguarding the finance, which the banks and other financial institutions make available to exporters. It would otherwise appear to be too risky a proposition to a bank if asked to make an advance without tangible security. ECGD. offered various types of policies, often as a result of long discussions between the Department, the Government and the banks. The result is that the amount of export finance available is increasing. The security offered by ECGD enabled exporters to offer better credit terms to buyers and to break into new markets.

The UK has for some time been playing a leading role in pushing forward initiatives to help the poorest developing countries emerging from debt and poverty burdens and return to the international trading community. ECGD had been committed to supporting productive expenditure for countries as they emerge from their debt problems.

ECGD derived its powers from the **Export and Investment Guarantees Act 1991** and undertook its activities in accordance with a specific consent from HM Treasury.

Role of ECGD: ECGD established in 1919 to promote UK exports lost during the submarine blockade of World War I. In recent years, ECGD had supported business in the aerospace, automotive, construction, healthcare, industrial processing, oil and gas, petrochemical, water treatment and satellite sectors.

Aim/Objective

ECGD's aim had been to benefit the UK economy by helping exporters of UK goods and services to win business, and UK firms to invest overseas, by providing guarantees, insurance and reinsurance against loss, taking into account <u>HM Government's</u> wider international policy agenda. ECGD is required by HM Government to operate on a slightly better than break-even basis, charging exporters premiums at levels that match the perceived risks and costs in each case.

The largest part of ECGD's activities involved <u>underwriting</u> long-term loans to support the sale of capital goods, principally for the export of aircraft, bridges, machinery and services; it helped UK companies take part in major overseas projects such as the construction of oil and gas pipelines and the upgrading of hospitals, airports and power stations. Support had been given for contracts as low as £1000, but some of the projects ECGD backs go well beyond the £1 billion mark.

As part of its <u>risk management</u> process, ECGD had to make a judgement on the ability of a country to meet its debt obligations. The department used a "productive expenditure" test, undertaken in consultation with the <u>Department for International Development</u>, that makes sure that the countries defined as <u>heavily indebted poor countries</u> and those exclusively dependent on <u>International Development Association</u> financing only get official export credits from the UK for projects that help social and economic development without creating a new unsustainable debt burden. ECGD continued to check that the proposed borrowing as a sustainable input.

Export Credits Guarantee Department (ECGD), the UK's export credit agency, now operates under the name of UK Export Finance (UKEF). The change was declared by ECGD Chief Executive Patrick Crawford at the SMEs' Export: Global Challenge event in London (UK) on 10 November 2016.

Mission

UK Export Finance mission is to ensure that no viable UK export fails for lack of finance or insurance, while operating at no net cost to the taxpayer.

How UKEF Operates

Export finance managers provide free and impartial consultations. They help UK companies to check they are getting the appropriate support and, if not, explore how to bridge gaps, if any.

Export finance managers are regional representatives of UKEF. They are valuable contacts for exporters and businesses with export potential.

UKEF Products

UK Export Finance policies are similar to the ECGD policies. For further information or inquiries interested parties need to contact UK Export Finance, for new business enquiries customer.service@ukexportfinance.gov.uk, Telephone 020 7271 8010

The information given in this book should be used as guidelines on each policy that is available at the time of publication from UK Export Finance for example:

Export Insurance Policy

Credit Insurance Services

Having accurate and reliable customer financial information it **reduces bad debts** and the time an entrepreneur spends dealing with it. It also gives reader the information and time to better **engage with new customers**. This allows you to stabilise your cash flow, protect your balance sheet against bad debts, expand sales, boost borrowing power and confidently **develop virgin grounds and or new markets**.

Professional Advice: Whether you are considering exporting or just expanding your business UKEF gives valuable advice to customers on **How to operate effectively**.

Credit insurance is one of the few insurance schemes that work not just for tomorrow; **it helps you to grow and protect your business today and keep it growing on an ongoing basis**.

Centrally Located: UKEF's dedicated team is based in Northampton and members have over rich and **long experience in the credit industry**.

Bond Support Scheme

Under the Bond Support Scheme UKEF provides partial guarantees to banks in support of UK exports. Where a bank issues a contract bond or indemnifies an overseas bank providing the bond in respect of a UK export contract, UKEF can guarantee up to 80% of the value of the bond. It means that the bank receives a guarantee from UKEF to cover an agreed percentage of the amount of the bond; if the exporter fails to reimburse the bank. The bank can also, for the duration of UKEF guarantee, increase its risk appetite for the exporter. There is no maximum value for each bond, and no maximum or minimum term for a guarantee.

Eligibility

To be eligible for support under the Bond Support Scheme an exporter must:

- be carrying on business in the UK, the Isle of Man or the Channel Islands;
- have entered, or be intending to enter, into a contract for the supply of goods and/or services with a company or other organisation that carries on business outside the UK, the Isle of Man or the Channel Islands;
- show that at least 20% of the value of the contract represents UK content.

How to Apply?

The scheme can only be accessed through lenders that have signed up to participate and access their Bond Support Scheme directly through the bank.
    Exporters need to get a form to completed, if bank with:

- Barclays Bank Plc
- HSBC
- Lloyds Banking Group/Bank of Scotland Plc
- The Royal Bank of Scotland Plc
- National Westminster Bank Plc
- Ulster Bank
- Santander UK Plc

The supporting banks have adequate arrangement in place for further guidance, if required by the exporter.

Bond Insurance Policy

Under the Bond Support Scheme UKEF provides partial guarantees to banks in support of UK exports. Where a bank issues a contract bond or indemnifies an overseas bank providing the bond in respect of a UK export contract, UKEF can guarantee up to 80% of the value of the bond. This means that the bank receives a guarantee from UKEF to cover an agreed percentage of the amount of the bond if the exporter fails to reimburse the bank. The bank can also, for the duration of UKEF guarantee, increase its risk appetite for the exporter. There is no maximum value for each bond, and no maximum or minimum term for a guarantee.

Eligibility

To be eligible for support under the Bond Support Scheme an exporter must:

- be carrying on business in the UK, the Isle of Man or the Channel Islands;
- have entered, or be intending to enter, into a contract for the supply of goods and/or services with a company or other organisation that carries on business outside the UK, the Isle of Man or the Channel Islands;
- Show that at least 20% of the value of your contract represents UK content.

How to Apply?

The scheme can only be accessed through designated lenders that have signed up to participate. The exporters access for Bond Support Scheme directly through their bank(s)

- Barclays Bank Plc
- HSBC
- Lloyds Banking Group/Bank of Scotland Plc
- The Royal Bank of Scotland Plc/National Westminster Bank Plc/ Ulster Bank
- Santander UK Plc

Under the Bond Support Scheme, UKEF provides partial guarantees to banks in support of UK exports. Where a bank issues a contract bond or indemnifies an overseas bank providing the bond in respect of a UK export contract, UKEF can guarantee up to 80% of the value of the bond. This means that the bank receives a guarantee from UKEF to cover an agreed percentage of the amount of the bond if the exporter fails to reimburse the bank. The bank can also, for the duration of their guarantee, increase its risk appetite for the exporter.

There is no maximum value for each bond, and no maximum or minimum term for a guarantee.

Eligibility

To be eligible for support under the Bond Support Scheme as an exporter, one must:

* be carrying on business in the UK, the Isle of Man or the Channel Islands;
* have entered, or be intending to enter, into a contract for the supply of goods and/or services with a company or other organisation that carries on business outside the UK, the Isle of Man or the Channel Islands;
* Show that at least 20% of the value of your contract represents UK content.

How to Apply

The scheme can only be accessed through lenders that have signed up to participate.

Access UKEF's Bond Support Scheme Directly Through Their Bank Viz.

* Barclays Bank Plc
* HSBC
* Lloyds Banking Group/Bank of Scotland Plc
* The Royal Bank of Scotland Plc
* National Westminster Bank Plc
* Ulster Bank
* Santander UK Plc

Export Working Capital Scheme

The scheme assists UK exporters in gaining access to working capital finance both pre- and post-shipment in respect of specific export related contracts. UKEF can provide partial guarantees to lenders to cover the credit risks associated with export working capital facilities. Where a lender provides such a facility in respect of a UK export related contract, UKEF can guarantee up to 80% of the risk.

This means UK exporters can be better enabled to support an export transaction in circumstances where their lender does not have sufficient risk appetite for the full facility amount. This is particularly useful in circumstances where a UK exporter wins an overseas contract that is higher in value than they can typically fulfil or succeeds in winning more overseas contracts than it has done before. There is no minimum or maximum value for the working capital facility.

Eligibility

To be eligible for support an exporter must:

- be carrying on business in the UK, Isle of Man or Channel Islands;
- have entered, or be intending to enter, into a contract for the supply of goods and/or services with a company or other organisation that carries on business outside the UK, the Isle of Man or the Channel Islands;
- show that at least 20% of the value of your contract represents UK content.

To be eligible for support as a direct supplier to an exporter, you must fulfil the above requirement for exporters and also have a supply contract that qualifies as export-related·

How to Apply?

The scheme can only be accessed through lenders that have signed up to participate and the access for Export Working Capital Scheme directly through your bank.

- Barclays Bank Plc
- HSBC
- Lloyds Banking Group/Bank of Scotland Plc
- The Royal Bank of Scotland Plc
- National Westminster Bank Plc
- Ulster Bank
- Santander UK Plc

Here is detail for contact at different designated banks for further guidance/queries:

Barclays Bank Plc	Mathew Enright, Vice President, Trade and Working Capital	020 7116 3999	mathew.enright@ barclays.com
HSBC Bank Plc	Su Lewis, Performance Director, Global Trade & Receivables Finance	07920 073256	sulewis@hsbc.com
	Ketan Gupta, Executive Manager, Global Trade & Receivables Finance	07468 704263	ketan.gupta@hsbc.com
Lloyds Banking Group/Bank of Scotland Plc	Barry George, Product Manager, Trade Product	N/A	barry.george@ lloydsbanking.com
National Westminster Bank Plc	Chris Duggan, SolutionsLine T team	0800 2100235	internationalbanking@ natwest.com
The Royal Bank of Scotland Plc	Chris Duggan, SolutionsLine T team	0800 2100235	internationalbanking@ rbs.co.uk
Ulster Bank	Gavin Murphy, Global Trade Finance	028 9027 6632	gavin.murphy@ ulsterbankcm.com
Santander UK Plc	Martin Hodges, Head of Trade	07827 872312	martin.hodges@ santander.co.uk

Letter of Credit Guarantee Scheme

Where a UK bank adds its confirmation to a Letter of Credit issued by an overseas bank to finance an export from the UK, UKEF can typically guarantee between 50% and 90% of the value of the Letter of Credit.

Eligibility Criteria

- The exporter must be carrying on business in the UK.
- The exports must be produced in and shipped from the UK, or imported into the UK before being re-exported.
- The foreign issuing bank must not be based in a country belonging to the European Union or certain other high-income countries.
- The period for presentation of documents under the Letter of Credit must not be longer than one year.
- Any deferred payment period under the Letter of Credit must be less than one year.

For longer presentation or deferred payment periods UKEF may be able to consider support outside the terms of the scheme on a case-by-case basis.

How the Scheme Works?

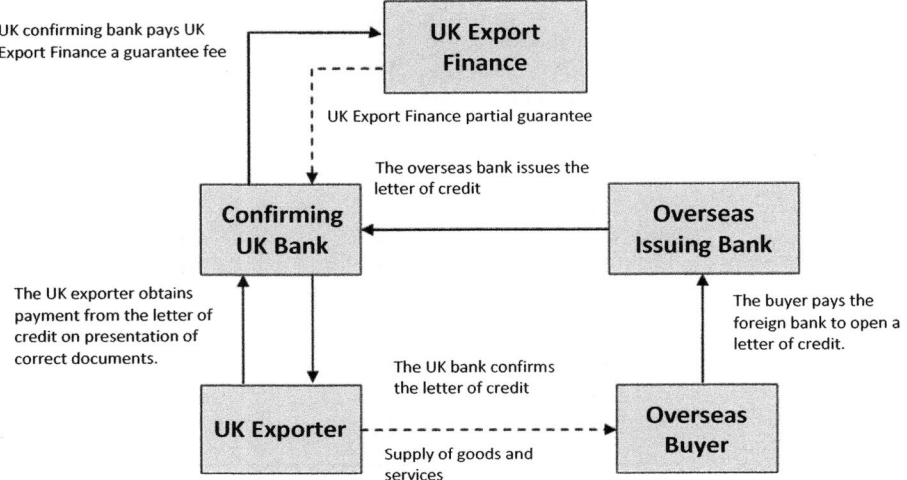

How to Apply?

Exporter would contact local export finance manager to discuss how UKEF can support the business.

Benefits of the Scheme

- The UK bank is able to confirm a Letter of Credit for the full amount where it doesn't have risk appetite on the foreign issuing bank.
- The UK bank receives a guarantee from UKEF to cover the percentage of the amount due to it if the foreign issuing bank fails to reimburse payments.
- The exporter is protected against a default of the foreign buyer and the foreign bank.

Risks Covered

The UK confirming bank is protected against the failure of the issuing bank to reimburse it for payments properly made by the confirming bank under the Letter of Credit. There is no minimum or maximum value of a Letter of Credit.

Cost

The UK confirming bank pays UKEF a guarantee fee, which is typically a proportion of the fee it receives for confirming the Letter of Credit.

Export Finance: Collections

- Documentary Collections: A documentary collection (D/C) is a transaction whereby the exporter entrusts the collection of payment to the exporter's bank (remitting bank), which sends documents to the importer's bank (collecting bank), along with instructions for payment. Funds are received from the importer and Remitted to the exporter through the banks in exchange for those documents. D/Cs involve using a bill of exchange (commonly known as a draft) that requires the importer to pay the face amount either at sight (document against payment [D/P] or cash against documents) or on a specified future date (document against acceptance [D/A] or cash against acceptance). The collection cover letter gives instructions that specify the documents required for the delivery of the goods to the importer. Although banks do act as facilitators (agents) for their clients under Collections, D/Cs offers no verification process and limited recourse in the event of non-payment. D/Cs are generally less expensive than letters of credit (LCs).

Key Points

D/Cs are less complicated and less expensive than LCs.

- Under a D/C transaction, the importer is not obligated to pay for goods before shipment.
- If structured properly, the exporter retains control over the goods until the importer either pays the draft amount at sight or accepts the draft to incur a legal obligation to pay at a specified later date.

- Although the goods can be controlled under ocean shipments, they are more difficult to control under air and overland shipments, which allow the foreign buyer to receive the goods with or without payment unless the exporter employs agents in the importing country to take delivery until goods are paid for.

Characteristics of a Documentary Collection

- Banks' role is limited and they do not guarantee payment.
- Banks do not verify the accuracy of the documents.

When to Use Documentary Collections

With D/Cs, the exporter has little recourse against the importer in case of non-payment. Thus, D/Cs should be used only under the following conditions:

- The exporter and importer have a well-established relationship.
- The exporter is confident that the importing country is politically and economically stable.
- An open account sale is considered too risky, and an LC is unacceptable to the importer.

Typical Simplified D/C Transaction Flow

1. The exporter ships the goods to the importer and receives the documents in exchange.
2. The exporter presents the documents with instructions for obtaining payment to his bank.
3. The exporter's remitting bank sends the documents to the importer's collecting bank.
4. The collecting bank releases the documents to the importer on receipt of payment or an acceptance of the draft.
5. The importer uses the documents to obtain the goods and to clear them at customs.
6. Once the collecting bank receives payment, it forwards the proceeds to the remitting bank.
7. The remitting bank then credits the exporter's account.

Documents Against Payment Collection

With a D/P collection, the exporter ships the goods and then gives the documents to his bank which will forward the documents to the importer's collecting bank, along with instructions on how to collect the money from the importer. In this arrangement, the collecting bank releases the documents to the importer only on payment for the goods. Once payment is received, the collecting bank transmits the funds to the remitting bank for payment to the exporter.

Supplier Credit Financing Facility

Under a Supplier Credit Financing Facility, UKEF provides a guarantee to a bank either:

- for a loan to an overseas buyer to finance the purchase of capital goods and/or services from a UK exporter—known as a Supplier Credit Loan Facility or
- to cover payments due under bills of exchange, or promissory notes, purchased by a bank from a UK exporter. The exporter will have received them in payment for capital goods and/or services supplied to an overseas buyer—known as a Supplier Credit Bills and Notes Facility

Finance can be made available in the main trading currencies (including sterling, US dollars and Euros). Other currencies as per requirement are considered by UKEF.

Eligibility

The following criteria must be met:

- The exporter must be carrying on business in the UK.
- The bank must be acceptable to UKEF.

How the Supplier Credit Loan Facility Works

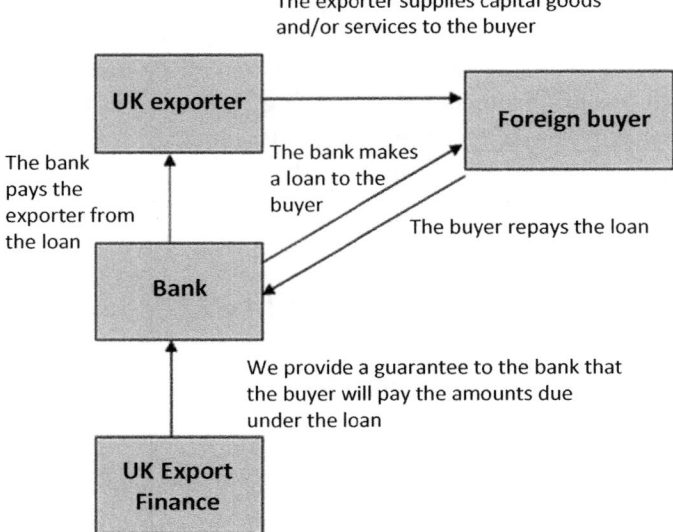

How the Supplier Credit Bills and Notes Facility Works

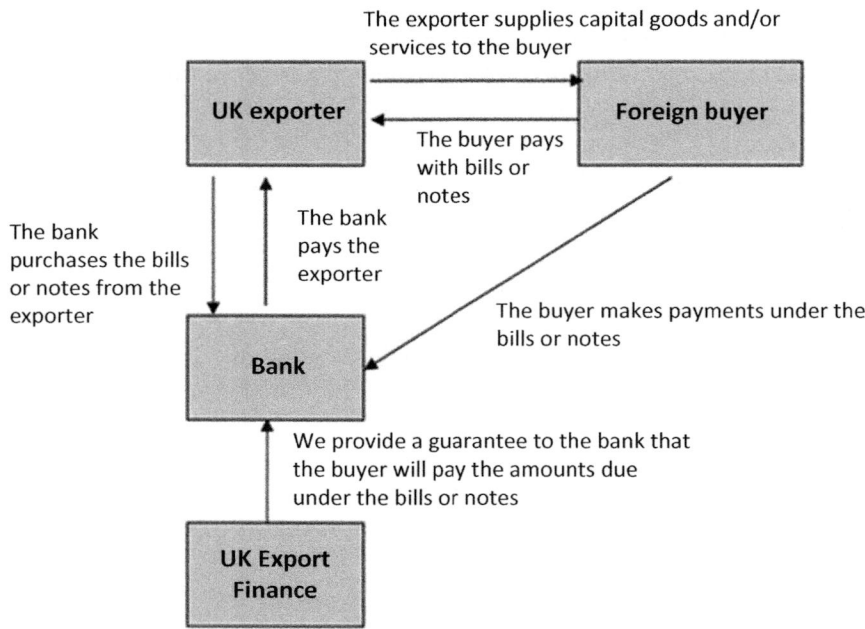

How to Apply?

The steps to apply for a Supplier Credit Financing Facility are:

(a) Know the laid down provisions as per UKEF guide to check this is the policy exporter need.
(b) Read the standard terms and conditions for the Supplier Credit Facility

1. Read the guide for applicants on business processes and factors and also to know how UKEF make decisions on applications.
2. Read the quick guide to credit terms relating to the export contracts UKEF are asked to support, which includes what is meant by credit terms, what terms can be agreed, the amount of credit that can be supported, starting point of credit, length of credit and repayments of credit.
3. Read the guide to recourse, which includes what recourse is, when it is sought and required, when UKEF exercise recourse, from which it is sought, the amount of recourse, release from recourse and the Lloyds recourse indemnity policy.
4. Use UKEF country cover indicators tool to find out what cover is available in the country you want to do business in.
5. Contact customer services, to obtain an indication of how much premium exporter will need to pay.
6. Fill in the prescribed Supplier Credit application form.
7. If an exporter wants supplemental export insurance with the Supplier fill in the sustainable lending questionnaire if necessary (the country cover indicator Credit Facility; fill in the supplemental export insurance policy application form as well.
8. This tool will tell exporter, if it is needed to fill in).
9. The application form and supporting documentation are to be sent to the Business Group. The address is as follows:

Business Group, UK Export Finance, 1 Horse Guards Road, London, SW1A 2HQ

Buyer Credit Facility

Under a Buyer Credit Facility UKEF provides a guarantee to a bank making a loan to an overseas buyer, so that capital goods and/or services can be purchased. Loans can be made in the main trading currencies (including sterling, US dollars and Euros) as well as some local currencies.

Eligibility

The following criteria must be met:

- The exporter must be carrying on business in the UK.
- The export contract must have a value of at least £5 million or the equivalent in foreign currency.
- The bank making the loan must be acceptable to UKEF.

How It Works?

The loan agreement is between the overseas buyer and the bank. UK Export Finance provides a guarantee to the bank that the loan will be repaid. The bank then uses the loan to pay the exporter for goods and/or services delivered. The UK exporter sells the capital goods and/or services to the overseas buyer.

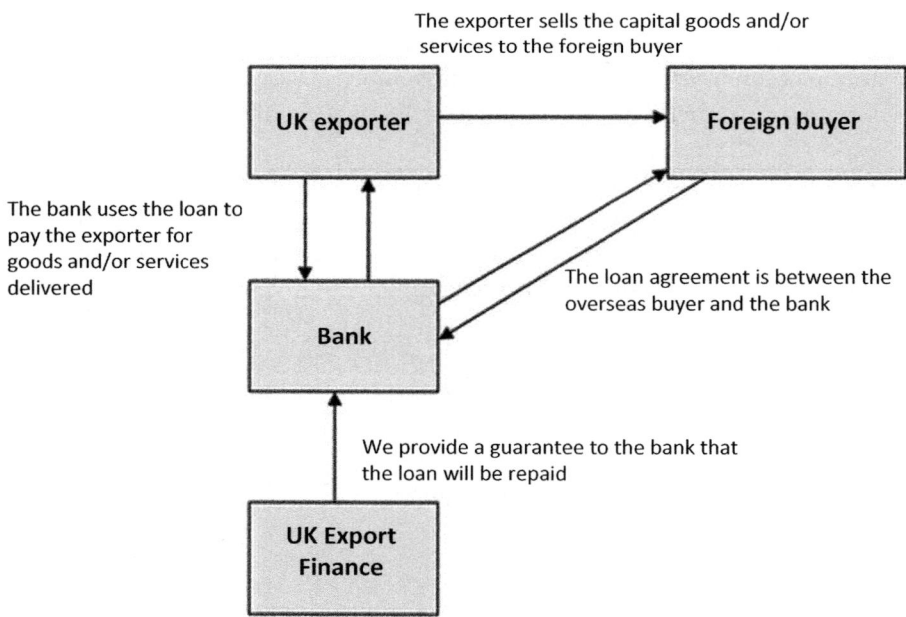

How to Apply?

The steps to apply for a Buyer Credit Facility are as follows:

1. Read UKEF guide to check if this is the facility an exporter needs.
2. Read the guide for applicants on business processes and factors to find out how UKEF make decisions on applications.
3. Read the quick guide to credit terms related to the export contract UKEF are asked to support, which includes what is meant by credit terms, what terms can be agreed, the amount of credit that can be supported, starting point of credit, length of credit and repayments of credit.

1. Read the quick guide to recourse which includes what recourse is, when it is sought and required, when UKEF exercise recourse, from which it is sought, the amount of recourse, release from recourse and the Lloyds recourse indemnity policy.
2. Read the guide on Local Currency Financing to find out details of eligible local currencies.
3. Use UKEF country cover indicators tool to find out what cover is available for the country you want to do business in.
4. Contact customer services using the details below, to obtain an indication of how much premium you will need to pay.
5. Fill in the buyer credit application form and schedule to the buyer credit application.
6. Fill in the sustainable lending questionnaire if necessary (the country cover indicators tool will tell exporter if there is a need to fill it in).
7. Send your application form and supporting documentation to the Business Group. The address is: Business Group, UK Export Finance, 1 Horse Guards Road, London SW1A 2HQ

Local Currency Financing

UKEF can guarantee a buyer credit loan to an overseas borrower in local currency, financing the purchase of capital goods and/or services from a UK exporter. Loans can be made in wide range of currencies.

A buyer credit in local currency follows the same format as a conventional buyer credit in a standard currency such as sterling, Euros or US dollars except that it is funded from a bank in the buyer's country.

Local Currency Financing is particularly suited to projects which do not usually generate foreign currency revenue, such as water/gas/electricity utilities, local transport and local municipalities/Councils and so on.

Eligible Currencies

As a good practice one needs to check with your bank or UKEF for eligible country and currency.

How It Works?

The diagram shows how UK Export Finance guarantees a loan to a buyer that is purchasing capital or semi-capital goods/services from a UK exporter, financed in a local currency.

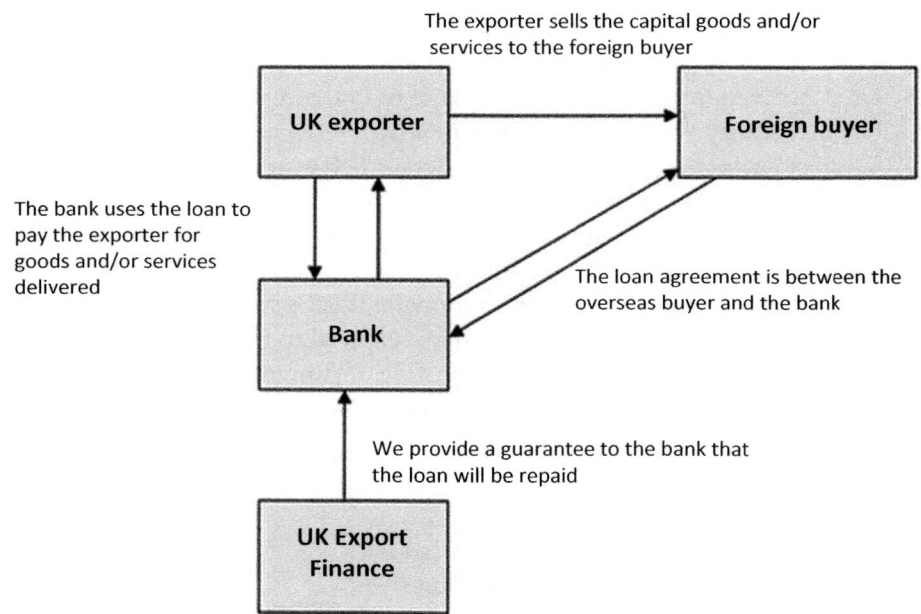

Benefits of Local Currency Financing

The benefits of a buyer credit denominated in local currency are that:

- the buyer/borrower has time to pay over a number of years at fixed or floating rates and repays in local currency;
- it is particularly suited to projects in sectors such as water/gas/electricity utilities, local transport and local municipalities/councils and so on which do not usually earn foreign currency revenue;
- it reduces foreign currency risk and eliminates a source of uncertainty over debt servicing cost of a loan for the overseas buyer/borrower;
- the bank in the buyer's country receives a guarantee from UKEF for full repayment of the loan plus interest.

LIMIT

The maximum amount of the loan is 85% of the contract value. A minimum of 15% of the contract value must be paid directly to the exporter by the buyer before the loan starts to be repaid. Of the 15%, a down payment of at least 5% should be received upon contract signature.

UKEF can consider support for foreign content (i.e. the cost to the exporter of purchasing goods or services from sub-contractors outside the UK) of up to 80% of the export contract's value. The period for repayment of the loan must be at least two years.

Cost

There is no fee for the application. Premium will be paid by the borrower through the loan agreement. The amount is determined on a case-by-case basis.

How to Apply?

Contact UKEF customer service team to get help with Local Currency Financing. customer.service@ukexportfinance.gov.uk

Read UKEF guide to the Buyer Credit Facility for details of how to apply.

Disclaimer by UKEF

"This information is not intended to be a comprehensive description of our products and procedures, and many details which are relevant to particular circumstances may have been omitted".

When considering applications, UKEF's underwriters will look at each case on its merits.

(The information is based on the guide by UKEF. It was last updated in March 2018.)

Published 24 November 2016 Last updated 27 March 2018).

UKEF is positive and willing to consider other currencies subject to satisfying eligibility standards.

How It Works?

The diagram shows how UK Export Finance guarantees a loan to a buyer that is purchasing capital or semi-capital goods/services from a UK exporter, financed in a local currency.

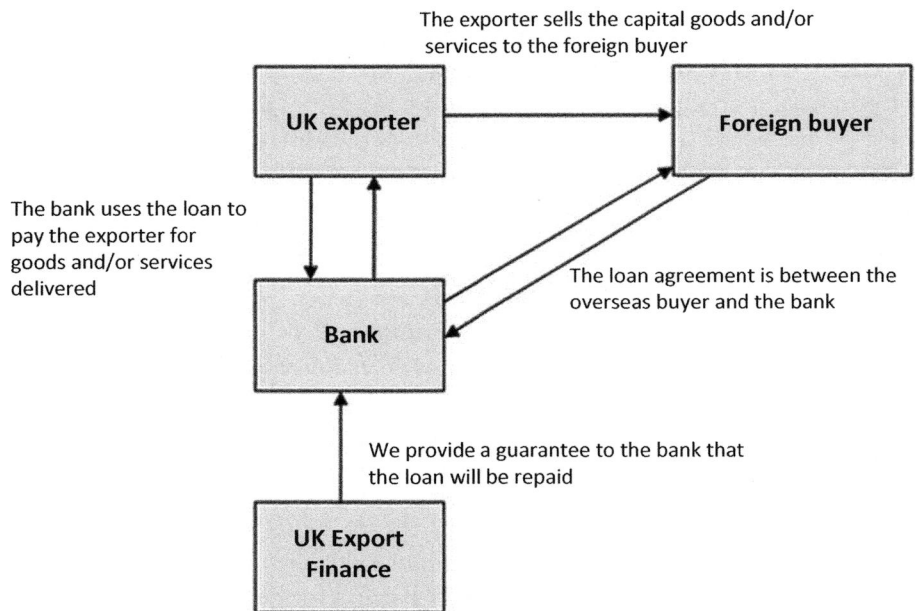

Benefits of Local Currency Financing

The benefits of a buyer credit denominated in local currency are that:

- the buyer/borrower has time to pay over a number of years at fixed or floating rates and repays in local currency;
- it is particularly suited to projects in sectors such as water/gas/electricity utilities, local transport and local municipalities/councils and so on which do not usually earn foreign currency revenue;
- it reduces foreign currency risk and eliminates a source of uncertainty over debt servicing cost of a loan for the overseas buyer/borrower;
- the bank in the buyer's country receives a guarantee from UKEF for full repayment of the loan plus interest.

Maximum Amount

The maximum amount of the loan is 85% of the contract value. A minimum of 15% of the contract value must be paid directly to the exporter by the buyer before the loan starts to be repaid. Of the 15%, a down payment of at least 5% should be received upon contract signature.

UKEF can consider support for foreign content (i.e. the cost to the exporter of purchasing goods or services from sub-contractors outside the UK) of up to 80% of the export contract's value. The period for repayment of the loan must be at least 2 years.

Cost

There is no fee for the application. Premium will be paid by the borrower through the loan agreement. The amount is determined on a case-by-case basis.

How to Apply?

Contact UKEF customer service team to get help with Local Currency Financing. customer.service@ukexportfinance.gov.uk
   Telephone +44 (0)20 7271 8010
   Read the UKEF guide to the Buyer Credit Facility for details of how to apply.

UKEF's Disclaimer

"This information is not intended to be a comprehensive description of our products and procedures, and many details which are relevant to particular circumstances may have been omitted".

When considering applications, UKEF underwriters will look at each case on its merits.

(The information is embodied based on the UKEF's guide that was last updated by them in March 2018, Published on 24 November 2016).

Direct Lending Facility

Under the Direct Lending Facility, UKEF provides loans up to £3 billion. In aggregate to overseas buyers, allowing them to finance the purchase of capital goods and/or services from UK exporters. Loans can be made in sterling, US dollars, Euros or Japanese yen. The Direct Lending Facility has no upper or lower loan value limit.

Interested exporters contact UKEF's customer service team in respect of enquiries for loans below £5 million, as an alternative product may be more appropriate.

Eligibility: The Following Criteria Must Be Met

- The exporter must be carrying on business in the UK.
- Agents/arrangers nominated by buyers or exporters will need to meet UK Export Finance's general eligibility criteria.

Initial Enquiry Form

Exporter can register business interest in applying for a loan under the Direct Lending Facility by completing the short enquiry form and returning it to customer.service@ukexportfinance.gov.uk

Based on the information provided, UKEF will aim to provide exporter with initial feedback on how best to proceed with the application.

How It Work?

UK Export Finance is not a bank, and cannot always offer exporters a full range of banking services. Therefore, UK Export Finance is willing to deliver Direct Lending in partnership with a private sector provider. The following diagram shows how UK Export Finance provides a loan in partnership with a bank or a suitable non-bank entity. In the absence of a partner bank, additional fees will be levied by UK Export Finance at times it is equivalent to the fee that a bank would charge.

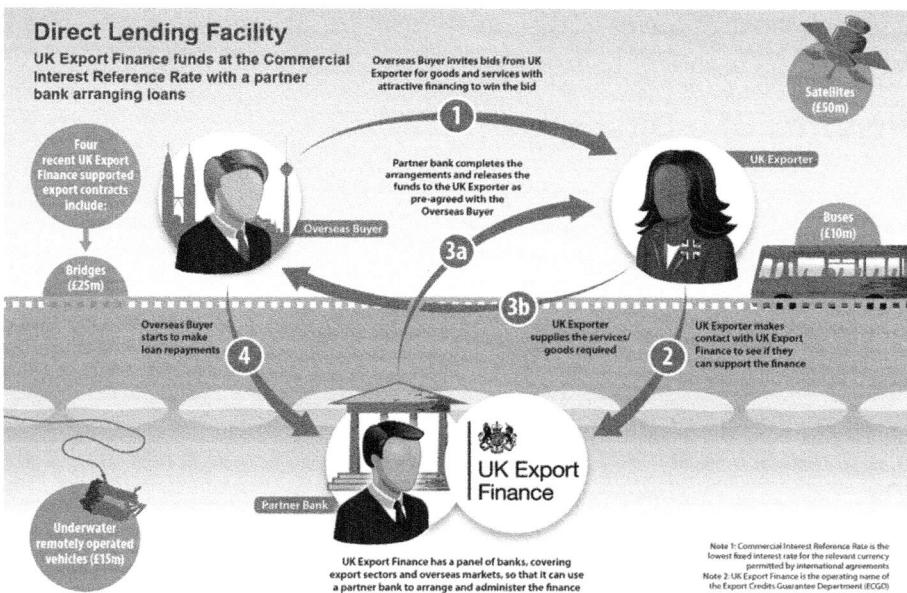

How to Apply?

The steps to apply for a Direct Loan are:

1. Entrepreneur need to go through and understand the UKEF's guide and the main features document to check this is the facility one needs.
2. Read the guide for applicants on business processes and factors to find out how UKEF make decisions on applications.
3. Read the quick guide to credit terms related to the export contract UKEF are asked to support, which includes what is meant by credit terms, what terms can be agreed, the amount of credit that can be supported, starting point of credit, length of credit and repayments of credit.

4. Read the quick guide to recourse which includes what recourse is, when it is sought and required, when we exercise recourse, from whom it is sought, the amount of recourse, release from recourse and the Lloyds recourse indemnity policy. (For the purpose of this note 'UK Export Finance' should be regarded as the 'lending bank'.)
5. Use UKEF country cover indicators tool to find out what cover is available for the country an exporter want to do business in.
6. Fill in the Direct Lending Facility application form.
7. The application form and supporting documentation are to be sent to the following address: Business Group, UK Export Finance, 1 Horse Guards Road, London, SW1A 2HQ

Benefits of a Direct Loan

The benefits are as follows:

- The exporter is paid as though it has a cash contract.
- The buyer or borrower has time to pay over a number of years and can borrow at a very competitive fixed rate of interest.

Maximum Amount

The maximum amount of the loan is 85% of the contract value. A minimum of 15% of the contract value must be paid directly to the exporter by the buyer before the loan starts to be repaid. Of the 15%, a down payment of at least 5% should be received upon contract signature.

UKEF can consider support for foreign content (i.e. the cost to the exporter of purchasing goods or services from sub-contractors outside the UK) of up to 80% of the export contract's value. UK Export Finance may vary this proportion if country limits are close to being filled and/or for large loan values (above £50 million). The period for repayment of the loan must be at least 2 years.

Cost

An administration charge will be specified in the Term Sheet for each transaction. In the absence of a partner bank, additional fees will be levied by UK Export Finance equivalent to those that a bank would charge.

Use UKEF's premium indicator tool to obtain an indicative premium rate for transactions where UKEF will be supporting a contract with an overseas sovereign buyer as the risk entity.

Interest Rate

Interest will be at a fixed rate based on the applicable Commercial Interest Reference Rates (CIRRs) set by the Organisation for Economic Co-operation and Development (OECD).

One can know the current CIRR from the OECD website.

For each currency, the minimum loan fixed rate will be (i) the appropriate CIRR, or (ii) the cost of government funds (NLF rates) if higher.

Disclaimer by the UKEF

"This webpage has been prepared for information purposes only and does not constitute legal, financial or investment advice. Any party entering into a legal agreement should obtain comprehensive legal and financial advice. This document does not constitute an offer or commitment of any kind on the part of Her Britannic Majesty's Secretary of State acting by the Export Credits Guarantee Department ("UK Export Finance") to provide a guarantee, to enter into any form of financing or other transaction or to otherwise act, and is not intended to create any legally binding obligations. Any decision to provide such a guarantee or enter into any such transaction will be subject to, among other things, all necessary internal approvals and consents (including credit approval), satisfactory due diligence and definitive final documentation. The terms set out in this document are indicative only. The final terms of any guarantee or commitment provided by UK Export Finance will be modified to reflect the individual circumstances of the transaction of which it forms part and of the parties thereto and will be subject to the final determination and approval of UK Export Finance. This document does not constitute nor does it form part of an offer to sell or purchase, or the solicitation of an offer to sell or purchase, any securities or an offer or recommendation to enter into any transaction.

This guide was last updated in October 2014"
customer.service@ukexportfinance.gov.uk
Telephone +44 (0)20 7271 8010

Export Refinancing Facility

The Export Refinancing Facility (ERF) is an add-on to UK Export Finance's standard Buyer Credit, in that it provides:

- an undertaking to the bank that UK Export Finance will purchase the export loan by a given time; and
- an undertaking to the borrower that UK Export Finance will provide a repayment guarantee for bonds issued (or other replacement refinancing) to refinance the loan.

The ERF is available to banks funding non-sterling Buyer Credit Loans, typically with values above £50 million that are intended to be refinanced through the debt capital markets (DCM) or other commercial loans. Such re-financings are priced competitively as a result of UK Export Finance's Guarantee of Payments Scheduled principal, and interest due under the bonds.

Should such commercial refinancing be unavailable, UK Export Finance provides certainty to the borrower and to the banks that it will fund the loan until such time as markets reopen.

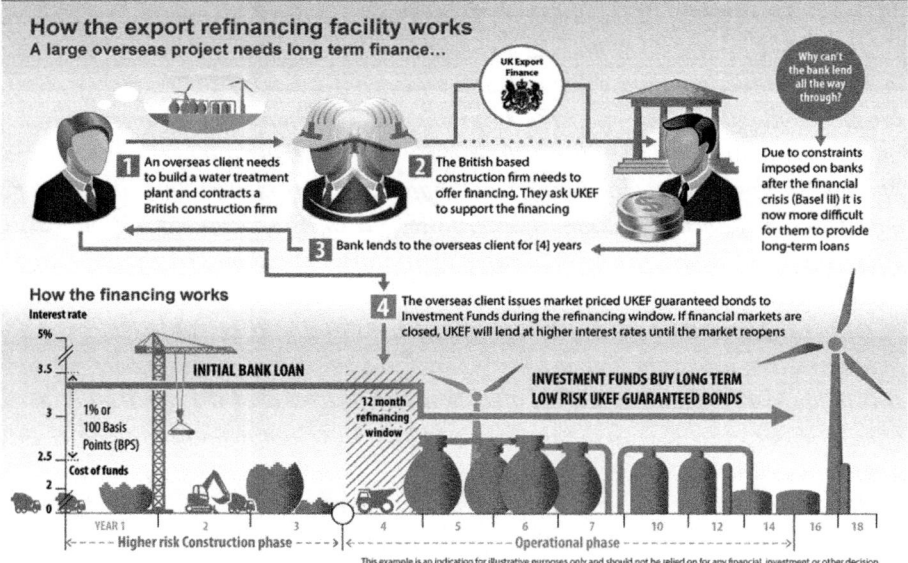

Eligibility

The following criteria must be met:

- The exporter must be carrying on business in the UK.
- Loans to overseas borrowers in the EU are not eligible under the scheme.
- The loan value must be the equivalent of at least £50 million in a commercial non-sterling currency with a substantial investor base.
- If UK Export Finance is required to purchase the loan, a higher rate of interest (agreed at the outset) will be applied.

How It Works?

The first diagram (below) shows how UK Export Finance provides a Buyer Credit Guarantee/ERF to a lender in support of the purchase by an overseas buyer of capital or semi-capital goods/services from a UK exporter.

The second diagram shows the expected refinancing arrangement, with the third diagram showing UK Export Finance taking out the loan, typically during a period of market disruption. For example, ERF provides the commercial bank confidence that one year after the final draw down, the loan will be taken out by UK Export Finance if it has not already been refinanced. Any UK Export Finance 'take out' is intended to be temporary, with the loan refinanced as and when markets return to normal.

STAGE 1 – DRAWDOWN (envisaged over [3] years)

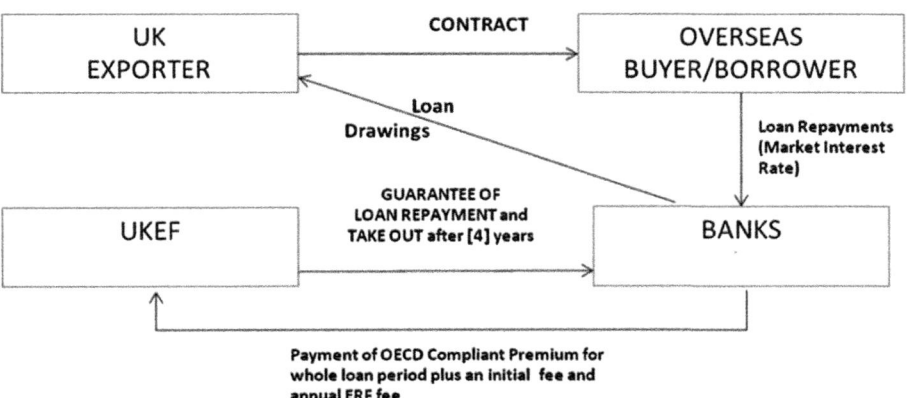

STAGE 2 – REFINANCING before [4] years

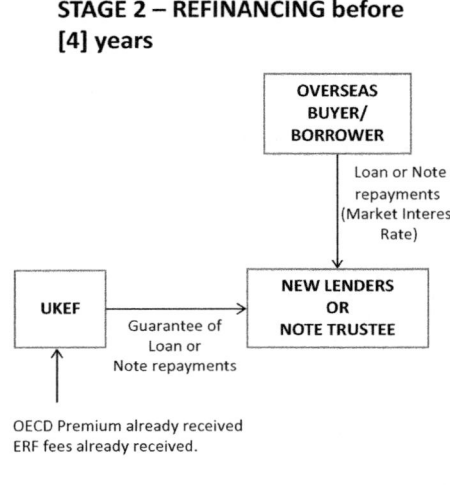

STAGE 2B – TAKE OUT FOLLOWING FAILURE TO REFINANCE

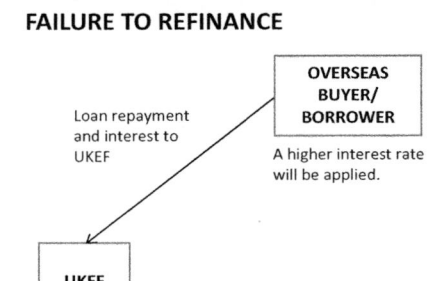

How to Apply?

It is recommended that the entrepreneur discusses the ERF with the bank before submitting an application.

The steps to apply for an ERF (Buyer Credit) facility are as follows:

1. Read the main features of the Export Refinancing Facility to check this is the facility one needs.
2. Read the guide for applicants on business processes and factors to find out how we make decisions on applications.
3. Read the quick guide to credit terms related to the export contract we are asked to support, which includes what is meant by credit terms, what terms can be agreed, the amount of credit that can be supported, starting point of credit, length of credit and repayments of credit.
4. Read the quick guide to recourse which includes what recourse is, when it is sought and required, when we exercise recourse, from whom it is sought, the amount of recourse, release from recourse and the Lloyds recourse indemnity policy.
5. Use our country cover indicators tool to find out what cover is available for the country you want to do business in.
6. Contact customer services using the details below, to obtain an indication of how much premium you will need to pay.

7. Fill in the Buyer Credit application form (for Export Refinancing Facility) and schedule to the Buyer Credit application.
8. Fill in the sustainable lending questionnaire if necessary (the country cover indicators tool will tell you if you need to fill it in).
9. Send your application form and supporting documentation to the Business Group to the address Business Group, UK Export Finance, 1 Horse Guards Road, London, SW1A 2HQ

It is to be noted that, as of 24 April 2017, UK Export Finance no longer offers the option for exporters to request Security of Information Arrangements ("Special Handling Arrangements") with regard to the provision of Agent's identities. Updated application forms can be obtained from UKEF, and applicants must therefore provide all the required information requested in respect of any agent.

Contact UKEF customer service team to get further help with regard to ERF from UKEF:

+44 (0)20 7271 8010 customer.service@ukexportfinance.gov.uk

Lines of Credit

A UK Export Finance-supported line of credit can provide UK exporters of capital goods with a quick way to access finance made available by a UK bank to assist an overseas buyer to purchase UK exports.

Lines of credit can be set up to enable:

* a variety of overseas buyers to purchase unrelated capital goods or services (known as a general purpose line of credit);
* an individual overseas buyer to purchase a wide range of capital goods or services for a particular project (known as a project line of credit).

Finance can be made available in the main trading currencies (including sterling, US dollars and euro).

How to Apply?

Contact UKEF +44 (0)20 7271 8010 or email customer.service@ukexportfinance.gov.uk

Line of Credit

The diagram shows how UK Export Finance provides a guarantee to the bank that the borrower will repay the loan. The banks pay the exporter from the loan. The UK exporter supplies the capital goods and/or services to the buyer. The buyer pays the bank which acts as the borrower. The bank extends a line of credit to the borrower, and the borrower repays the loan under the line of credit.

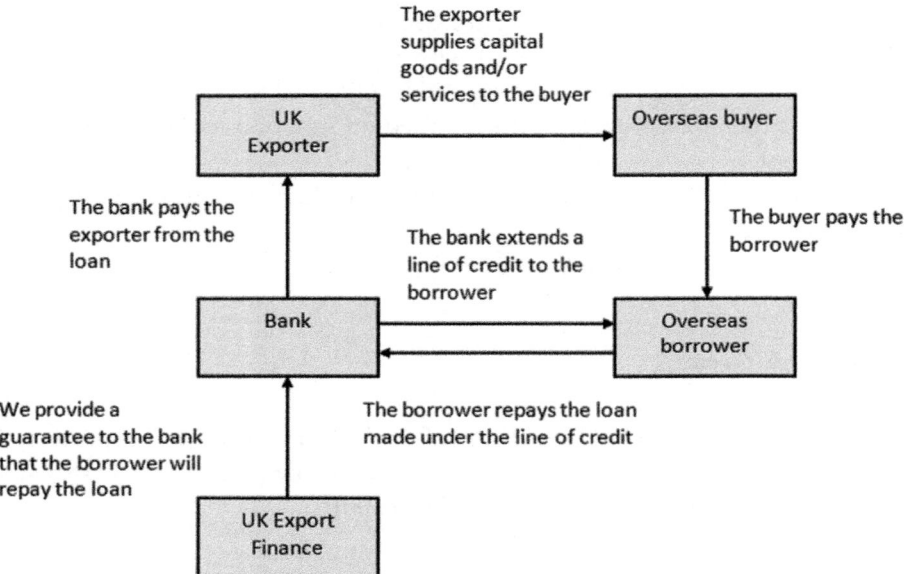

The buyer may also act as borrower in its own right (if this is acceptable to UKEF), otherwise an acceptable bank in the borrower's country will need to act as borrower. A foreign bank will almost always act as borrower in the case of a general purpose line of credit.

The Benefits of a Line of Credit

- The line will usually be put in place before an export contract is signed, which means that the exporter should be able to gain access to the facility quickly.
- The exporter is paid as soon as the goods have been shipped and/or services performed.

- The buyer or borrower has time to pay over a number of years and can borrow at fixed or floating rates of interest.
- The bank receives a guarantee from UKEF for the amounts due under the line of credit.

Risks Covered

The bank is protected against non-payment by the borrower under the loan.

Eligibility Criteria

- The exporter must be carrying on business in the UK.
- Each export contract value must be at least £25,000 or the equivalent in another currency.
- The bank which is to provide the line of credit must be acceptable to UKEF.

LIMIT

The maximum amount that can be made available for each contract financed by the line of credit is 85% of the contract value. A minimum of 15% of the contract value must be paid directly to the exporter by the buyer before the loan starts to be repaid. We can consider support for foreign content (the cost to the exporter of purchasing goods or services from sub-contractors outside the UK) of up to 80% of the export contract value.

Term

The period for repayment of the loan made under the line of credit must be at least two years.

Cost

The premium is payable on the amount of support provided. The premium is determined on a case-by-case basis.

Disclaimer by the UKEF

"The information available in this book is not intended to be a comprehensive description for lines of credit and many details which are relevant to particular circumstances may have been omitted. Underwriters will look at each case on its merits". Contact UKEF for a query customer.service@ukexportfinance. gov.uk, Telephone +44 (0)20 7271 8010.

Overseas Investment Insurance

Overseas Investment Insurance (OII) can protect a UK investor against potential losses on overseas investments due to defined political events that may arise in a non-OECD country.

Eligibility

Any UK-based entity investing overseas is eligible, as long as:

• you are carrying on business in the UK, not simply acting as a conduit for investment outside the UK;
• there is a lack of availability of cover from the private market on normal terms;
• where cover is requested for a guarantee in respect of an overseas investment, the party giving the guarantee must have an interest in that enterprise.

How It Works?

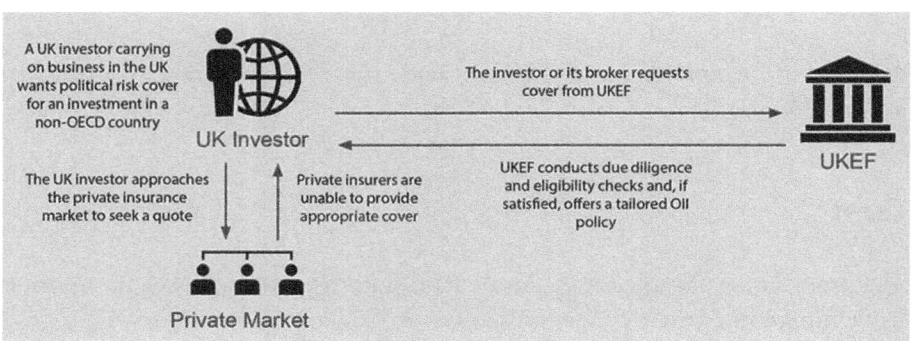

1. A UK investor carrying on business in the UK wants political risk cover for an investment in a non-OECD country.
2. The UK investor approaches the private insurance market to seek a quote.
3. Private insurers are unable to provide appropriate cover.
4. The investor or its broker requests cover from UKEF.
5. UKEF conducts due diligence and eligibility checks and, if satisfied, offers a tailored OII policy.

How to Apply?

The steps for applying for OII are as follows:

1. Check UKEF country cover policy and indicators to find out what cover is available in the country Exporter want to do business in.
2. Contact customer.service@ukexportfinance.gov.uk to obtain an indication of how much premium exporter will need to pay.
3. Fill in and send the Overseas Investment Insurance application form, if exporter is required to by UKEF country cover indicators, fill in the sustainable lending questionnaire.
4. Send your application form and supporting documentation to Business Group, UK Export Finance, 1 Horse Guards Road, London, SW1A 2HQ

For further guidance, entrepreneur can get in touch with the local export finance manager and seek help for Overseas Investment Insurance +44 (0)20 7271 8010 customer.service@ukexportfinance.gov.uk.

Debt Conversion Scheme

UK Export Finance Debt Conversion Scheme allows a proportion of outstanding debts owed to UK Export Finance by a number of countries to be converted into local currency, at a discount, for investment in local projects approved by UKEF and the government of the country concerned.

How to Apply?

1. Read the UKEF guide and check this is the scheme an entrepreneur need, and to verify eligibility.
2. Fill in the Debt Conversion Application Form.

3. Send the application form and supporting documentation to: Business Group, UK Export Finance, 1 Horse Guards Road, London, SW1A 2HQ

Contact +44 (0)20 7271 8010 customer.service@ukexportfinance.gov.uk.

How It Works?

An entrepreneur approaches UKEF with an offer to purchase debt and at the same time provides details of the project entrepreneur intend to invest the debt in. We then assess the project and the price which entrepreneur has offered for the debt and notify you of the initial acceptability of the proposals.

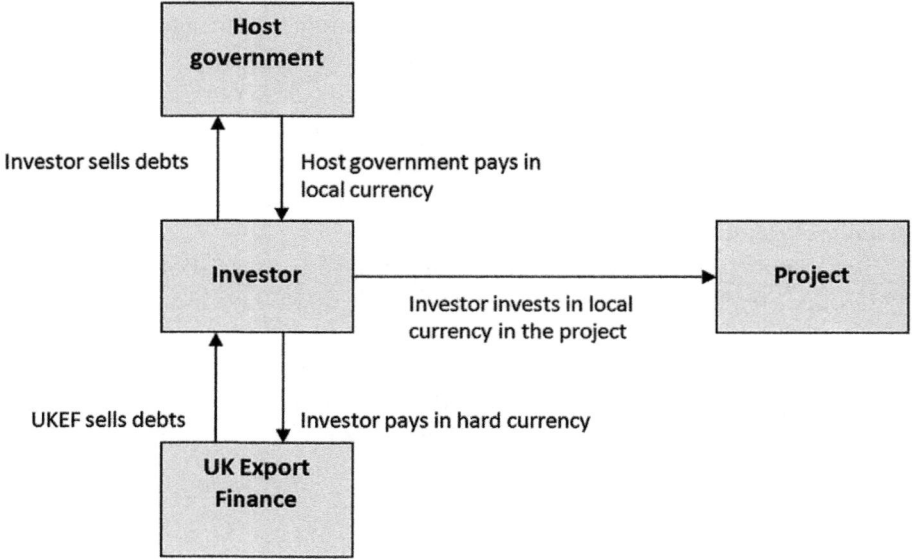

The Benefits of the Debt Conversion Scheme

The benefits are as follows:

- UK Export Finance receives recoveries for payments which UKEF has made under its guarantees.
- The investor (who purchases the debt) can obtain local currency at a good rate of exchange to finance the acquisition of assets for use in a local project.

- The debtor country is able to settle outstanding debts, but in its local currency and at a discount—the local currency is invested in approved and beneficial projects and it may attract investment that might not otherwise take place.

Eligible Countries

The Debt Conversion Scheme can be capitalised and drawn upon in the following countries:

- Bosnia
- Burma (Myanmar)
- Cuba
- Ecuador
- Egypt
- Grenada
- Indonesia
- Iraq
- Kenya
- Pakistan
- Serbia
- Seychelles
- Vietnam

Eligibility

UK Export Finance considers the following factors:

- whether the purchase price you offer for the debt is acceptable;
- the nature of the proposed project or investment that would be financed by the purchase of the debt;
- the contribution the project will make to the social, economic and environmental development of the country;
- your ability, and that of any other participants in the project, to buy the debt and undertake the project;
- whether the project is consistent with UKEF policies, including those on combating bribery and corruption.

Cost

There is no fee for the application.

Disclaimer by the UKEF: "The information available in this book is not intended to be a comprehensive description of UKEF debt conversion scheme, and many details which are relevant to particular circumstances may have been omitted".

When considering applications, UKEF underwriters will look at each case on its merits. (The guide was last updated in May 2012 and published on 17 April 2013.) Further queries entrepreneurs need to contact customer.service@ ukexportfinance.gov.uk, Telephone +44 (0)20 7271 8010.

Source: www.UKExport Finance.Gov.uk

21

Marine Insurance

Introduction

Marine insurance began in the cities of Northern Italy, about the end of the twelfth century. Italian merchants came to the UK in the thirteenth and fourteenth centuries and brought with them their trading customs, including marine insurance. Initially merchants entered into marine insurance contracts as incidental to their general trading activities and later specialised in this business.

Do we need marine insurance? There are various risks of loss and damage to goods when transported from one place to another, depending upon mode of transport. The loss could be partial or total loss of goods and this could cause financial loss to the importers and/or to other parties involved such as banks.

To protect the importers/parties involved, especially in international trade, insurance companies are prepared to offer protection against such risks, on payment of a premium to the insurers according to the protection required for loss or damage to the goods.

Importance of Marine Insurance

Most ship owners and those responsible for cargo, resort to marine insurance for the protection of their ships, goods, freight and other interests against marine perils. Very heavy capital values are locked up in ships, the loss of which might easily prove financially crippling for the strongest shipping

© The Author(s) 2019
T. Bhogal, A. Trivedi, *International Trade Finance*, Finance and Capital Markets Series,
https://doi.org/10.1007/978-3-030-24540-5_21

companies. Marine insurance, therefore, occupies an important position in international trade business. By affording protection against accidental losses, it enables those engaged in overseas trade to venture their capital more freely, without keeping large reserves of their own to meet disasters, and to expand the scope of their operations.

Business transactions, whether internal or international, necessarily involve movement of goods by sea, air, and/or land from one place to another. In the course of the journey the goods sustain various types of loss or damage including non-delivery. The marine insurance policy is the best means to protect the owner against possible loss or damage to cargo in transit. With a view to understanding the implications of a policy of marine insurance, in particular the person who can effect insurance, it is necessary to understand the terms and conditions of a contract of sale and also whether the person will stand to gain by the safe arrival of the cargo or sustain loss by damage to the cargo. When the seller executes an order as per directions of the buyer the contract of sale is performed and the property in the goods passes from the seller to the buyer. With the transfer of ownership the risk of loss also passes from the seller to the buyer and the terms of the contract of sale determine when the ownership of the goods passes on to the buyer.

Definition

Marine insurance is a contract uberrimae fidei representing an agreement whereby the insurer undertakes to indemnify the insured, in the manner and to the extent agreed, in terms of space-time and risk clauses subject to the principle of proximate clause, for insurable property lost or damaged by maritime perils, incidental to marine adventure. The contract can be assigned by endorsement and delivery to the other party.

Classification of Marine Insurance Cover

Marine insurance against loss of or damage to property by the perils of the sea, may be classified under these headings:

HULL: This refers to the insurance of the ship (i.e. hull and machinery), by the ship owners against maritime perils, which are briefly, perils of the sea, such as heavy weather, stranding or collision, fire and similar perils. Such insurance is normally arranged for a period of 12 months.

CARGO: This refers to goods and/or merchandise imported or exported to and from various ports of the world. Insurance interest exists on behalf of both buyer and seller. Cargo is normally insured against all maritime and transit risks, including war perils.

FREIGHT: Freight is the sum paid for transportation of goods to the ship owners. When goods are lost or damaged by marine perils, freight, or a proportion of it, will be lost. The person involved therefore, has an insurable interest. If the freight is prepaid, it is merged with the insurable value of the cargo. If it is payable at destination it is a ship owner's risk.

Marine Insurance Associations

- British Insurance Association
- Lloyd's Underwriters' Association
- The Institute of London Underwriters
- Liverpool Underwriters' Associations

Types of Insurance Instruments

BROKER'S NOTE: It is issued by an insurance broker/agent. Usually it is not acceptable to banks because its validity is for a short period only (say 28 or 30 days).

COVER NOTE: It is issued by an insurance company/broker or insurance agent. Generally it is not acceptable to banks unless issued under an "open policy".

INSURANCE CERTIFICATE: It is issued by an insurance company and is acceptable to banks.

MARINE INSURANCE POLICY: It is issued by an insurance company and is acceptable to banks.

Marine Insurance Policy

Marine insurance plays a very important role in overseas trade as it affords protection against accidental losses and enables the various trading interests to deploy their capital freely and thus helps them to expand the scope of their activity. It is very important to insure the goods against the risks of loss or damage. It depends upon the sale contract as to who will take the insurance policy (the buyer or the seller of the goods). An insurance policy explains in detail the terms and conditions of the risks covered. An insurance policy covers cargo, hull freight or any other insurable interest allied to these, against marine perils or perils incidental to a marine adventure.

As per the Institute of London Underwriters Cargo Clauses policies can be classified into three types viz. Clause (A) Clause (B) and Clause (C).

Institute Cargo Clauses (A) Risk Covered

This insurance policy covers all risks of loss of or damage to the subject matter insured except as provided in clauses 4, 5, 6 and 7 of the policy.

This insurance covers general average and salvage charges, adjusted or determined according to the contract of affreightment and/or the governing law and practice, incurred to avoid or in connection with the avoidance of loss from any cause except those excluded in Clauses 4, 5, 6 and 7 or elsewhere in this insurance.

This insurance is extended to indemnify the assured against such proportion of liability under the contract of affreightment "Both to Blame Collision" clause as is in respect of a loss recoverable hereunder. In the event of any claim by ship owners under the said clause the assured agree to notify the underwriters who shall have the right, at their own cost and expense, to defend the assured against such claim.

Institute Cargo Clauses (B) Risks Covered

This insurance covers, except as provided in clauses 4, 5, 6 and 7 in the policy, loss of or damage to the subject-matter insured reasonably attributable to, fire or explosion, vessel or craft being stranded, grounded sunk or capsized, overturning or derailment of land conveyance, collision or contact of vessel craft or conveyance with any external object other than water, discharge of cargo at a port of distress, earthquake, volcanic eruption or lightning, loss of or damage to the subject-matter insured caused by general average sacrifice, jettison or washing overboard, entry of sea lake or river water into vessel craft hold, conveyance container lift-van or place of storage. Total loss of any package lost overboard or dropped whilst loading on to, or loading from, vessel or craft.

Institute Cargo Clauses (C) Risks Covered

This insurance covers, except as provided in clauses 4, 5, 6 and 7 of the policy, loss of or damage to the subject-matter insured reasonably attributable to fire or explosion, vessel or craft being stranded, grounded, sunk or capsized, overturning or derailment of land conveyance, collision or contact of vessel craft or conveyance with any external object other than water, discharge of cargo at a port of distress, loss of or damage to the subject-matter insured caused by general average sacrifice, jettison clauses.

This insurance covers general average and salvage charges, adjusted or determined according to the contract of affreightment and/or the governing law and practice, incurred to avoid or in connection with the avoidance of loss from any cause except those excluded in clauses 4, 5, 6 and 7 or elsewhere in this insurance.

This insurance is extended to indemnify the assured against such proportion of liability under the contract of affreightment "Both to Blame Collision" clause as is in respect of a loss recoverable hereunder. In the event of any claim by ship owners under the said clause the assured agree to notify the underwriters who shall have the right, at their own cost and expense, to defend the assured against such claim.

Contents of a Marine Insurance Policy

A marine insurance policy may be issued at the time when the contract is concluded or afterwards. It should give the following information, which must be checked by a banker dealing with documentary credits.

1. Amount of Insurance
2. Currency of Policy Money
3. Name of the Insurance Company
4. Name of the Assured
5. Name of the Carrier
6. Merchandise Description
7. Ports of Loading and Discharge
8. Party to Whom Insurance is Payable
9. Place of Payment of Policy Money
10. Technical Information
11. Number of Copies, Original, Duplicates and so on
12. What Risks are Covered
13. Signature/countersignature
14. Facsimile Signature
15. Date of Issue

Insurance Certificate

The credit will indicate what insurance cover is required and will call for either an insurance policy or insurance certificate.

An insurance policy may only be issued by the insurer and is usually in standard form covering the customary risks for any voyage. The form of policy in general use today is Lloyd's SG (Ships and Goods) policy.

Regular exporters normally arrange an open contract to cover all exports during a specific period. This provides insurance cover at all times within the agreed terms and conditions of the contract and avoids having to obtain separate cover and a new policy for each shipment.

Insurance certificates are issued for each shipment by either the insurers and/or by the exporters.

The certificate must contain the same details as the policy with the slight difference that it will carry a shortened version of the provisions of the policy under which it is issued. An insurance certificate should be issued and signed by the insurance company or its agent.

Insurance Documents Normally Show the Following Details

- The name and signature of the insurer;
- The name of the assured;
- A description of the risks covered;
- The sum or sums insured expressed in the same currency as that of the credit;
- A description of the consignment;
- The place where claims are payable together with details of the agent to whom claims may be directed;
- The declaration of the assured together with his designation where applicable his endorsement on the reverse of the document is also required so that the right to claim may be transferred to another party (usually the importer);
- The date of issue. This must be the same as or earlier than the date of the document evidencing despatch, except where warehouse-to-warehouse cover is indicated.

Insurance, particularly marine insurance, is a complicated subject, and exporters should arrange cover for their shipments through a professional insurance broker.

Source: Marine Insurance Acts

22

Innovative Non-traditional Finance

Supply Chain Finance

What Is a Supply Chain?

Supply Chain Finance is an innovative way of financing where large companies help their supply chain access credit at a much lower cost and improve cash-flow. It has already been successfully implemented by companies including Rolls Royce and Vodafone in the UK scenario. The arrangement has full support and backing of the UK Government to encourage and promote jobs and boost growth of SMEs in the UK and enabling such establishments to compete in the global spectrum.

Mechanism

Under Supply Chain Finance, a bank is notified by a large company that an invoice has been approved for payment; the bank is then able to offer a 100% immediate advance to the supplier at lower interest rates, knowing well that the invoice will ultimately be paid by the large company. Under Supply Chain Scheme larger firms are identifying a variety of different ways to support their supply chains, normally through improved payment terms, direct collaboration and investment. It's self-encouraging to note that the UK Government lead the front by setting up its own supply chain

© The Author(s) 2019
T. Bhogal, A. Trivedi, *International Trade Finance*, Finance and Capital Markets Series,
https://doi.org/10.1007/978-3-030-24540-5_22

finance scheme for NHS pharmacists. Banks have for a number of years structured Supply Chain finance programmes for corporate to support the financing needs of their suppliers.

UK Government Support

The UK Government is keen to ensure that SMEs have the widest range of credit options available to them and is taking action on a number of fronts to deliver:

The Funding for Lending scheme to encourage banks to boost lending in the UK economy;

The Enterprise Finance Guarantee—A loan guarantee programme which has helped a large number of small firms obtain bank finance;

More than £160 m invested in high-growth UK firm through support for the UK Venture Capital industry as per authentic information;

Generous tax schemes for people investing in start-ups and growing companies in UK; and,

A new £82.5 m start-up loan programme to help young people start their own businesses.

Large Companies vs. SMEs

Experiencing the perspective, the major UK companies generally have strong credit ratings and excellent access to finance. In contrast the SME suppliers to those major UK companies often have relatively more expensive finance and more limited access to equity capital to finance their operations.

The largest component of SME financing is "working capital" funding. SMEs generally fund their working capital via overdrafts, invoice discounting or factoring or similar products. These products are generally more expensive than their customer's cost of credit and provide the SME with an advance rate of around 80%—with the rest coming from equity capital and or outside financiers. This makes it relatively more challenging and expensive for SMEs to grow.

Supply Chain Finance: Benefits

It provides funding to suppliers at a comparatively lower cost based on the credit quality of their customers.

It allows suppliers to receive 100% of the invoice value, less a small finance fee, rather than the 70 to 90% generally offered through traditional finance products for SMEs. This can help free up money for growth, boost cash-flow or allow businesses to refinance existing debt.

It can help supply chains to become more efficient as the overall cost of finance is reduced.

It allows banks to provide finance to SMEs in a significantly more capital efficient manner. Rather unlocking capital for them to potentially provide yet more lending to SMEs.

Tim Breedon Taskforce on Non-Bank Lending

Supply Chain Finance was recommended by the Breedon Taskforce on Non-Bank Lending.

Pharmacist Scheme

Community pharmacies dispense around 80 million NHS prescription items every month. They then claim payment from the NHS for the products and services provided. The amount they are owed is calculated by the NHS Business Services Authority (NHSBSA). Such high voluminous flow to process, it takes time. Typically, pharmacy contractors receive an estimated 80% of their payment within four weeks of sending their prescriptions to the NHSBSA with the balance being paid the following month. It can therefore take eight weeks before payment is made in full. However, in the meantime, suppliers need to be paid and many pharmacy businesses use commercial loans—which are often expensive—to maintain cash flow.

NHSBSA

Under the Supply Chain Finance system, a bank will make the NHSBSA's estimated payment available to the pharmacist in a week. This means they will have access to money more quickly instead of having to wait for the first payment at the end of the month. In accessing the money early, they will need to pay interest, but it will be at comparatively lower cost than any borrowing arrangement they could usually access.

The Supply Chain Finance scheme does help reduce this cost of borrowing. Around 4500 pharmacy businesses will be able to get access to approximately £800 million of credit at a much lower cost than they do now. This means pharmacies will have access to cost-effective finance to help cover their suppliers' bills.

GSFC Role

The role of Global Supply Chain Finance (GSCF) is to optimize both the availability and cost of capital within a given buyer–supplier supply chain. It does this by aggregating, packaging, and utilizing information generated during supply chain activities and matching this information with the physical control of goods. The mitigation of risk allows more capital to be raised, capital to be accessed sooner or capital to be raised at lower rates.

The requirement to increase capital or inject capital into the supply chain more quickly is supported and backed by factors:

Market trends with respect to the global supply chain have caused companies to demand an integrated approach/solution to physical and financial supply chain challenges:

1. Buyers—looking to optimize their balance sheet by delaying inventory ownership;
2. Suppliers—looking to obtain funds earlier in the supply chain at favourable rates, given buyers' desire to delay inventory ownership;
3. Middle market companies—looking to monetise non-US domiciled inventory to increase liquidity;
4. There is wide interest in integrated supply chain finance solutions by the users.

Globalization of the US's and Western Europe's manufacturing bases has resulted in fewer domestic assets that can be leveraged to generate working capital.

Most small and medium suppliers to US and European businesses are located in countries that lack well-developed capital markets. Without access to efficient and cost-effective capital, production costs increase significantly or the suppliers go out of business.

Letters of credit, a long-standing method of obtaining capital for suppliers in less developed countries are on the decline as large buyers are forcing suppliers to move to open account.

There is a desire to ensure stability of capital as supply chains elongate. Another Asian financial crisis (such as the one in 1997) would severely disrupt US buyers' supply chains by making capital unavailable to their suppliers.

The market is expected to continue to expand strongly in the coming years at a rate of approximately 15–25% per annum and 10% per annum by 2020. The highest growth of supply chain finance programmes currently originates from the US and Western Europe. Asian countries, India and China in particular, are considered the markets with most potential in the years to follow.

The driving forces behind growth of supply chain finance programmes are:

Globalisation has increased the risk in supply chains and the impact on the financials of corporations.

Working Capital Management has risen at the top of the Finance Head's and credit dispensers agenda.

Strong interest from suppliers regarding the provision of liquidity and enabling lower financing costs.

In order for Supply Chain Finance to take off on a broad scale, an initiative with focus is needed. A moot point has to be thought of and route would be easy to reach if think tanks in the field address and solve the challenges are mentioned as under:

On-boarding of Supplier. In a Supplier Financing programme, the servicer needs to be on board the buyer's trading partners—the suppliers. The multitude of such platforms generates operational issues for suppliers wishing to benefit from various Supply Chain Finance offerings via their buyers' funders.

Know-Your-Customer (KYC). Most funders require KYC checks to be performed on suppliers being enlisted as new trading partners. This procedure not only increases the total processing cost, but it also puts the business case for all parties including the service provider, funder, buyer and ultimately the supplier at risk besides other implications.

Available Capital and Liquidity and BASEL III. With 90% of liquidity in Supply Chain Finance programmes provided by large, global commercial banks, there is a large amount of trade assets, which cannot be covered by such financial institutions. Further regulations such as Basel III might impact the risk appetite and funding capacity of banks and make it more attractive for non-bank funders to step in and support Supply Chain Finance facilities limited to large buyers.

Currently Supply Chain Finance offerings are mainly addressing the large buyers with sound credit ratings whereas the real Supply Chain Finance opportunity extends to large suppliers as well, in particular in terms of payment assurance and risk mitigation.

Legal documentation. Current Supply Chain Finance offerings use proprietary legal documentation, which makes the signing of non-standard agreements a costly, complex and time-consuming process for corporate clients and their suppliers. Therefore, the market is currently facing challenges related to the absence of interoperability and legal standards.

Standardisation. The naming and definitions of the various Supply Chain Finance solutions vary from one market player to the other, which makes it difficult for corporations to compare offerings and consider switching from one provider to another.

Structures

Supply Chain Finance practices have been operating for over a decade. With the passage of time distinctive supply chain finance structures have stabilised.

Buyer managed system. In this structure the buyer owns and runs the supply chain finance platform. Some large retailers such as Carrefour or Metro Group are using this structure and managing the finance programme, supplier on boarding, and liquidity themselves.

Bank operations. The supply chain finance structure is managed by large commercial banks providing the technology-based platform, services and funding. This structure is used by several large buying organisations such as Carlsberg, Boeing, Marks & Spencer and Procter & Gamble to quote in specific.

Multi-bank platforms. The structure that has exhibited the strongest growth rate is represented by independent third-party supply chain finance providers offering multi-bank platforms. In this structure the funding in Supply Chain Finance is uncommitted, no bank can fund in every jurisdiction or currency and due to the general limitations in terms of credit risk appetite and funder concentration risk.

Market share. In terms of market share, programmes are serviced and funded by a handful of players including large commercial banks. Together they manage over 40% of the market share. The rest of the Supply Chain Finance is serviced and funded by a variety of local banks and smaller, independent service providers.

Considering need, mechanism, government's backing and trade bodies support there is a wide scope for Supply Chain Finance to flourish further.

Structured Finance

Structured Finance: Structured finance is a highly involved financial instrument offered to large financial institutions or companies that have complex financing needs that don't match with conventional financial products.

Ever since the mid-1980s, structured finance has become visible in the financial industry. Well collateralised debt obligations, synthetic financial instruments, collateralised bond obligations (CBOs), syndicated loans, bridge finance and mezzanine finance are modes of structured finance instruments.

Structured Finance-Anatomy

Structured finance is typically indicated for borrowers—mostly extensive corporations—that have unique or highly specified needs. A simple loan or other type of conventional financial instrument will not suffice to resolve such need. In most cases, structured finance involves one or several discretionary transactions to be completed and thus evolved and often risky instruments must be implemented.

Structured Finance-Products/Instruments

When a standard loan is not enough to cover unique transactions dictated by a corporation's operational needs, for example, a number of different structured finance products may be implemented. Along with CDOs and CBOs—instruments such as collateralised mortgage obligations (CMOs), credit default swaps (CDSs), and hybrid securities combining elements of debt and equity securities are often resorted out.

Benefits

Structured Products: Non-transferable

Structured financial products are typically not offered by traditional lenders. Generally, because structured finance is required for major capital injection into a business or organisation, investors are required to provide such financing. Structured financial products are almost always non-transferrable, meaning that they cannot be transferred between various types of debt in the same way that a standard loan is.

Structured financing and securitisation are used by corporations, governments and financial intermediaries in advancing, evolving and complex emerging markets to manage risk, develop financial markets, expand business reach and design new funding instruments. For these entities, using structured financing transforms cash flows and reshapes the liquidity of financial portfolios.

Securitisation

Securitisation is mechanism through which a financial instrument is created by combining financial assets. Various tiers of these repackaged instruments are then sold off to investors. Securitisation, much like structured finance, promotes liquidity and is also used to develop the structured financial products used by uniquely qualified businesses and other customers.

A mortgage-backed security (MBS) is a model example of securitisation. Mortgages may be grouped into one large pool, leaving the issuer the opportunity to divide the pool into pieces that are based on the risk of default inherent to each mortgage. The smaller pieces may then be sold to investors.

Bridging Loan

Bridging loans are a short-term funding option secured against a property, usually residential but they can also be taken out on a commercial property. They are used to bridge the gap between the purchase and either sale or re-mortgage of a property collateralising an underline business and or otherwise. Bridging loans are also used as a short- to medium-term loan until the borrower can repay the debt.

High Street Banks

After the banking crisis more and more property developers started to use them due to paucity or non-availability of funding from the high street banks. Bridging Loans can be arranged up to 100% with additional security, and also on a First, Second or Third charge basis.

Bridging Loans Work Mechanism

Bridging loans can help to complete the purchase of a property before selling the existing one, by offering you short-term access to funds, for anything from a month to eighteen months. Bridging Finance can also be used if you are property trading thereby stating that you can make a quick purchase of a property, before arranging a traditional mortgage after six months or simply sell the property on.

Auction Purchase

Auction purchase Bridging loans are also often used when making an auction property purchase before arranging a mortgage these are available for both commercial and residential.

Development and Refurbishment of Property

Bridging loans are widely used by both new and experienced developers alike. After the financial crash of 2008 the high street lenders virtually pulled out of the property development market, the slack as an opportunity was quickly taken up by bridging loan lenders, although significantly more expensive than traditional development loans, bridging loans allowed developers to continue building and refurbishing properties.

Cash Buy and Opportunity

It is of significance to envisage that with residential bridging for home sellers, the extra cost over traditional lenders can be absorbed partially by the fact that they become in effect a cash buyer or they can make a purchase that they may otherwise have missed out on.

Exit Strategy

With bridging loans borrower will need a clear exit strategy, for the comfort of lender. Crucially a caution for the borrowers who have not used this type of finance before is that they need to tread carefully and take professional advice, also if the borrower intend to move into the property at any point then it becomes a regulated loan and there would be an obligatory requirement to appoint an FCA approved advisor in order to deal with the loan for applicant/ borrower. If the applicants are not moving in to the property then this is not necessary as it is deemed a purely commercial transaction.

Bridging Finance-Interest

Bridging finance is often resorted to/utilised to address a temporary cash flow problem. A common example of this type of situation is when a person wishes to purchase a property but still needs to sell their existing residence or arranged finance entail delay due to procedure/formalities to be completed. Bridging finance can, in these circumstances, provide a solution by offering short-term funding. The loan will be secured against property and can bridge the gap to an exit through the sale or refinancing of the asset.

Quantum of Finance

Bridging loans may be offered in amounts ranging from £25,000 to several million, depending on your personal circumstances, project nature and who are the lenders, standing of lender and risk appetite.

Bridging Finance Is Basically to

Beat the competition—Secure a property quickly before it is snapped up by another buyer—even if you have not yet sold the property in hand.

Mortgage chain issue—Secure your ability to buy even in the event that the home buying chain breaks down—for example, if the sale of your old house falls through, bridging finance can allow you to still have sufficient funds to purchase the new house.

Buying an auction property—Use bridging finance to pay the required percentage needed to secure the property on the day of the auction.

Time factor—Get a fast, temporary cash injection when it is needed during the property purchasing process. The ability to move quickly can make the difference on any property transaction. Hence, time factor is essential.

Development finance—If you are buying property to redevelop and you need finance to get your project off the ground, then a bridging loan would help making the difference.

Bridging Finance Providers

A bridging loan, or bridge mortgage nomenclature, can be used for almost any purpose and can be secured on many different types of property. In some cases you may be able to borrow up to 80% of the value of the property. The borrower needs to compare bridging loan companies to get competitive terms including the best interest rate. Here market surveillance/standing of brokers and repute is key factors and must be considered.

Mezzanine Finance

Mezzanine finance is a type of top-up funding to help fill a gap between a developer's equity and the amount that the main lender will provide. This is normally secured by having a second charge over the property in question, as the bank or initial lender would hold a first charge on the asset.

By taking out mezzanine funding, the developer is able to obtain maximum return with minimum cash contribution. Often with busy developers, having a strong cash flow and good contribution levels can be the key to a project's success and give the developer the ability to potentially invest in other opportunities.

Debt and Equity vs. Mezzanine Finance

Debt, equity and mezzanine finance are the three broad categories of business funding, and many are familiar with the first two as these are often utilised.

Debt Finance

Debt finance is a technical term generally used to describe most borrowing, it is immaterial that it's a business loan, invoice finance or a commercial mortgage. The details vary, but the underlying concept is that the business is taking on a debt—the lender gives you cash in return for regular repayment that adds up to the principal amount borrowed plus interest. Therefore, with debt finance the lender usually has a clear idea of how much they'll get back, often with a set and agreed timeframe too and reflect cash-flow and fund-flow accordingly.

Equity fundraising, meanwhile, sells shares in your business to investors, and your new stakeholders will benefit from any growth in your company (sometimes suffer losses). The portion of the business they own can go up and down in value depending on how your firm does in the future, which means it's a riskier proposition and usually part of a longer-term strategy for venture capitalists and private investors.

In other words, unlike debt finance lenders, equity investors are usually in it for the long haul.

Mezzanine's: Importance

Mezzanine is the third way. The mechanics vary between lenders, but the overall idea is that it's a combination of some of the risk and reward of equity investment, combined with the more predictable middle-term income of a loan.

Equity-Business Participation

One common arrangement is a loan that "converts" to an equity share after a set timeframe elapses, or at the lender's discretion; which means if things go well, the business can pay back the money, but if it can't, the lender can recover costs via shares in the business that increase in value. In other scenarios, mezzanine funding uses shares in the business as a form of collateral for a loan, so the future growth of the business enables it to borrow more than it would get from a "senior debt" with a regular lender.

Illustration

Mezzanine finance is best thought of as a kind of "top up" funding for big projects. Say you want to raise Euro 10 million, and you've agreed a loan for Euro 7 million with a standard lender. Through a mezzanine agreement you might secure another Euro 1.5 million, meaning you need to put in Euro 1.5 million yourself instead of Euro 3 million. Or alternatively, you could put in the same amount yourself but have a project fund of Euro 11.5 million instead of Euro 10 million. In this way, mezzanine finance allows you to leverage future profits for the maximum return with the available cash.

Mezzanine finance is often used for management buy-outs. In such situations, it's an entire business being financed rather than a specific project or expansion. Using mezzanine for an objective based project depends heavily on the specific circumstances of the businesses and individuals involved so it's hard to make generalisations, but overall the value of the business being bought is the main factor in the amount raised. It's also a common method of funding property development, where projects won't realise any revenue until the work is complete.

For

If the company continues to grow, it's unlikely that the owners will lose out-right control.

It's flexible, offering various repayment schedules and structures to suit the business.

Mezzanine finance as an input can make the difference in unlocking the funding needed for a project or acquisition.

Against

If the company's fortunes don't go as planned, the business owners may lose some control over its future.

The requirements of mezzanine lenders can be restrictive, for example in terms of security or personal guarantees requirement.

It's often more expensive than similar amounts of debt finance.

Mezzanine finance can take time to arrange (say 3–6 month).

Final Word

However, mezzanine finance is a complex area of business funding, but it can be a useful way for companies to raise more money than would other-wise be possible based on the strength of the current business/personal and professional reputation alone sometime. Or, it offers an alternative to sell-ing large amounts of equity outright, which may be preferable for business owners wishing to keep as much control as possible. Overall, it's worth exploring if business is considering an acquisition, management buy-out, or a large new project based on capability and business acumen behest the venture.

Entrepreneurs (importers/exporters) do look for structured finance, securi-tisation, bridge finance and mezzanine finance depending plan/project in hand, funds available and requirement of further cash to mitigate gap, if any.

23

BREXIT

The second decade of twenty-first century acknowledge many a political and economic developments all over the world including, "BREXIT" in Europe and "NAFTA" in North Americas. This chapter address a few features and facts that have surfaced relating to the subject matter.

The people of Britain had voted for Britain Exit or BREXIT, from the European Union (EU) in a holistic referendum (51.9%) in June, 2016. A referendum—a vote in which everyone (or nearly everyone) of voting age can take part—was held on Thursday, 23 June 2016, to decide whether the UK should leave or remain in the European Union. Leave won by 51.9% to 48.1%. The referendum turnout was 71.8%, with more than 30 million people voting.

England voted for BREXIT, by 53.4% to 46.6%. Wales also voted for BREXIT, with Leave getting 52.5% of the vote and Remain 47.5%. Scotland and Northern Ireland both backed staying in the EU. Scotland backed Remain by 62% to 38%, while 55.8% in Northern Ireland voted Remain and 44.2% Leave.

The word BREXIT seems to have been coined on the analogy of "Grexit"—Greece exiting from Euro Zone. Going by the referendum, the UK is scheduled to depart at 11 pm (UK time) on Friday, 29 March 2019 from the EU. After declaration of the referendum results the GB pound the currency of the UK fell to its lowest level ever since 1985; an important development in the financial market. It is true that the pound slumped the day after the referendum—but it has now regained its losses against the dollar, while remaining 15% down against the euro. Predictions of immediate doom were wrong, with the UK economy estimated to have grown 1.8% in 2016, second

© The Author(s) 2019
T. Bhogal, A. Trivedi, *International Trade Finance*, Finance and Capital Markets Series,
https://doi.org/10.1007/978-3-030-24540-5_23

only to Germany's 1.9% among the world's G7 leading industrialised nations. The UK economy continued to grow at almost the same rate in 2017 although there was slower growth, of 0.1% in the first three months of 2018. Inflation rose after June 2016 but has since eased to stand at 2.4%. Unemployment has continued to fall, to stand near a 40-year year low of 4.2%. Annual house price increases have steadily fallen from 9.4% in June 2016 but were still at an inflation-beating 4.2% in the year to March 2018.

However, referendum results and its acceptance by the Government resulted into the political development that David Cameron resigned from his position as the Prime Minster of the UK.

Theresa May

Theresa May took over as the Prime Minister of the UK. Ever since then she is endeavouring to manage the dead lock in the EU negotiations and the counterparts have agreed to move on the trade talks. In between new words were coined and necessary processes were initiated viz. "Hard and Soft BREXIT", "Divorce Bill", "Brexiteer", "Remainer", "Invocation of Article 50", "White Paper", "Chequers Plan"—short name/nomenclature narrated by the media to "the future relationship between the UK and the European Union" and so on.

Divorce Issues

The UK and the EU have discussed at length and agreed on the three "divorce" issues of how much the UK owes the EU, what happens to the Northern Ireland border and what happens to UK citizens living elsewhere in the EU and EU citizens living in the UK in addition many other but directly related knit-grit issues. Talks during rounds of discussion are now focusing on the detail of the defined issues—there is yet to be final agreement on how to avoid having a physical Northern Ireland border—and on future relations. To buy more time, the two sides have agreed on a 21-month "transition" period to smooth the way to post-BREXIT relations. The UK Cabinet has discussed and agreed to an extent how it sees the future relations working and will now be seeing if the EU agrees. Negotiations after negotiations through structured meetings, debates, seminars and summits about future relations between the UK and the EU are taking place. Both sides hope they could agree by October 2018 on the outline of future relations on things like trade, travel and security. If all goes to plan this deal could then be given the go ahead by both sides in time on 29 March 2019.

Key EU Summit

Theresa May presented the Government's thoughts on the UK and the EU's future relations on 2 March 2018. Both sides hope to agree outline of future relations to allow time for UK parliament and EU members to ratify deal by BREXIT day.

13 December 2018: EU summit. If deal not done by October 2018, this is the fall back option if the two sides still want to reach agreement. The House of Commons and The House of Lords vote on withdrawal treaty—MPs could reject the deal but it's not clear what would emerge if that is the case. The UK Parliament also needs to pass an implementation bill before BREXIT day, that is, 29 March 2019; as things stand, situations are "deal or no deal", BREXIT is due to happen at 11 pm the UK time.

31 December 2020: If all goes as anticipated to plan a transition period will then last until midnight on this date.

The UK government and the main UK opposition party both say BREXIT will happen. There are some groups campaigning for BREXIT to be halted, but the focus among the UK's elected politicians has been on what relationship the UK has with the EU after BREXIT, rather than whether BREXIT will happen at all. Nothing is ever certain, but as things stand Britain is leaving the European Union as per sanctity of referendum and the Government is to deliver the mandate to the voters of the UK.

Brexit: The Britain's Stand

Theresa May was against BREXIT during the referendum campaign but is now in favour of it because she says it is what the British people want. Her key message has been that "BREXIT means BREXIT" and she triggered the two-year process of leaving the EU finally on 29 March, 2019. She set out her negotiating goals in a letter to the EU Council President Donald Tusk. She outlined her plans for a transition period after BREXIT. She then set out her thinking on the kind of trading relationship the UK wants with the EU through her speeches.

The Labour Party and Brexit?

The Labour Party say it accepts the referendum result and that BREXIT is going to happen. Leader Jeremy Corbyn opines that he would negotiate a permanent customs union with the EU post BREXIT, which would be very similar to the one it has now. This is the only way to keep trade flowing freely and protect jobs. He has ruled out staying a member of the single market, as some of his pro-EU MPs want, so he can carry out his plans to nationalise key industries without being hampered by EU competition rules. He says the UK should have a very close relationship with the single market. Labour accepts that some form of free movement of people might have to continue. Optimistically he also insists he could persuade Brussels to let the UK have a say in its rules post-BREXIT.

"Soft" and "Hard" BREXIT: Implications

These terms are used during debate on the terms of the UK's departure from the EU. There is no strict definition of either, but they are used to refer to the closeness of the UK's relationship with the EU post-BREXIT.

So at one extreme, "hard" BREXIT could involve the UK refusing to compromise on issues like the free movement of people even if it meant leaving the single market or having to give up hopes of aspects of free trade arrangements. At the other end of the scale, a "soft" BREXIT might follow a similar path to Norway, which is a member of the single market and has to accept the free movement of people as a result of that.

Standards and Level Playing Field

The European Union single market, which was completed in 1992, allows the free movement of goods, services, money and people within the European Union, as if it was a single country. It is possible to set up a business or take a job anywhere within it. The idea was to boost trade, create jobs and lower prices.

But it requires common law-making to ensure products are made to the same technical standards and imposes other rules to ensure a "level playing field".

Critics

Critics are of the opinion that the European Union as a single market generates too many petty regulations and robs members of control over their own affairs. Mass migration from poorer to richer countries has also raised questions about the free movement rule.

The customs union ensures EU member states all charge the same import duties to countries outside the EU. It allows member states to trade freely with each other, without burdensome customs checks at borders, but it limits their freedom to strike their own trade deals.

It is different from a free trade area. In a free trade area no tariffs, taxes or quotas are charged on goods and services moving within the area but members are free to strike their own external trade deals.

The UK Government is planning to leave the customs union after the transition period but internal system have yet to decide on what will replace it amid divisions in cabinet over the two options—a customs partnership and a technology based "maximum facilitation" arrangement.

Reality Check: The Government's Customs Options

Britain's Exit from the EU

Theresa May set up a government department, headed by veteran Conservative MP. Dominic Raab, BREXIT secretary, and Jeremy Hunt, foreign secretary, in conjunction with Prime Minster Theresa May would negotiate BREXIT with the EU Council.

EU Citizens Living in the UK and the UK Citizens in the EU - Status

An agreement between the UK and the EU provides what Theresa May advocate is certainty to the 3.2 million EU citizens in the UK—as well as citizens of Iceland, Liechtenstein, Norway and Switzerland that they would be able to carry on living and working in the UK as they have done with their rights enshrined in the UK law and enforced by British courts. The UK citizens in the EU will also retain their current rights with what the EU's Jean-Claude Juncker called a cheap and simple administration procedure.

The proposal provides a cut-off date of Brexit day—29 March 2019—for those to be covered by the rules. Babies born after that date to people who have qualified under these rules will be included in the agreement. Under the plan EU citizens legally resident in the UK and the UK citizens in the EU will be able to leave for up to five years before losing the rights they would have as part of the proposed BREXIT deal.

Health Care

Healthcare rights will continue as now although it is not clear yet what status an EHIC card would have for other travellers after BREXIT and minute details are mentioned in the UK–EU agreement.

BREXIT Deal: Parliament Vote

The Prime Minister had promised that both houses of the parliament would vote to approve whatever deal the UK and the rest of the EU agree at the end of the two-year process. This vote was proposed as a "take it or leave it" one, after the deal was done; despite some anti-BREXIT MPs believe that they could then persuade enough of their colleagues to back a second referendum.

UK Residents: Visa to Travel to the EU

The UK government wants to keep visa-free travel to the UK for EU visitors after BREXIT, and it is expected to be on reciprocal basis; meaning the UK citizens would continue to be able to visit the EU countries for short periods without seeking official permission to travel.

Work/Study: Issues

If visitors from the EU countries wanted to work, study or settle in the UK they would have to apply for permission under the proposals. No agreement has been reached yet, however. If it is decided that the EU citizens would need visas to come to the UK in the future, then the UK citizens will need visas to travel to the EU.

Pensions, Savings, Investments and Mortgages

State pensions are set to continue increasing by at least the level of earnings, inflation or 2.5% every year—whichever is the highest, no matter what happens in the BREXIT negotiations.

Interest rates going up generally make it more expensive to pay back a mortgage or loan—but a silver lining for savers as they would get more interest on their investments.

UK to Leave: Reasons

Britain was being held back by the EU and imposed too many rules on business and charged billions of pounds a year in membership fees for little in return. They also wanted the UK to make all of its own laws again, rather than being created through shared decision making with other the EU nations.

Immigration

Immigration was also a big issue for BREXIT supporters. They wanted Britain to take back full control of its borders and reduce the number of people coming here to live and/or work.

One of the main principles of EU membership is "free movement", which means you don't need to get a visa to go and live in another EU country. The Leave campaign also objected to the idea of "ever closer union" between EU member states and what they see as moves towards the creation of a "United States of Europe".

UK–EU: Remainers

The then Prime Minister David Cameron was the leading voice in the Remain campaign, after reaching an agreement with other European Union leaders that would have changed the terms of Britain's membership had the country voted to stay in.

He used to say that the deal would give Britain "special" status and help sort out some of the things British people said they didn't like about the EU, like high levels of immigration—but critics said the deal would make little difference.

Sixteen members of Mr Cameron's Cabinet, including the woman who would replace him as PM, Theresa May, also backed staying in. The Conservative Party was split on the issue and officially remained neutral in the campaign. The Labour Party, Scottish National Party, Plaid Cymru, the Green Party and the Liberal Democrats were all in favour of staying in.

The then US President Barack Obama also wanted Britain to remain in the EU—contrary to his successor, Donald Trump, who is an enthusiastic champion of BREXIT—as did the leaders of other EU nations such as France and Germany.

UK to Remain in EU: Reasons

Those campaigning for Britain to stay in the EU said it got a big boost from membership—it makes selling things to other EU countries easier and, they argued, the flow of immigrants, most of whom are young and keen to work, fuels economic growth and helps pay for public services.

They also said Britain's status in the world would be damaged by leaving and that we were more secure as part of the 28 nation club, rather than going it alone.

Businesses

Big business—with a few exceptions—tended to be in favour of Britain staying in the EU because it makes it easier for them to move money, people and products around the world.

Given the crucial role of London as a financial centre, there's interest in how many jobs may be lost to other hubs in the EU. Some UK exporters say they've had increased orders or enquiries because of the fall in the value of the pound. There are others who are less optimistic; fearing products for the European market may have to be made at plants in the EU.

UK: Political Influence

There are views including one is that the UK projects power and influence in the world, working through organisations such as the EU and that on our own means the UK it would be a much diminished force. Simultaneously there is a view that unencumbered by the other 27 members, the UK can get on with things and start adopting a much more independent, self-confident, assertive role on the world stage.

How BREXIT will reveal the outcome of the efforts at the level of the UK Government and the EU by 29 March, 2019 is indeed a reality test. However, there may be sparking indicatives intermittently.

NAFTA (North American Free Trade Zone): Historical Perspective

The boosting encouragement for a North American free trade zone began with the US President Ronald Reagan, who made the idea as part of his presidency campaign in November 1979. Canada and the US signed the FTA in 1988, and followed by Mexican President Carlos Salinas de Gortari who decided to approach US President George H. W. Bush proposing a similar agreement in an effort to bring in foreign investment following the Latin American debt crisis. The two leaders began negotiating; the Canadian government under Prime Minister Brian Mulroney feared that the advantages Canada had gained through the Canada–US FTA would be undermined by a US–Mexican bilateral agreement. He offered to become a party to the US–Mexican talks. Negotiations dating back to 1990 among the three nations, the three leaders signed the agreement in their respective Countries on 17 December 1992. The signed agreement then needed to be ratified by each nation's legislative or parliamentary system. Rather the earlier Canada–US Free Trade Agreement attained controversy and was divisive in Canada, and featured as an issue in the 1988 Canadian election.

Goal

The goal of NAFTA had been to eliminate barriers to trade and investment between the US, Canada and Mexico. The implementation of NAFTA on 1 January 1994, brought the immediate elimination of tariffs on more than one-half of Mexico's exports to the US and more than one-third of US exports to Mexico. Within a decade of the implementation of the agreement, all US–Mexico tariffs were to be eliminated except for some US agricultural exports to Mexico to be phased out within 15 years. Most US–Canada trade was already duty free. NAFTA also sought to eliminate non-tariff trade barriers and to protect the intellectual property rights on traded products.

Intellectual Property

The North American Free Trade Agreement Implementation Act made some changes to the copyright law of the US, foreshadowing the Uruguay Round Agreements Act of 1994 by restoring copyrights (within the NAFTA nations) on certain motion pictures which had entered the public domain.

NAFTA has two supplements:

The North American Agreement on Environmental Cooperation (NAAEC),
The North American Agreement on Labour Cooperation (NAALC).

2016 US Presidential Candidates: Criticism

In a sixty minute interview in September 2015, 2016 Presidential candidate Donald Trump called NAFTA "the single worst trade deal ever approved in the United States", and said that if elected, he would "either re-negotiate it, or will break it".

Trade Expert

A range of trade experts have said that pulling out of NAFTA would have a range of unintended consequences for the US, including reduced access to its biggest export markets, a reduction in economic growth, and higher prices for gasoline, cars, fruits and vegetables.

Mexico: WTO

Members of the private initiative in Mexico noted that to eliminate NAFTA many laws must be adapted by the US Congress. The move would also eventually result in legal complaints by the World Trade Organisation.

Bernie Sanders

Democratic candidate opposed the trade agreements, like NAFTA, Central American Free Trade Agreement (CAFTA) and permanent normal trade relations with China. He believed that free trade agreements have caused a loss of American jobs and depressed American wages. Sanders has said further that America needs to rebuild its manufacturing base using American factories for well-paying jobs for American labour rather than outsourcing to China and elsewhere.

Re-negotiation

Soon after his election, US President Donald Trump clearly said that he would begin renegotiating the terms of NAFTA, to resolve trade issues he had campaigned on. The leaders of Canada and Mexico have indicated their willingness to work with the Trump Administration. Although vague on the exact terms he seeks in a re-negotiated NAFTA, Donald Trump stated further to withdraw from NAFTA, if negotiations fail.

In July 2017, the Trump administration provided a detailed list of changes that it would like to see to NAFTA with top priority of reduction in the US's trade deficit. The list also alleged subsidised state-owned enterprises and currency manipulation.

NAFTA moves, saying the "issues affect real jobs, real lives and real people". Kansas is a major agricultural exporter, and farm groups warn that just threatening to leave NAFTA might cause buyers to minimize uncertainty by seeking out non-US sources.

A fourth round of talks included a US demand for a sunset clause that would end the agreement in five years, unless the three countries agreed to keep it in place, a provision US propose.

At the very least, US–Mexico relations would be impactive, with adverse implications for cooperation on border security, counterterrorism, drug-war cooperation, deportations and managing Central American migration.

Trade Policy

The US Government announced a sharp break from US trade policy, vowing it may ignore certain rulings by the World Trade Organisation if those decisions infringe on US sovereignty. The 336-page report included a section entitled "The President's Trade Policy Agenda", which outlined some of the possible breaks from the WTO.

President Trump's Approach

The approach offers President Trump an opportunity to make good on his campaign promises of an "America first" economic nationalism, as he has already declared that the US economic policy needs to create new jobs for American workers and prevent companies from moving operations overseas and the president has been found sticking to vow and planning to pull back from multinational trade agreements and seek bilateral trade deals, alleging other countries that use tariffs and subsidies to disadvantage US companies. He has threatened to withdraw from the North American Free Trade Agreement unless Mexico agrees to renegotiate the deal.

Threats/Retaliation

Trump's threatened tariffs and other trade barriers could violate WTO rules and bring blowback from other countries in the trade organisation. Emphatic insight by the Donald Trump regime could simply ignore those complaints. Several trade experts said Trump's decision to work outside of the WTO in some cases could create a chain reaction, with countries deciding to impose sanctions and tariffs to help their own businesses and penalise US manufacturers. It has proved to be true in case of a few countries like China where the US has to retaliate with sanction/levy load. In case of the retaliatory reaction the economists and industry groups fear that could trigger a global trade war that could disrupt international business and growth.

WTO Effectiveness

If the Trump administration follows through on the proposals, it would be a body blow to the multinational trade system that the US has helped to build up and the WTO will lose effectiveness and credibility in trade resolutions soon the US decides to walk away.

Manipulating Currency

Charges against China were made frequently during his campaign by the President Donald Trump include accusations that the country manipulates its currency to gain a trade advantage over the US. Chinese officials have operated defensively denying such accusations.

WTO

The WTO provides a forum for countries to settle trade-related disputes, and the Trump administration has said that the organization's reach hamstrings the ability of the US and others to respond to unfair trade practices. There are more than 150 countries in the WTO, and they often accuse one another of violating trade agreements. The US has brought more than 100 complaints through the WTO process since 1995, and other countries have filed 129 cases against the US. For example, the WTO sided with the US in 2014 about duties China had imposed against US automobiles imported into China. China had accused the US of "dumping" automobiles at unfairly low prices in China, but the WTO panel found that China's dumping accusations were calculated improperly. Separately, India filed a case against the US over renewable energy subsidies established by a number of US states, including California, Montana and Washington. That dispute is pending for resolution.

The President Donald Trump has assigned the task of negotiating trade deals arrangements to high-powered functionaries who had been a long-time critic of China's trade practices.

The thoughts by the world powers coupled with proposed action are envisaged to bring cataclysmic changes to the world trade flows, imbalances created by different economies due to trade practices and manipulations thereto.

24

Blockchain Technology and Trade Finance

Blockchain Technology

A basic question before a student interested to know the subject of international trade finance is what really the blockchain technology is and how this technology has relevance to this subject? And also the related queries of an inquisitive learner of international trade inter alia, how blockchain mechanism operates, parties thereto, can the system reshape trade finance and ensure safe and secure conduct of business, envisage future state vision and regulatory support, scalability, inherent or probable advantage with concern to disadvantages/limitations of the system.

There are three principal technologies that combine to create a blockchain viz.

(a) Private key cryptography,
(b) Distributed network with a shared ledger,
(c) Record-keeping and security to service the network's transactions.

Virtually blockchain is in no way distinct technology. Rather, it is the orchestration and application that is new.

Here is an explanation of how these technologies work together to establish and secure digital relationships with the help of a grid that is self-explicit.

© The Author(s) 2019

T. Bhogal, A. Trivedi, *International Trade Finance*, Finance and Capital Markets Series,

https://doi.org/10.1007/978-3-030-24540-5_24

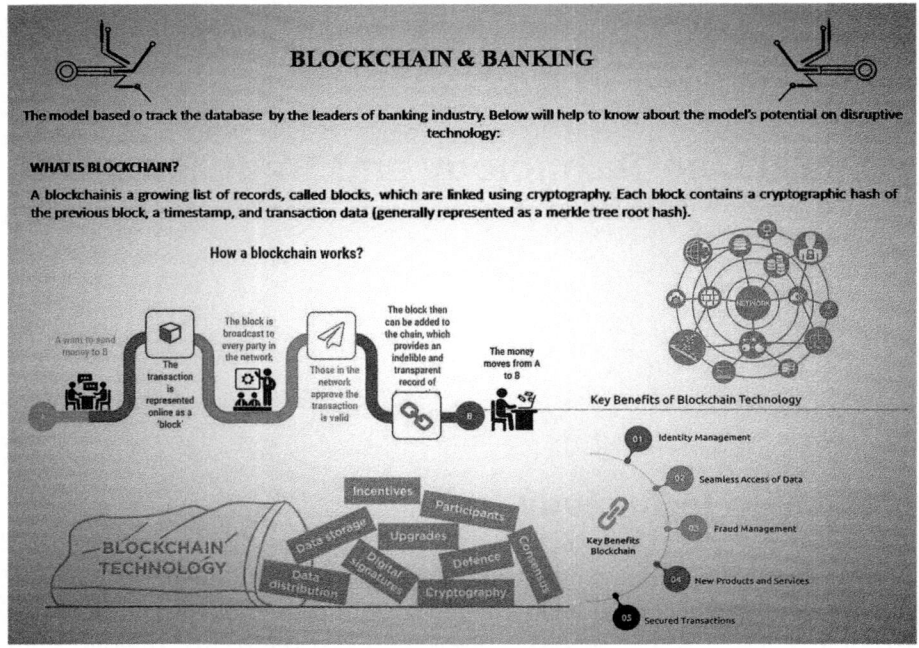

Source: Ninit Ltd. (www.cloudguru.academy)

Cryptographic Keys

Two persons/traders wish to transact over the internet. Each of them holds a private key and a public key. The main purpose of this component of blockchain technology is to create a secure digital identity reference. Identity is based on possession of a combination of private and public cryptographic keys. The combination of these keys can be seen as a dexterous form of consent, creating an extremely useful digital signature. In turn, this digital signature provides strong control of ownership.

Relationship and Belief of Architects

Technology architects believe that a strong control of ownership is not enough to secure digital relationships. While solving the authentication, it has to be combined with a means of approving transactions and permissions (authorisation). For blockchains, the process begins to operate with a distributed network.

Distributed Network

The requirement for a distributed network can be simply understood by the experience as a result of thought "if an electric pole falls in the forest".

If an electric pole falls in a forest, with cameras to record its fall, we can be pretty certain that the electric pole had fallen. We have visual evidence, despite the particular reasons for fall of electric pole may not be meticulously clear.

Bitcoin Blockchain: To be more candid in thought let us know that much of the value of the bitcoin blockchain is a large network where valuators', like the cameras in the assumption, reach a consensus that they witnessed the same thing at the same time. Instead of cameras, they use mathematical verification. In short, the size of the network is important to secure the blockchain network.

That is one of the bitcoin blockchain's most attractive qualities. A section of players in the market believe in technology size and find it is large and has amassed computing power, and is secured by 3,500,000 TH/s, combined together by more than the 10,000 participating banks across the world.

Ethereum: It is a system which is not mature enough and is secured by about 12.5 TH/s may be it is two-years old and in fact still at testing stage.

Blockchain: A System of Record

Technology practitioners reveal that when cryptographic keys are combined with this network, a super useful form of digital interactions emerges. The process begins with person A taking their private key, making an announcement of some sort—in the case of bitcoin, that one is sending a sum of the cryptocurrency—and attach it to person B's public key.

Protocol

A protocol is designed with the help of technology. In a layman's understanding A block—containing a digital signature, timestamp and relevant information—is then broadcast to all nodes in the network.

Network Servicing Protocol

A realist might challenge the electric pole falling in the forest thought experiment with the following question: Why would there be a million computers with cameras waiting to record whether an electric pole fell? In other words, how do you attract computing power to service the network to make it secure—are a few lurking questions to satisfy.

With blockchains, by offering your computer processing power to service the network, there is a reward available for one of the computers. A person's self-interest is being used to help service the public need.

With bitcoin, the goal of the protocol is to eliminate the possibility that the same bitcoin is used in separate transactions at the same time, in such a way that this would be difficult to detect.

This is how bitcoin seeks to act as gold, as property. Bitcoins and their base units (satoshis) must be unique to be owned and have value. To achieve this, the nodes serving the network create and maintain a history of transactions for each bitcoin by working to solve proof-of-work mathematical problems. They basically interface with their CPU power, expressing their agreement about new blocks or rejecting invalid blocks. When a majority of the miners arrive at the same solution, they add a new block to the chain. This block is time stamped, and can also contain data or messages.

Verification vs. Blockchain

The type, amount and verification can be different for each blockchain. It is a matter of the blockchain's protocol—or rules for what is and what is not a valid transaction, or a valid creation of a new block. The process of verification can be designed for each blockchain. Required rules and incentives are created when enough nodes arrive at a consensus on how transactions ought to be verified.

Though the thoughts are at a taster's choice situation, and traders have started to experiment as it is an era of blockchain development where many such experiments are being run simultaneously. The only conclusions drawn so far are that we are yet to fully understand the dexterity of blockchain protocols.

Blockchain and Trade Finance

Trade financing, where banks/financial institutions provide credit facilities, in order to guarantee exchange of goods, is an age-old industry that has not seen much change with the growth of global trade flows. As per market reports the trade finance market was more than $15 trillion in 2015 with addition by more and more traders contributing to the trade finance flows.

Current Scenario and Perspective

Importers

Manual Contract/Agreement Creation: The import bank manually reviews the financial agreement provided by the importer and sends financials to the correspondent bank.

Exporters

Invoice Factoring means exporters use invoices to achieve short term financing from multiple banks, adding additional risks in the event the delivery of goods fails.

Timeline

The shipment of goods is delayed due to the multiple checks by the intermediaries and numerous communication points.

Anti-money Laundering (AML) Checks

The export bank has to manually conduct anti-money laundering (AML) checks drawing upon the financials provided by the import bank.

Multiple Platforms

As the parties across the continents operate on different platforms, scope for miscommunication is common and scope for propensity for frauds cannot be ruled rather quite high.

Shipping Documents

Duplicate shipping documents including bill of lading are financed multiple times due to the inability of the banks to verify authenticity of the documents.

Facts/Truth

As financials are sent from one entity to another, significant version control challenges exist as changes are made during the process.

Payment/Settlement

Multiple intermediaries have to verify that funds stand delivered to the importer as agreed prior to the disbursement of funds to the exporting bank.

Trade Finance: Future State Version (Blockchain)

Upon purchase, the agreement of sale between the importer and exporter is shared with import bank using a "smart contract" on the blockchain.

In real time, the import bank will have capability to review purchase agreement, draft terms of credit and submit obligation to pay to the export bank.

Export bank will review the provided payment obligation and once approved, a smart contract will be generated on the blockchain to cover terms and conditions and lock-in obligations.

On receiving the obligations, the exporter will digitally sign blockchain equivalent letter of credit within the smart contract to initiate shipment.

Goods will be inspected by third parties and the customs authorities or their agent in the exporting country—with all providing their respective digital signature of approval on the blockchain smart contract.

In transit period, goods will be delivered from one place to destination.

Upon delivery, importer will digitally acknowledge receipt of goods and trigger payment.

Using acknowledgement thus provided, blockchain will automate payment from importer to exporter in pursuant of smart contract.

Blockchain: Advantages

Advocates favouring the blockchain mechanism put forward the advantages as under:

Reduced cost.

Faster Settlement-Financial documents linked and accessible through blockchain are reviewed and approved, in real time, reducing the time it takes to initiate shipment of goods/services.

Reduction in counter-party risk—Shipping documents (Bill of lading) is tracked through blockchain, eliminating the potential scope for double spending.

Reduced reliance on third-party intermediation—Banks facilitating trade finance through blockchain do not require a trusted intermediary to assume risk, eliminating necessity for correspondent banks as intermediaries.

Collateral Demand Reduced—The title available within blockchain provides transparency into the location and ownership of the goods.

Fraud Prevention—Regulatory transparency—Regulators are provided with a real-time view of essential documents to assist in enforcement and anti-money laundering issues, if any.

Simplicity in Data Collection and Reporting—As contract terms are adhered to, status is updated on blockchain in real time, reducing the time and headcount required to monitor the delivery of goods thereby simplifying the data collection and reporting thereof in a straightforward way, in any given situation and so on.

Disadvantages

There is a section of financial engineers who are critics of the mechanism and outline disadvantages as under:

Lack of scalability;

Lack or no co-ordination between various parties to the transaction as compared to international trade practices/procedures hitherto;

Significant investment in setting up blockchain technology, awareness, marketing and training to the user system;

Lack of clarity, monitoring and raising ethical risks by regulators (jurisdiction issues in case of a dispute).

Blockchain: Issues and Limitations

There are treacherous passes in a technological revolution at a given point of time. Critical commentary about blockchain technology is not an exception. There are critics who say that blockchain has become overhyped when in reality, the technology has limitations and is inappropriate for many digital interactions/interfaces.

However, through research and development, success and failure, and trial and error, it has been learned that here are issues and limitations of blockchain as under:

Complexity
New vocabulary

It has made cryptography more mainstream, but the highly specialised industry is chock-full of jargon; maybe there are several efforts at providing glossaries and indexes that are thorough and easy to understand as per those who advocate blockchain technology and its application.

Network Size

Blockchains (like any distributed system) are not so much resistant to bad actors as they are "antifragile"—that is, they respond to attacks and grow stronger.

This requires a large network of users, however. If a blockchain is not a robust network with a widely distributed grid of nodes, it becomes more difficult to reap the full benefit.

Costs and Speed

Bitcoin currently has notable transaction costs after being propagated as "near free" for the first few years of its existence. As of late 2016, it can only process about seven transactions per second and each transaction costs about $0.20 and can only store 80 bytes of data.

Human Error

Using blockchain as a database, the information going into the database needs to be of high quality. The data stored on a blockchain is not inherently trustworthy as per critics of the system, so events need to be recorded accurately in the first place. The phrase "garbage in, garbage out" holds true in a blockchain system of record, just as with a centralised database.

Security Flaw

There is one notable security flaw in bitcoin and other blockchains: if more than half of the computers working as nodes to service the network tell a lie, the lie will become the truth. This is called a "51% attack" and was highlighted by Satoshi Nakamoto at the time of launch of bitcoin. Hence bitcoin mining pools are monitored closely by the community, ensuring no one unknowingly gains such network influence.

Regulatory Provisions

These disagreements are a notable feature of the blockchain industry and are expressed most clearly around the question or event of "forking" a blockchain, a process that involves updating the blockchain protocol when a majority of a blockchain's users have agreed to it. The critics further argue that use of blockchain technology done in BITCOIN is largely restricted to few countries and had created significant doubts on its acceptability and scalability. The debates by the subject pundits/ panellists claim to be quite technical, and at times heated, but are informative for those interested in the mixture of democracy, consensus and new opportunities for governance experimentation that blockchain technology is opening up. Blockchain protocols offer an opportunity to digitise governance models, and because miners are essentially forming another type of incentivised governance model, there have been ample opportunities for public disagreements between different community sectors. Growing artificial intelligence-based or even otherwise fast approaches to accept technology like blockchain regulators such as Fed, Bank of England, FCA, European Central Bank and RBI have proactively planned to enforce necessary regulatory provisions/practices to be adhered to by the market participants.

Bolero

BOLERO is an entity established in 1998 by SWIFT and the global logistics and insurance industry, with global headquarters at Walton-on-Thames (UK); it claims to have a strong combination of trade finance expert knowledge, technology and legal framework to deliver digital solutions across the entire global supply chain. Through the Software as a Service (SaaS) application and services, the organisation helps the users to optimise working capital, secure trade finance and reduce the risks and costs of global trade.

Goal

- To digitise global trade;
- Seamlessly connect the trading community;
- Assist buyers and sellers in digital business conduct.

BOLERO has a history of working in partnership with banks, financial institutions to drive operational efficiencies and deliver value-added services to their clients; it includes managing guarantees and trade instruments to enabling automated accounts payable and receivable services.

Bolero's solutions help banks to deliver safer, smarter and faster trade finance products to their corporate clients. Solutions can be deployed as stand-alone services or integrated and white-labelled to support the bank's go-to-market strategy. Bolero is expanding their coverage and value-added services as per their Chairman Mr. Daniel Cotti.

25

Money Laundering and Sanctions

Money Laundering

Money laundering poses international and national security threats through corruption of officials and legal systems, undermines free enterprise by crowding out the private sector, and threatens the financial stability of countries and the international free flow of capital. Undeniably, the revenue produced by some narcotics-trafficking organizations can far exceed the funding available to the law enforcement and security services of some emerging market countries.

Since 11 September 2001, the threat posed by money laundering's closely related corollary, terrorist financing, has also been more widely recognized. The amount of damage through loss of life and economic after-effects from a relatively small amount of operational funding can be devastating. While terrorist financing shares most of the fundamental attributes of money laundering, and while the legal and regulatory regimes needed to control both are essentially the same, terrorist financing does exhibit some significant differences.

Terrorist Financing

Most crime is committed for financial gain by intent and design. The primary motivation for terrorism, however, is not financial. While traditional narcotics-traffickers and criminal groups seek monetary gain, terrorist groups usually seek non-financial goals as well viz. to attain publicity for their cause and to influence the environment. Ordinarily, criminal activity produces funds and

© The Author(s) 2019
T. Bhogal, A. Trivedi, *International Trade Finance*, Finance and Capital Markets Series,
https://doi.org/10.1007/978-3-030-24540-5_25

other proceeds that traditional money launderers must disguise by taking large cash deposits and facilitates entering such funds into the financial system without detection.

Contribution

Funds that support terrorist activity may come from illicit activity but are also generated through means such as fundraising through legal non-profit entities. In fact, a significant portion of terrorists' funding comes from contributors, some who know the intended purpose of their contributions and some who may not be aware of. Because terrorist operations require relatively little money (e.g. the attacks on the World Trade Centre and the Pentagon are estimated to have cost approximately $500,000), terrorist financiers need to place funds into the hands of terrorist cells and their members. This is a significantly easier task than seeking to disguise the large amounts of proceeds generated by criminal and drug traders.

Funding Sources

Transnational organised crime groups have long relied on criminal proceeds to fund and expand their operations, and were pioneers in using corporate structures to pool funds to disguise their origin. In particular, it is the terrorists' use of social and religious organizations, and to a lesser extent, state sponsorship, that differentiates their funding sources from those of traditional transnational organised criminal groups.

International Terrorist Groups

Actual terrorist operations require comparatively modest funding, while international terrorist groups need significant amounts of money to organise, recruit, train and equip new adherents, and otherwise support their activities. In addition to direct costs, some terrorist organizations also fund media campaigns, invite and or even buy political influence, and undertake social projects that help maintain membership and attract supporters' sympathy.

Because of these larger organisational costs, terrorists often rely in part on funds gained from traditional crimes such as kidnapping for ransom, narcotics trafficking, extortion, credit card fraud, currency and merchandise counterfeiting, and smuggling. In this respect al-Qaeda is an anomaly as, at least initially, it was largely self-financed by Osama Bin Laden. In most cases, terrorists engage in some criminal activity and then use a portion of the proceeds to finance their terrorism efforts. Like narcotics-related money launderers, terrorist groups also utilise front companies, that is, commercial enterprises that engage in legitimate enterprise, but which are also used to commingle illicit revenues with legitimate profits. Front companies are frequently established in offshore financial centres/tax heavens that provide anonymity, thereby insulating the beneficial owners from law enforcement. In addition to commingling the proceeds of crime, terrorist front companies also pool donations from sympathisers.

Money Movements

The methods used to move money to support terrorist activities are nearly identical to those used for moving and laundering money for general criminal purposes. In many cases, criminal organisations and terrorists employ the services of normal professionals (including accountants and lawyers) seeking help to move funds.

Intermediaries/Professionals

Both terrorists and criminal groups have used and continue to use established mechanisms in the formal financial sector, such as banks, primarily because of their international linkages. Both terrorist organisations and narcotics-trafficking groups have exploited poorly regulated banking systems and their built-in impediments to international regulatory and law enforcement cooperation, and have made use of their financial services to originate wire transfers and establish accounts that require minimal or no identification or disclosure of ownership.

Money Changers/Couriers

In addition to the formal financial sector, terrorists and traffickers alike employ informal methods to move their funds. One common method is smuggling cash, gems or precious metals across borders either in bulk or through the use of couriers. Likewise, both traffickers and terrorists rely on currency or moneychangers. Moneychangers play a major role in transferring funds, especially in countries where currency or exchange rate controls exist and where cash is the traditionally accepted means of settling commercial accounts. These systems are also commonly used by large numbers of expatriates to remit funds to families abroad. Traffickers and terrorists have become adept at exploiting the weaknesses and lack of supervision of these systems to move their funds.

Hawala or Hundi and Underground Banking

Both terrorists and traffickers have used alternative remittance systems, such as "hawala" or "hundi", and underground banking; these systems use trusted networks that move funds and settle accounts with little or no paper records. Such systems are prevalent throughout Asia and the Middle East as well as within expatriate communities in other regions.

Trade-Based Activities

Trade-based money laundering is used by organised crime groups and, increasingly, by terrorist financiers as well. This method involves the use of commodities, false invoicing and other trade manipulation to move funds. Examples of this include the Black Market Peso Exchange in the Western Hemisphere, the use of gold in the Middle East and the use of precious gems in Africa.

Investment Houses

Some terrorist groups use Islamic banks to move funds. Islamic banks operate within Islamic law, which prohibits the payment of interest and certain other activities. They have proliferated throughout Africa, Asia and the Middle East since the mid-1970s. Some of the largest Islamic financial institutions now operate investment houses in Europe and elsewhere. Many of these banks are not subject to a wide range of anti-money laundering regulations and controls normally imposed on secular commercial banks nor do they undergo the regulatory or supervisory scrutiny by bank regulators via periodic bank examinations or inspections. While these banks may voluntarily comply with banking regulations, and in particular, anti-money laundering guidelines, there is often no control mechanism to assure such compliance or the implementation of updated anti-money laundering policies.

Like money laundering, terrorist financing represents a potential exploitable vulnerability. In money laundering, transnational organized crime groups deliberately distance themselves from the actual crime and the jurisdiction in which it occurs, but they are never far from the eventual revenue stream. By contrast, funds used to finance terrorist operations are very difficult to track.

Capacity Building

Building the capacity of our coalition partners to combat money laundering and terrorist financing through cooperative efforts, and through training and technical assistance programmes, is critical to our national security. While there are some important differences between how money laundering and terrorist financing is conducted, in terms of capacity building through training and technical assistance, there is no appreciable difference.

Cleaned to Give

Money laundering is generally understood as the process by which assets illegally obtained are "cleaned" to give them apparent legitimacy to enable their subsequent use. It involves the purported legitimisation of any asset that is illegitimately obtained, through disguising its true origin. The proceeds of crime, and the true ownership of those proceeds, are changed so that the proceeds appear to come from a legitimate source.

The process typically involves three stages—(1) placement, (2) layering and (3) integration—but these are not clear-cut distinctions and money laundering may become a seamless blend of all three.

Placement—Cash or assets generated from crime are placed in the financial/banking system. The intention is to change the identity of the illegitimate cash/asset. This is the point when proceeds of crime are most apparent and at risk of detection. As banks and financial institutions have developed anti-money laundering procedures, criminals look for other ways of placing cash/assets within the financial/banking system. Professionals, such as solicitors and accountants, can be targeted because they commonly deal with client money.

Layering—Once proceeds of crime are in the financial system, layering obscures their origins by passing the money through complex transactions. These often involve different entities like companies and trusts and can take place in multiple jurisdictions. Sometimes the transactions may have no legitimate economic purpose, but simply result in money/assets moving around.

The intention is to hide the origins of the illegitimate asset, making it difficult to trace and recover.

Integration—Once the origin of the funds has been obscured, the criminal seeks to make the funds reappear as legitimate funds or assets. They will invest funds in legitimate businesses or other forms of investment, often using professionals to buy a property, set up a trust, acquire a company or even settle litigation, among other activities in practice. This is the most difficult stage of money laundering to detect.

UK Law

In UK law the definition of money laundering is broader and more subtle than how it may commonly be understood. It includes all forms of handling of or possessing "criminal property", including possessing the proceeds of one's own crime, and facilitating any handling or possession of criminal property. Criminal property is property which is, or represents, a person's benefit from "criminal conduct", where the alleged offender knows or suspects that it is such. Criminal conduct is conduct which constitutes an offence in any part of the UK or world, in most cases, constitute an offence in any part of the UK, if it has occurred there. Criminal property may take any form and may be in the UK or abroad.

Tax Evasion

An accumulation of small amounts obtained or retained by tax evasion, regulatory breaches or benefit fraud (for instance) would be criminal property for these purposes.

Single/Multiple Act

Money laundering activity may range from a single act, for example being in possession of the proceeds of one's own crime, to complex and sophisticated schemes involving multiple parties, and multiple methods of handling and transferring criminal property as well as concealing it and entering into arrangements to assist others to do so.

The Terrorism Act 2000

The Terrorism Act 2000 (as amended) criminalises not only the participation in terrorist activities, but also the provision of monetary support for terrorist purposes and certain other types of involvement in the funding of terrorist activities or dealings with funds intended or likely to be used for terrorist purposes or funds that represent the proceeds of terrorist activities. All dealings with funds or property which are likely to be used for the purposes of terrorism, even if the funds are "clean" in origin, is a terrorist financing offence under the Act.

US Sanctions: Perspective and Implications

Perspective

The US employs sanctions as a critical component of their national security from a foreign policy perspective. The US's State Department work closely with their allies and partners to ensure that diplomatic pressure is applied with strength, unity and consensus.

Objective

The US president's National Security Strategy is declared from time to time that they would deploy economic pressure on security threats and use existing and also pursue new economic authorities and mobilise international actors to increase pressure on threats to peace and security in order to resolve confrontations short of military action.

Economic Power Strategy

Sanctions are a central component of their economic pressure strategies. When utilised effectively, these are a significant source of power which can be used to shape the behaviour of rogue regimes and malicious global actors.

The US has expanded and strategically deployed their sanctions authorities in response to a wide array of destructive activity around the world.

There are specific instances explained as under.

Russia

Russia poses a threat to its national security on many fronts and sanctions have imposed substantial costs on the Russian Government and the president, and serves to deter the nefarious activities under his regime. The US has witnessed Russian aggression globally, threatening its partners and allies and also threatening its own democratic process. Cogently, the present US Administration has sanctioned a total of 229 individuals and entities for their involvement in Russia's malign activities. Notably, 136 of these designations were imposed under Ukraine-related sanctions authorities codified by the Countering America's Adversaries Through Sanctions Act (CAATSA). The US has also relied on a broad range of other tools, including the Sergei Magnitsky Rule of Law Accountability Act, the Global Magnitsky Human Rights Accountability Act, cyber-related sanctions and transnational criminal organisation sanctions. These actions have sent a stark message that those who support election interference, aggression against other countries, human rights abuses, and other malign activity will suffer severe consequences, as per the US sanction process.

Government of the US is actively engaging its transatlantic allies to seek a resolute, strong, and unified approach. They have made clear that there would be no relief from Eastern Ukraine-related sanctions until Russia meets its commitments under the Minsk agreements, and Crimea-related sanctions would remain in place until Russia returns control of the Crimean peninsula to Ukraine.

Iran

Another regime where economic penalties are a key tool to force behavioural change is Iran. Sanctions on the Iranian regime have attempted to cripple their government by preventing access to the global financial system and deterred companies from investing in Iran and that country's capacity stand destabilised.

Plan of Action

President Trump announced that the US was ceasing its participation in the Joint Comprehensive Plan of Action (JCPOA). The flawed deal failed to protect America's national security interests while enriching the Iranian regime and enabling its malign behaviours and have formed an Iran Action Group and outlined 12 changes they seek in Iranian behaviour. To name a few

(1) Iran must end support to Middle East terrorist groups, including Lebanese Hizballah, Hamas and the Palestinian Islamic Jihadi. (2) Iran must respect the sovereignty of the Iraqi Government and permit the disarming, demobilisation and re-integration of Shia militias. (3) Iran must also end its military support for the Houthi militia and work towards a peaceful political settlement in Yemen. (4) Iran must withdraw all forces under Iranian command throughout the entirety of Syria. (5) Iran must end support for the Taliban and other terrorists in Afghanistan and the region, and cease harbouring senior al-Qaeda leaders. (6) Iran must end its threatening behaviour against its neighbours. This certainly includes its threats to destroy Israel, and its firing of missiles into Saudi Arabia and the United Arab Emirates.

Strong Sanctions

To compel Iran to change its behaviour, the US is putting in place some of the strongest sanctions in history that include sanctions on Iran's trade in gold, sanctions on the sale, supply, or transfer to or from Iran of certain metals, sanctions related to the Iranian Rial and sanctions on Iran's automotive sector, are back in place already, and also include those on Iran's energy sector, port operators, shipping and shipbuilding sectors and on the Central Bank of Iran and other designated Iranian financial institutions.

Iran Regime

In the given scenario, the Iranian regime has a choice to make—either to discuss and resolve these issues diplomatically or face unrelenting economic pressure. If Iran demonstrates a commitment to make the fundamental desired changes in its behaviour, the US Government is prepared to consider easing the pressure of sanctions.

North Korea

Severe orders impose powerful sanctions, including secondary financial sanctions, meaning the US can cut off from the US financial system and/or block the property of any foreign financial institution that knowingly facilitates transactions in connection with trade with North Korea or knowingly facilitates transactions on behalf of certain designated persons. The US' severe economic pressure continues and has yielded the outcome of the first meeting between a North Korean leader and a US president.

Orders/Sanctions

The US has rolled out fourteen tranches of North Korea-related designations, sanctioning a total of 78 individuals, 92 entities, and numerous vessels in response to North Korea's ongoing development of weapons of mass destruction, continued violation of United Nations Security Council resolutions (UNSCRs), and serious human rights abuses.

Venezuela

In Venezuela the use of sanctions to address the Maduro regime's authoritarian rule and economic mismanagement remain a top regional priority for the US, and they are using sanctions to address the Maduro regime's undermining of democratic institutions, abuses of human rights, and rampant endemic corruption and also covering to the designation of 52 individuals and three entities. In tandem with these measures, the US Government have further prevented Maduro's regime from misusing the US financial system to support its rule. The US is bringing the full weight of American economic and diplomatic power to bear to help create the conditions for the restoration of democracy for the Venezuelan people.

Global Magnitsky

The US Administration launched this programme in December 2017 to target serious abuses of human rights and corrupt actors worldwide. The US has used Global Magnitsky to respond to extrajudicial killings in Nicaragua, the ethnic cleansing in Burma and human rights abuse in Turkey to name a few instances. Economic sanctions against Burundi, Central African Republic, Cuba, Democratic Republic of Conga, Somalia, South Sudan, Sudan, Syria and Zimbabwe, due to untoward type of actions the US Administration has to inflict sanctions pressure as an instrument of powerful diplomacy envisaging things go better and ensure orderly conduct of behaviour by the persons and nations in future.

Annexures

Annexure A

SPECIMEN OF APPLICATION FOR L/C

(Banks do have their own style of format but the information required for issue of a L/C is usually similar.)

Dear Sirs,

Please issue by Airmail/Brief or Full Cable/SWIFT your Irrevocable Documentary Letter of Credit available by negotiation/payment/acceptanceas per details below

Name of Issuing Bank Branch	L/C Number	Application to Issue Irrevocable ------------------------------- Documentary Credit
--------------------------	--------------	--------------------------------------

Date of Application: Date LC issued: Date of Expiry (for negotiation in the country of beneficiary)

Applicant's full name and address	Beneficiary's full name and address
Advising Bank's name and address (Issuing Bank to write)	Amount in words and figures –State *FOB, FAS, CIF, C&F asapplicable
Partial Shipments:allowed/forbidden*	
Trans-shipment: permitted/prohibited*	

© The Author(s) 2019
T. Bhogal, A. Trivedi, *International Trade Finance*, Finance and Capital Markets Series,
https://doi.org/10.1007/978-3-030-24540-5

Shipment from ---------------- to --------------- not later than ------------------
Documentary credit to be available by draft(s) at -------------------- drawn on us/yourselves for full invoice value of shipment purporting to be
   Accompanied by the following signed documents marked (X)

- Commercial invoice in ---------- copies certifying goods to be of -------origin
- Full set of clean "shipped on board" marine bills of lading made out or endorsed to your order showing "Freight prepaid"/and marked notify us and you
- Air Waybill bearing your Credit number showing the goods consigned to and showing 'Freight prepaid*/Freight to pay ---------------------------- and marked notify you and us.
- Insurance policy/certificate in duplicate issued to beneficiary's order and bank endorsed covering goods for the invoice value plus 10% covering marine and war risks including Institute Cargo Clauses (All risks) and Institute Strike Riots and Civil Commotion. Claims payable in -----------------------Additional Risks:
- Insurance covered by --------------. The details of the shipment under your credit must be advised by the beneficiary by air mail/telex immediately after shipment to us and referring to cover note number----------of-----------------
- Two copies of this advice should accompany the original set of documents.
- Certificate of origin issued by a Chamber of Commerce.
- Packing list in ------------------copies.

   Additional conditions:

1. short form of Bills of Lading not acceptable.
2. ---------------------------------
3. ---------------------------------

- Advising and Negotiating Bank charges are for ( ) our account ( ) Beneficiary's account

N.B. If any special documents (over and above those termed "shipping documents" are required such as health, inspection certificate and so on or certificate covering any special or unusual class of insurance, such documents should always be included in the application and specifically mentioned
   Documents to be presented within --------------------days after the date of issuance of the shipping documents but within the validity of the credit.

- We request you to arrange/not to arrange the forward exchange cover subject however to your rights under your terms and conditions.

We agree that the documentary credit issued by you is subject to Uniform Customs and Practice for Documentary Credits (2007 Revision, International Chamber of Commerce, Publication No. 600) except as otherwise stated herein.

The Documentary Letter of Credit shall be deemed to have been issued when an advice thereof has been despatched to the beneficiaries.

In consideration of your issuing the Documentary Credit in accordance with the details set out above we agree to be bound by the above terms and conditions and without prejudice to the generality of the same we specifically instruct you to pay or accept, as the case may be, for our account all drafts drawn pursuant thereto.

Applicant's Signature--------------------------Date: -------------------

Account No. ------------------------------------

(Please note the applicant's signature(s) on the application must be in accordance with the customer's mandate for the operations of the account)

Basic Terms and Conditions for Issuing of Letters of Credit

The applicants agree to be bound by the following terms and conditions (in addition set out on the application form)

The applicant undertakes to:

1. pay at maturity in legal tender of the place of payment or in any currency in which the drafts are drawn at any offices of the bank or its agents all or any of the drafts together with interest that may be due there-under or the terms of the said letter of credit;
2. reimburse you with the amounts required to effect such payments together with interest at such rate as may be currently charging or as may be obtainable at the due date or the date of payment and so on;
3. pay on demand commission, which shall be determined from time to time of the full amount of the credit;
4. to acquire sufficient foreign currency for delivery immediately thereafter or at such time as may be necessary or as may appear necessary to effect such;
5. to repay all indebtedness and the discharge of all liabilities absolute or contingent which may be now or hereafter, may be due or owing or become due or owing in respect of any transaction now or subsequently entered into;
6. to transfer all rights and interests that customer may acquire in goods and chattels relating to the credit and when such goods or chattels are at sea or in foreign ports;

7. that all goods be fully insured against all risks including war risks with insurers approved by the bank, that the insurance policies shall be assigned to the bank until all amounts due to in respect of the said credit or discharge of all liabilities;

8. acknowledge that all documents or goods pertaining to the said credit at any time held by the bank or its agents may be regarded as deposited with the bank or its agents as pledges in the absence of specific contrary arrangements and that as such you are entitled to sell or otherwise dispose of the said goods or documents in such way and on such terms as you think fit;

9. to assign to the bank his right in the said goods or chattels as unpaid sellers on the bank's first demand;

10. pledge or any other security at such time as the bank may think fit and in particular not withstanding that drafts relating to the said credit may not have matured;

11. to obtain relevant instructions from the applicant, or the bank or its agent may in its discretion (without having any obligation so to do) accept as tender in lieu of Bills of Lading any documents issued by a carrier (including a lighter age receipt), which acknowledges receipt of goods for transport;

12. be responsible for the risks arising for the bank's acts or any other person acting or purporting to act on bank's behalf together with all responsibility for the character, kind, quantity, delivery or existence of the merchandise purporting to be represented by any document and/or for any difference of character quality or quantity of merchandise shipped under this credit from that expressed in any invoice accompanying any of the said drafts and/or for the validity genuineness sufficiency from or correctness of any documents;

13. ensure that all necessary export and import authorisation is obtained in respect of the transaction to which the letter of credit relates;

14. to give the bank on demand any further security that may be required and further agree that all the other funds, credit instruments and securities including proceeds thereof, now or hereafter handed to the bank or left in its possession by the applicant or by any other person for his account or held by the bank for transit to or from the bank by mail or courier are hereby made security for this obligation;

15. continue in force notwithstanding any change in the constitution of the undersigned whether arising from the death or retirement of one or more partner or partners or the accession of one or more new partners, or otherwise howsoever;

16. to debit the account with all charges on account of this credit including amendments or extensions of this credit, as well as charges levied by the

overseas correspondents or agents. We also authorise you to make payments of the premium to the insurance company concerned by debiting our account;

17. this letter of credit can be revoked or altered only with consent of all parties interested;

18. irrespective of the port to which shipment is effected the applicant shall retire the bills on demand of payment;

19. the documents accepted in connection with the credit may be those which are generally acceptable in accordance with the laws, customs and usages at the place of negotiation;

20. this will also constitute an agreement between the undersigned and your correspondent whom you employ (as you are at liberty to do so) for the purpose and in connection with this letter of credit agreement;

21. it is a term of this letter of credit agreement that it is to be subject to and interpretation in accordance with English law and that it is to be subject to the exclusive jurisdiction of the English courts (save and except that you are not thereby to be prevented from commencing proceedings before any other court);

22. we agree that the address mentioned on the application is an effective address for service in respect of any proceedings commenced in the English courts as hereinbefore described.

I/WE request you to *arrange / *do not arrange the forward exchange cover subject however to your rights under the terms and conditions of your bank.

We agree that the documentary credit issued by you is subject to Uniform Customs and Practice for Documentary Credits (2007 Revision, International Chamber of Commerce, Publication No. 600) except as otherwise stated herein.

The Documentary Letter of Credit shall be deemed to have been issued when an advice thereof has been despatched to the beneficiaries.

In consideration of your issuing the Documentary Credit in accordance with the details set out above we agree to be bound by the above terms and conditions and without prejudice to the generality of the same we specifically instruct you to pay or accept, as the case may be, for our account all drafts drawn pursuant thereto.

Applicant's Signature----------------------Date: ------------------

Account No. -----------------------------

(Please note the applicant's signature(s) on the application must be in accordance with the customer's mandate for the operations of the account)

Annexure B

GENERAL GUIDANCE FOR COMPLETION OF L/C APPLICATION FORM

The application forms for letters of credit are usually designed by most banks using the same format as the bank's letter of credit. This facilitates the easy transfer of details from the application to the letter of credit itself.

When completing the application the following information should be given:

1.	L/C number	This is a serial number assigned by the issuing bank. Some banks may allocate a block of serial numbers to authorised branches of the bank.
2.	Date of application	The date should be written as follows: 22 December 2006, that is, date in figures, month in words and year in figures.
3.	Date of expiry	Date of expiry is written in the same style as in paragraph (2) above.
4.	Mode of issue	Applicant should state the method of issue of letter of credit, that is, by airmail or telex, SWIFT and so on.
5.	Applicant	Applicant should state full name and postal address including postcode. This information will be incorporated on the L/C by the bank in the letter of credit when issued.
6.	Beneficiary	Beneficiary's full name and postal address including post code should be mentioned.
7.	Advising bank	This is written by the issuing bank. In countries where there is a branch of the issuing bank, the letter of credit should be advised through that branch. In other places, the bank would advise through its correspondent banks.
8.	Amount	Amount of the credit should be written in figures and words e.g. US$50,000. CIF (US Dollars fifty thousand only). The currency should be mentioned in words together with the appropriate "incoterm".
9.	Partial shipment/ trans-shipment	The appropriate term/clause must be clearly stated. Trans-shipment should be allowed when multimodal transport is to be used.
10.	Port of shipment	The following should be clearly mentioned on the application form; i) Port of loading ii) Port of destination iii) Latest date of shipment. The date should be mentioned in the same style as in paragraph (2) above.
11.	Tenor of bill of exchange	The tenor (Period relating to payment i.e. 30 days, 60 days etc) of the bill of exchange should be written in the space provided on the form.
12.	Drawee	Under the Article No. 6(c) of the UCP 600 the bill of exchange is required to be drawn on the issuing bank. If the bill of exchange is to be drawn on the applicant or on any other party it will be considered as an additional document, the drawee's name should be written in the space provided.

(continued)

(continued)

13.	Description	The brief but precise description of the goods concerned should be given. If the space provided is too small to accommodate the description then it should be continued on a separate sheet to form part of the application. It may be more convenient for the applicant to refer to the pro-forma invoice number, date and so on than to a list of different items.
14.	Invoice	Number of copies required should be indicated.
15.	Country of origin	Required country of origin of the goods covered in the credit should be stated, if necessary.
16.	Shipment	Tick the appropriate box for shipment of goods or state the shipment: By sea or By Air
17.	Terms of shipment	"Freight prepaid" or "Freight to pay" shipment according to the incoterms.
18.	Name of the consignee	Name of the consignee should be stated. Usually the IB insists that the goods are consigned to its order to protect its security position. Air waybills are non-negotiable receipts and not documents of title.
19.	Terms of air freight	If freight has not been prepaid the term "Freight prepaid" should be deleted and applicable term inserted, that is, "Freight payable at destination".
20.	Insurance cover	a) If the insurance is to be covered by the beneficiary e.g. under CIF term, it should be stated. b) If the insurance is to be covered by the applicant e.g. under FOB term, it should be stated. Prior arrangements in this respect should be made. c) The name and address of the insurance company/broker should be stated so that insurance can be arranged in time
21.	Where claims payable	Country/place where claims under insurance are payable should be clearly indicated.
22.	Cert. of origin	It should be stated, if required.
23.	Other documents	Details of other documents that may be required to cover the risks relating to goods, should be mentioned.
24.	Other conditions	Any other condition(s) to be fulfilled should be written clearly. Write condition No.1—Short form bill of lading not acceptable.
25.	Advising and/or negotiating banks charges	Mention who should bear these charges, that is, negotiating banks the applicant or the beneficiary.
26.	Period for presentation of doc	The number of days allowed for presentation of documents after the issuance of transport document should be stated. If this period is not stated on the L/C then documents must be presented within 21 days after the issuance of the transport documents under Article No. 14(c) UCP 600. The presentation of documents must be within the expiry date of the L/C
27.	Applicant's signature on application form	Applicant should sign the application form in accordance with the mandate held by the bank.

Annexure C

NEGOTIATION OF DOCUMENTS UNDER RESERVE

Form of an Indemnity for Discrepancies (Amend wording to suit requirements)
The Manager Date -------------------- Bank's name ------------------------------
----- Address ---
Dear Sir,
Re:--- In
consideration of your *negotiating/accepting/paying on presentation a Bill of
Exchange (*delete as appropriate) dated -------------- for ------------------
amount in words ----------------------

Drawn under letter of credit no.--------------------dated ----------------Issued
by --notwithstanding that the documents tendered therewith fail to conform with the requirements of the said
letter of credit by reasons of (State here specifically the irregularities in documents tendered together with the relative precise requirements of the letter of
credit) We undertake to indemnify you from and against all losses or damage,
which you may incur or sustain because of the above irregularities in the
documents. Provided that any claim upon us hereunder shall be made before
the expiration of six months from the date hereof.

Yours faithfully
Signature(s) -------------------------------

Annexure D

Form of an Indemnity for Discrepancies (Amend wording to suit requirements)
The Manager ------------------------------Date: ----------------------Bank's name
---------------------------Address -----------------------------------
Dear Sir,
Letter of Credit No. -------------------issued by --------------------------------In
consideration of your paying us the sum of ----------(amount in words and
figures)   --
Under the above-mentioned credit we hereby indemnify you from all conse-
quences, which may arise notwithstanding the following discrepancies in the
documents.

Signed by the beneficiary Signed by the beneficiary's bank or third party

Glossary

Acceptance A word sometimes used to denote an accepted bill of exchange, but strictly the writing across the face of a bill by which the drawee assents to the order of the drawer.

Accommodation Bill A bill to which a person adds his name to oblige or accommodate another person, without receiving any consideration for so doing (in other words to lend the person money).

ACH (Automated Clearing House) An electronic clearing system in which payment orders are exchanged among financial institutions, primarily via magnetic media or telecommunication networks and handled by a data processing centre.

ACH Return An item not accepted by the receiving bank and returned to the originator.

AD Valorem According to the value, generally in connection with taxes or duties.

Airway Bill A document issued in the case of transport by airfreight.

All Monies Debenture A deed of debenture expressed to cover all monies owing by a company at any time on any account.

AML Anti-money laundering.

ANSI (American National Standards Institute) ANSI is a private non-profit organisation that administers and coordinates the US voluntary standardization and conformity assessment system. It is the official US representative on the International Organization for Standardization (ISO). It has approximately 1000 company, organisation, government agency, institutional and international members.

APACS (Association for Payment Clearing Services) APACS is the umbrella body for the UK payments industry. Three autonomous clearing companies operate under the umbrella of APACS—Voca, CHAPS Clearing Company and the Cheque and Credit Clearing Company.

Appreciation Describes a currency strengthening in response to market demand rather than by official action such as revaluation.

© The Author(s) 2019

333

T. Bhogal, A. Trivedi, *International Trade Finance*, Finance and Capital Markets Series,
https://doi.org/10.1007/978-3-030-24540-5

APS (Assured Payment System) An arrangement in an exchange-for-value system under which completion of timely settlement of a payment instruction is supported by an irrevocable and unconditional commitment from a third party (typically a bank, syndicate of banks or clearing house).

Arbitrage Buying a currency in one centre and selling it in another to take advantage of temporary rate discrepancies. Preferably the two transactions should take place simultaneously, but this is not essential. Arbitrage transactions can take place over many centres and through many currencies before being brought (hopefully) to a satisfactory conclusion.

Assignment A transfer or making over of a right to another person, as in the assignment of the proceeds of a life policy as security to a lending banker.

Authentication The methods used to verify the origin of a message or to verify the identity of a participant connected to a system and to confirm that a message has not been modified or replaced in transit.

Authorised Depository A person authorised by an order of the Treasury to keep bearer securities in safe custody. The term arose under the Exchange Control Act, 1947, and included banks, members of the Stock Exchange, solicitors practising in the UK, and certain other financial institutions.

Back Office The part of a firm that is responsible for post-trade activities. Depending upon the organisational structure of the firm, the back office can be a single department or multiple units (including documentation, risk management, accounting or settlements, etc.). Some firms have combined a portion of these responsibilities usually found in the back office, particularly those related to risk management, into what they term a middle office function.

BACS Bankers Automated Clearing Services

Bacstel-IP The delivery channel, which provides vocal customers with a secure, and direct online telecommunications access to the payment network.

Bank Bill A bill of exchange drawn on a bank or bearing the endorsement of a bank.

Bank Draft This is an instrument drawn by the buyer's bank, normally on a correspondent bank in the exporter's country. The buyer sends the draft to the exporter, who then obtains payment via his own bank. It is possible for the buyer's bank to draw a draft on itself, which is less convenient to an exporter in the UK if he wants payment in GB Pounds, and, in any case, will not finally be paid until it is presented to the bank on which it is drawn.

Bank Rate Formerly the advertised minimum rate at which the Bank of England would discount approved bills of exchange, or lend against certain securities. Bank Rate was discontinued in October 1972 and replaced by the minimum lending rate.

Barge B/L A Bill of Lading issued for transportation of goods by barge, that is, small boat.

Barratry It is a wrongful act wilfully committed by the master or crew of the ship.

Bear A speculator on the Stock Exchange who anticipates a fall in the value of a certain security and therefore sells stocks which he does not possess in the hope of buying them back more cheaply at a later date, thus making a profit.

Beneficiary One entitled to receive the benefit such as cash or goods. In case of a letter of credit the beneficiary is the seller or exporter of goods.

Berth B/L The term used to distinguish a B/L issued by a liner, or a vessel trading under liner conditions, from a B/L issued by a vessel carrying cargo under a charter party.

BIC (Bank Identifier Code) A unique address that identifies precisely the financial institutions involved in international financial transactions. A BIC consists of eight or eleven characters comprising the first three or four of the following components: Bank Code, Country Code, Location and Branch Code. BIC are allocated by SWIFT.

BID Normally the rate at which the market in general, or market-maker in particular, is willing to buy a currency. "Bid", "pay" "take" and "buy" all mean that the quoting or contracting party is interested in buying a currency. Beware, however, when the quotation is a cross-rate for two foreign currencies; then the currency, which is of interest should always be specified.

Bilateral Net Settlement System A settlement system in which participants' bilateral net settlement positions are settled between every bilateral combination of participants.

Bilateral Netting An arrangement between two parties to net their obligations. The obligations covered by the arrangement may arise from financial contracts, transfers or both.

Bill Broker A merchant engaged in buying and selling bills of exchange.

Bill of Exchange An unconditional order in writing, addressed by one person to another, signed by the person giving it, requesting the person to whom it is addressed to pay, on demand or at a fixed or determinable future time, a sum certain in money to, or to the order of, a specified person, or to the bearer.

Bill of Lading A receipt for goods upon shipment, signed by a person authorised to sign on behalf of the owner of the ship. The bill of lading is also a document of title to the goods. It is capable of ownership being transferred by endorsement and delivery.

Bimetallism A currency system having a double standard, under which gold and silver coins are in circulation, containing the full weight of metal represented by their face value.

Biometric This term refers to a method of identifying the holder of a device by measuring a unique physical characteristic of the holder, for example, by fingerprint matching, voice recognition or retinal scan.

BIS (Bank of International Settlements) The BIS is an international organisation which fosters co-operation among central banks and other agencies in pursuit of monetary and financial stability, its banking services are provided exclusively to central banks and international organisations.

Blue Chip A term used to describe the ordinary shares of first-class industrial companies.

Bolero Bolero is a secure platform, which enables paperless trading between buyers, sellers and their logistics service and bank partners.

Both to Blame Collision Clause When damage may be caused by collision of goods into one and another.

Bottomry Bond Borrowing of money to complete the voyage by ship owners by offering the ship as security. The lenders lose the money if the ship is lost.

Breaking Bulk To open hatches and commence discharge.

Broker Intermediary who negotiates foreign exchange deals between banks. In most money centres brokers do not act as intermediaries between banks and commercial users of the market.

Brokerage Commission charged by a broker for his services. In some countries, this fee is referred to as "commission". Brokerage charges can vary depending on currency amount and maturity of the foreign exchange contract.

Bull A speculator on the Stock Exchange who anticipates a rise in the value of a certain security and therefore buys such stocks, not intending to pay for the purchase, but hoping to sell them later, at a profit.

Bullion Gold or silver in bars or in species. The term is also used to describe quantities of gold, silver, or copper coins when measured by weight.

Business Day Also Banking Day, Clear day, Market day and open day. A day on which foreign exchange contracts can be settled, e.g. a foreign exchange contract covering the sale of US dollars against GB Pound can be finalised only on a day when both New York and London are open for normal banking business (of course, other cities in the US and UK are suitable for payment, but only if they are acceptable to both parties to a transaction).

Buyer's Option A beneficial holder of a buyer's option can take delivery at any time between first day and last day of the option, e.g. between a spot and a forward date or even between two forward dates, without incurring further costs or for that matter gaining extra profits.

Buying Rate The rate (see Bid) at which the market in general, or a market-maker in particular, is willing to buy a foreign currency.

Capital Money contributed/used to run a business, often raised by an issue of shares; sums of invested money; the amount of money used or available to carry on a concern.

Carrier's Agent An agent of the shipping company.

Carrier's Lien The shipping company has a "Lien" on the goods for any unpaid freight.

Cash Deposits with the central bank, banknotes and coin.

Caspiana Clause Where the ship owners are permitted to discharge the cargo at a port other than the destined port stated in the B/L.

Chain of Title The proof of title to land, the sequence of deeds and documents from the good root of title to the holding deed.

CHAPS (Clearing House Automated Payment System) The UK electronic transfer system for sending same-day value payments from bank to bank. It operates with the Bank of England in providing the payment and settlement service.

Charter Party B/L A Bill of Lading issued by a charter party, that is, the party to whom the owner has leased the vessel for a certain period or a certain voyage.

Cheque A bill of exchange payable on demand drawn on a banker. The buyer could draw a cheque payable at his own domestic bank, and forward it to the exporter. It may take some weeks for such a cheque to be cleared through the banking system, though it is sometimes possible for the exporter to obtain funds against the cheque by having it purchased by his own bank.

CHIPS Clearing House Inter-bank Payment System is a computerized funds transfer system for international dollar payments linking over 140 depository institutions with offices or subsidiaries in New York. Funds transfers through CHIPS, operated by the New York Clearing House Association, account for over 90% of all international payments relating to international trade. Final settlement occurs through adjustments in special account balances at the Federal Reserve Bank of New York.

Claused B/L See Unclean B/L below

Clean B/L When the goods received on board are in good order and no adverse remark, such as "boxes broken", is marked on the Bill of Lading.

Clean Bill A bill of exchange having no documents attached.

Clean Float When an exchange rate reflects only normal supply and demand pressures, with little or no official intervention.

Clearing Bank A bank, which is a member of the London Banker's Clearing House.

Clearing House A central location or central processing mechanism through which financial institutions agree to exchange payment instructions or other financial obligations, for example securities. The institutions settle for items exchanged at a designated time based on the rules and procedures of the Clearing House. In some cases, the Clearing House may assume significant counterparty, financial or risk management responsibilities for the clearing system.

Combined Transport Document A Bill of Lading issued by a transporting authority covering more than one mode of transport of goods.

Combined Transport Operator A transporter who provides for the cargo to be transported through more than one mode of transport.

Commercial Deals or Transactions Foreign exchange deals between a bank and a non-banking party.

Commission Charges made by a bank to execute a foreign exchange contract with a commercial organisation. (In some countries, this charge is made in the exchange rate).

Conference Liner B/L A Bill of Lading issued by a shipping company running cargo vessels on regular line or regular schedule basis.

Confirmation After transacting a foreign exchange deal over the telephone or telex, the parties to the deal send to each other written confirmation giving full details of the transaction.

Consideration The price paid. The term has been defined as "some right, interest, profit or benefit, accruing to one party, or some forbearance, detriment, loss, or responsibility given, suffered or undertaken by the other".

Consignee One who is to receive the consignment.

Consignor One who sends or forwards the consignment.

Consolidation A person or company (Freight Forwarder) undertaking Consolidation of Consignments.

Consumer Spending The current expenditure of individuals, including purchases of so-called "consumer durable" articles, such as television, radios, washing machines and machinery for use in the home.

Containerised Cargo When the goods are transported duly packed in special large sized containers (20 × 8 × 8 feet) for handling cargo more efficiently.

Contract of Affreightment An undertaking to carry the goods to the agreed port of destination. Bill of Lading is a contract of affreightment.

Convertible Currency A currency, which can be freely exchanged for other currencies or gold without special authorisation from the appropriate central bank.

Copy Bill of Lading An unsigned additional copy of a B/L, which is of no value but may serve the purpose of evidence of shipment of goods.

Correspondent Banking An arrangement under which one bank holds deposits owned by other banks and provides payment and other services to those respondent banks. Such arrangements may also be known as agency relationships in some domestic contexts. In international banking, balances held for a foreign correspondent bank may be used to settle foreign exchange transactions. Reciprocal correspondent banking relationships may involve the use of so-called Nostro and Vostro accounts to settle foreign exchange transactions.

Cover Foreign exchange deal which protects the value of an import or export transaction against exchange rate fluctuations.

Cross-Border Settlement A settlement that takes place in a country other than the country in which one trade counterparty or both are located.

Cross-Rate An exchange rate between two foreign currencies, in particular, other currencies against dollars outside the US. For example, when a dealer in London buys (or sells) Euros against US Dollars, he uses a cross-rate.

Currency The recognised means of making payments, which circulate from hand to hand, or pass current, in a country.

Currency Band The margin within which a currency is allowed to fluctuate by the monetary authorities.

D/A Bill A bill with documents attached, presented for acceptance by the drawee. The documents must be surrendered against such acceptance.

D/P Bill A bill with documents attached, presented for payment by the acceptor or drawee, the documents to be surrendered against such payment.

Dated Stock Gilt-edged stock issued by the government having a date by which it will be repaid.

Dealer (Trader) A specialist in a bank or commercial company authorised to effect foreign exchange transactions and allowed to take speculative positions.

Debenture An acknowledgement of indebtedness, usually given under seal incorporating a charge on the assets of an incorporated company.

Deed A written document executed under seal, evidencing a legal transaction.

Demand An authoritative claim or request. A demand draft is one payable on presentation. Current account balances are repayable on demand.

Demurrages Extra charge to be paid if a vessel is not loaded or unloaded within a time allowed.

Deposit Bank A bank taking money from customers on current deposit or other accounts on the terms that the money is to be repaid on demand or at the end of an agreed term: usually confined to banks which take any sum on deposit, and do not specify any minimum amount.

Deposit Rate The rate of interest paid by a bank on a deposit account.

Depreciation A currency, which loses in value against one or more other currencies, especially if this happens in response to natural supply rather than by an official devaluation.

Depreciation Loss in value of assets by wear and tear, obsolescence and so on; or normal deterioration in value which takes place during the life of an asset.

Depreciation of a Currency A diminution or lessening of the power of the monetary unit over the market, the diminution being shown by a rise in prices.

Details All information required for a foreign exchange transaction—name, rate, date(s) and where payment is to be effected.

Devaluation The reduction of the official par value of the legal unit of currency, in terms of the currencies of other countries. Deliberate downward adjustment of a currency in relation to gold or other currencies.

Deviation Clause The shipping company may change the route to reach the agreed destination.

Direct Debit It is a pre-authorised payment system used in collecting recurring bills by electronic means. Generally, the borrower signs a pre-authorisation agreement giving his bank the right to debit an account for the amount due on a designated day.

Direct Quotation A foreign exchange rate, which values a foreign currency in terms of the national currency, for example, dollars quoted in Frankfurt in Euros terms.

Dirty Float When the value of a floating currency is influenced by the intervention of the central bank.

Discount Usually refers to the value of a currency in the forward market. When a currency is at a discount compared to the spot rate, it is worth less, or in other words, is cheaper to buy in the forward market than for spot settlement.

Documentary Bill A bill of exchange which is accompanied by various documents, such as a bill of lading, invoice and insurance policy.

Domestic Banking The normal course of business between a banker and his customer (as opposed to "wholesale" banking), or the banking business in this country (as opposed to international foreign banking).

Domicile A place of permanent residence; the place at which a bill of exchange is made payable.

Drawee The person or company on whom a bill of exchange or cheque is drawn. When the person has accepted a bill he is known as the acceptor.

Drawer The person who writes out and signs a cheque or bill of exchange.

EBA (European Banking Association) A discussion forum for payments practitioners, the Euro Banking Association plays a major role in the financial industry as a developer of European payment infrastructures. The initiation and coordination of a cost effective and efficient euro clearing system are core activities of the association and have led to the creation of Europe's leading private large-value clearing system EURO 1, the low-value payment system and STEP 1, and the first pan-European automated clearing house, STEP 2.

EBPP (Electronic Bill Presentment and Payment) The process by which companies bill customers and receive payments electronically over the internet. There are two types of presentments model: the direct model, in which a biller delivers the bill to customers via its own website or via a third-party's site; and the consolidator model, in which bills multiple billers are delivered to a single website, to be presented in aggregate to the consumer for viewing and payment.

ECB (European Central Bank) The ECB is the central bank for Europe's single currency, the Euro. The ECB's main task is to maintain the Euro's purchasing power and thus price stability in the Euro area. The ECB was established as the core of the Euro-system and ESCB (European System of Central Banks). The ECB and the national central banks together perform the task they have been entrusted with. The ECB has legal personality under public international law.

EDI (Electronic Date Interchange) The electronic exchange between commercial entities (in some cases also between public administrations), in a standard format, of data relating to a number of message categories, such as orders, invoices, customs documents, remittance advices and payments. EDI messages are sent through public data transmission networks or banking system channels. Any movement of funds initiated by EDI is reflected in payment instructions flowing through the banking system. EDIFACT, a United Nations body, has established standards for electronic data interchange.

EDIFACT (Electronic Data Interchange for Administration Commerce and Transport) Along with ANSI X12, EDIFACT was one of the first information standards created for e-business transactions.

EFT (Electronic Fund Transfer) A service which routes payments to the appropriate bank or building society.

EFTPOS (Electronic Fund Transfer at Point of Sale) The term refers to the use of payment cards at a retail location. The payment information is captured either by paper vouchers or by electronic terminals, which in some cases are designed also to transmit the information. Where this is so, the arrangement may be referred to as "electronic fund transfer at the point of sale".

Eligible Liabilities The GB Pound deposits of the banking system as a whole, excluding deposits having an original maturity or more than two years, and any GB Pound resources gained by switching foreign currencies into GB Pound. Interbank transactions and GB Pound certificates of deposit (both held and issued) are taken into the calculation of individual banks' liabilities on a net basis, irrespective of the term.

Endorsement in Blank An endorsement in blank consists of the name only of the payee or endorsee of a bill of exchange, written on the back of the bill. Such an endorsement specifies no endorsee, and the bill becomes payable to bearer.

Euro-Currency Currency held by non-residents and placed on deposit with banks outside the country of the currency. Major Euro-markets exist in Germany, Switzerland, France and the UK, and, from time to time, there are active dealings in Netherlands and Belgium and even Japan. The Euro element is of less importance now that deposit markets have been established in the Far East (the Asian currency market) and in the Western hemisphere.

Euro-Dollars Dollars belonging to non-residents of the US, which are invested in the money markets in Europe, particularly in London. Side by side with the Euro-dollar market, there exist the Asian and the Western hemisphere markets. Euro-dollar settlements are made over the banking accounts in the US and form an integral part of the US money supply.

Exchange Contract Verbal or written agreement between two parties to deliver one currency in exchange for another for a specific value date, or sometimes a specific period, as in the case of an option contract.

Exotic Currencies Currencies in which there is no active exchange market. Most of the currencies of the underdeveloped world would fall within this category.

FATF (Financial Action Task Force) It is an inter-governmental body whose purpose is the development and promotion of policies, both at national and international levels, to combat money laundering and terrorist financing. It is a "policy-making body" which works to generate the necessary political will to bring about national legislative and regulatory reforms in these areas.

Fed Wire Federal Wire is a high-speed electronic communication network linking the Federal Reserve Board of Governors, the 12 Federal Reserve Banks and 24 branches, the US Treasury Department and other federal agencies.

Finance Bill A bill drawn by a firm or company for the purpose of arranging a short-term loan. The bill is drawn by arrangement on another firm or on a bank or accepting house. No sale of goods is involved. When the bill is accepted, it is discounted.

Firm Quote (Quotation) When a foreign exchange dealer gives a firm buying or selling rate, or both, for immediate response or with a definite time limit.

Fixed Exchange Rate Official rate set by monetary authorities for one or more currencies. In most instances, even fixed exchange rates are allowed to fluctuate between definite upper and lower intervention points.

Flexible Exchange Rates Exchange rates with a fixed parity against one or more currencies but with frequent up or down valuations.

Floating Exchange Rate When the value of a currency is decided by supply and demand only.

Floating Pound The GB Pound left to find its own level on the Foreign Exchange through the operation of the laws of supply and demand.

Fluctuations Up and down movements of an exchange rate in response to supply and demand.

Foreign Bill A bill of exchange drawn abroad and payable in this country; or drawn in this country and payable abroad.

Foreign Exchange Conversion of one currency into another.

Foreign Exchange Market Worldwide network which connects the various national exchange markets by telephone and telex, either direct or via the brokers, to transact foreign exchange business.

Forward Book Various net exposures for forward maturities which a bank has incurred by deliberate policies or as a result of dealing activities.

Forward Contract Exchange agreement between two parties to deliver one currency in exchange for another at a forward or future date.

Forward Exchange Buying or selling currencies for delivery later than spot. Also called "future".

Forward Margins Discounts or premiums between the spot rate and the forward rates for a currency.

Forward Maturities Business days for which deals can be transacted later than the spot date.

Forward Purchase Engagement to buy a currency in exchange for another at a future date.

Forward Rate The rate at which foreign currency can be bought or sold for delivery at a future time.

Forward Rates Discounts or premiums between the spot rate and the forward rates for a currency.

Forward Sale Agreement to deliver a currency in exchange for another on a future date.

Forward/Forward Simultaneously buying and selling the same currency for different maturity dates in the forward market. This also describes a dealer's forward book when he has long and short positions for different maturities, for example, long of Euro three months and short of Euro in the six months maturity.

Forwarding Agent's B/L A certificate of shipment issued by a shipping company's agent stating that the named consignment has been forwarded.

Freehold An estate in land, which is properly described as an estate in free simple absolute possession, signifying the highest type of land ownership, which anyone can possess.

Freight Paid/Prepaid It is a clause when the freight is paid to the carrier prior to the transportation of the consignment.

Freight Prepayable/To Be Prepaid Freight to be paid before shipment of the cargo.

Gilt-Edged Securities of the highest class (e.g. government stocks) which are readily realizable.

Good Root of Title A document, which deals with the whole legal and equitable interest in land, describes the property in detail and shows no adverse factor influencing the title. It is the starting point of the chain of title when proving title to land.

Green Clause This clause is written on a letter of credit and is distinct to Red Clause, primarily covers the degree to which each one ties up the applicant's funds and exposes him to a foreign exchange risk. The merchandise is taken as collateral security against the advance of funds allowed by this clause. The advance funds may be given against warehouse receipts. Such clauses are not common these days and are of academic interest.

Ground Rent The rent paid to a freeholder who has granted a lease on his land and/or buildings.

Hedge Against Inflation An investment in land or shares, which are expected to appreciate in value in times of inflation, thus protecting the investor against loss due to the fall in the value of money.

Hedging Act of buying or selling the currency equivalent of a foreign asset or liability in order to protect its value against depreciation (appreciation) or devaluation (revaluation).

Holding Deed The deed, which transferred the ownership of land to the person who is now holding it.

House Air Waybill A document issued by a consolidator for instruction to the break bulk agent.

House Bill of Lading A Certificate of Shipment of a specified consignment usually issued by a Freight Forwarder in association with a group age or consolidated international consignment.

Hull Loading It is where the vessel is loaded away from the port or a small ship goes into the other big ship.

Inconvertible Currency Currency, which cannot be exchanged for other currencies, either because this is forbidden by the foreign exchange regulations or because there are no buyers who wish to acquire the currency.

Indication (Indication Rate) When a dealer states "for indication" or "indication rate", this means that he does not want to transact business at the given rate or rates. The use of this expression can lead to confusion and it is preferable to substitute the less ambiguous term "for information only".

Indirect Quotation Foreign exchange rate, which values the local or national currency in terms of the foreign currency. For example, in London foreign exchange rates show the value of £1 in other currency terms.

Inflation The result of the excessive issue of paper money, so that too much money is chasing too few goods, with the result that the value of the money in terms of goods steadily falls (i.e. prices rise).

Inherent Vice Deterioration of perishable goods by the passage of time or period.

Inland Bill A bill of exchange both drawn and payable within a country.

Interest Arbitrage Switching into another currency by buying spot and selling forward, and investing the proceeds in order to obtain a higher interest yield. Interest arbitrage can be inward, that is, from foreign currency into the local one, or outward, that is, from the local currency to the foreign one. Sometimes better results can be obtained by not selling the forward interest amount, but in that case, if the exchange rate moved against the arbitrageur, the profit on the transaction might be less and even turn into a loss.

Interest Parity One currency is in interest parity with another when the difference in the interest rates is equalized by the forward exchange margins. For instance, if the operative interest rate in the US is 5% and in the UK 6%, a forward premium of 1% for US Dollars against GB Pounds would bring about interest parity.

Intervention When central banks operate in the exchange markets to stabilize the rates and sometimes to influence the external value of a currency.

Intrinsic Value Genuine or real value. When used of a coin it means that the metal in the coin is worth the face value of the coin.

Investment Using money to buy something which, it is hoped, will bring in some return and will not lose its value.

Jettision Means the throwing overboard of cargo or ship's gear to save the ship.

Jobber A dealer on the Stock Exchange who carries on business with the public and with other jobbers through the medium of stockbrokers.

L.A.S.H. B/L (Lighter Abroad Ship) A smaller ship that goes into mother ship.

Leads and Lags Process of accelerating or delaying foreign exchange cover when a currency adjustment seems imminent.

Leasehold Granting of the use of land by the freeholder to a lesser for a term of years.

Legal Tender The authorised notes and coin which may be lawfully offered in payment of a debt in a country.

Lien Lien is a legal right to obtain goods belonging to someone else until the charges on them have been paid, or until some pecuniary claim against the owner has been satisfied.

Limited Liability The limitation of the shareholders of a company of their liability for the debts of the company to the nominal amount of the shares they hold or to the amount they have guaranteed.

Liner B/L A Bill of Lading issued by a shipping company operating passenger ships.

Long Bill A long bill is a bill of exchange having a usance of three months or more.

Long Position (or just Long) Incurred when a dealer purchases a currency in excess of his immediate requirements. Obviously a long position in one currency is compensated by a short position in another, even if the other currency is the national one.

Mail Transfer (MT) In this case, the buyer's bank sends instructions by airmail to a correspondent bank, asking it to credit the exporter or his bank with GB Pound or foreign currency. Bank charges for remitting funds by MT are to be met by either the buyer or exporter and depend on what the parties have agreed. This method is slower than other methods of transfer of funds between banks in two different countries.

Managed Float When the monetary authorities intervene regularly in the market to stabilize the rates or to aim the exchange rate in a required direction.

Margin (Spread) Difference between the buying and selling rates, but also used to indicate the discounts or premiums between spot and forward.

Maritime Lien Shipping company's lien over the cargo for freight not paid and the captain and the crew also have lien over the cargo for not being paid their salary by the shipping company.

Market-Maker The bank which makes buying and selling quotations in one or more currencies, either for spot and/or forward, to most comers.

Master Air Waybill An air waybill covering a consolidated shipment showing the consolidator as the shipper.

Master of the Vessel Captain of a merchant vessel.

Mate Receipt Is an acknowledgement of the goods issued by the wharfinger or master of the ship when the goods are delivered on the wharf before the arrival of the ship named to carry the goods.

Maturity Date Due date of an exchange contract, that is, the day that settlement between the contracting parties will have to be effected.

Mortgage The conveyance of a legal or equitable interest in real or personal property as security for a debt or for the discharge of an obligation.

Near Money A term sometimes applied to bills, cheques, promissory notes, postal and money orders.

Negotiable Bill of Lading Original copy of B/L duly signed by the ship owner or his authorised agent which gives the transferee a good title to goods.

New Jason Clause Means the ship owners will not be responsible for any accidental damage to the goods, before or after the shipment but in their custody.

Ocean B/L When the buyer names a particular ocean-going vessel to transport the consignment.

Offer for Sale An invitation to the public to buy shares of a new issue from an Issuing House, which has bought the issue from the company concerned.

Offshore Funds A name given to mutual investment funds registered abroad in countries which offer tax advantages.

On-Board B/L A Bill of Lading indicating that the goods named therein have been received on board of the ship.

On-Deck Shipment Received on the deck for shipment. It is similar to "On Board B/L".

Open Day Also known as Banking day, Business day, Clear day and Market day. A day on which foreign exchange contracts can be settled; e.g. a foreign exchange contract covering the sale of US dollars against GB Pounds can be finalised only on a day when both New York and London are open for normal banking business (of course, other cities in the US and UK are suitable for payment, but only if they are acceptable to both parties to a transaction).

Open Market Operations The purchase or sale of securities in the Stock Exchange or Money Market by the central bank for the purpose of expanding or contracting the volume of credit.

Option Forward Rate The rate at which foreign currency can be bought or sold for delivery between two future dates at the option of the buyer or seller. The option is as to the precise day of completion.

Over-Valuation Describes the exchange rate of a currency, which is in excess of its purchasing power parity. This means that the country's goods will be uncompetitive in the export markets.

Overnight Limit Net long or short position in one or more currencies that a dealer can carry over into the next dealing day.

Package Deal When a number of exchange and/or deposit orders have to be fulfilled simultaneously.

Palletised Cargo Cargo of heavy weight placed on wooden frame and so on to facilitate lifting.

Paper Money Documents representing money, such as banknotes, promissory notes, bills of exchange or postal orders. (The last three of these are sometimes referred to as "quasi-money").

PAR The nominal value of securities, or the exact amount, which has been paid for them.

Paramount Clause Bills of Lading issued in the UK bear the "Paramount Clause" which means that the carriage of goods is subject to the terms and conditions of the "Carriage of Goods Act of 1924".

Partial Shipment Shipment of the cargo in part of the entire or complete consignment for shipment.

PIP The fifth place after the decimal point, for example $/£1.72105. The last digit represents five pips.

Pledge A delivery of goods or the documents of title to goods, by a debtor to his creditors as security for a debt, or for any other obligation. It is understood that the subject of the pledge will be returned to the pledgor when the debt has been paid or the obligation fulfilled.

Point The fourth place after the decimal point is called a "point", for example $/Euro1.4012. The last digit (2) represents two points.

Port Bill of Lading It is a Bill of Lading, which is signed by an authorised person after the receipt of goods/shipment by the person at the port of shipment.

Port Congestion Surcharge Extra charges for causing congestion at the port by over staying in the port.

Premium A currency is at a premium, especially in the forward market, when fewer units can be bought for a forward maturity than on the spot.

Prime Bank Bill A bill of exchange drawn on and accepted by a first-class bank.

Qualitative Control Directives from the Bank of England to the lending banks and financial institutions as to classes of customers who may be allowed to borrow.

Quantitative Control Directives from the Bank of England to the lending banks and financial institutions as to the total amount of money which they may lend.

Quarantine Isolation imposed on a passenger while travelling.

Quasi Negotiable B/L It is a Bill of Lading that if the transferor has a defective title the transferee does not get good title to the B/L.

Railway Receipt A Railway Receipt is document issued by Railway authorities for transportation of goods by railway.

Red Clause It is a clause added to a letter of credit, which authorises the advising/confirming bank to advance a certain specified percentage of the credit amount to the beneficiary before the beneficiary is in a position to present documents.

Received For Shipment B/L A document issued by a shipping company acknowledging the receipt of goods for shipment.

Reserve Assets These assets, to be held by banks and other financial institutions, are those which the Bank of England is ready to convert into cash, either directly or through the discount market. They comprise Treasury Bills, (Repos), cash held with Bank of England, investments in Gilt Edged Securities and so on.

Respondentia Bond An instrument by which the owner of the ship hypothecates the cargo as security for repayment of money borrowed at a foreign port.

Restraint of Princes Action by a Government or King for arresting the ship or the cargo and so on.

Restrictive Endorsement One which prohibits the further negotiation of a bill or cheque.

Retail Banking The traditional course of business between a banker and his domestic customers, as opposed to "wholesale" banking.

Revaluation When the official value of a currency is updated by a deliberate decision of the monetary authorities.

Rights Issue The offer by a company of new shares direct to its existing members. The price is usually set below the market price of the existing shares in order to make the offer attractive. The rights to subscribe, therefore, have themselves a market value, and can be sold.

Rollover Prolongation of a maturing contract by swapping it onto a forward date.

Sailing Vessel B/L Bill issued by the owner of the "sailing vessel" (S.V.)

Scrip The document or provisional certificate which is given to a person who has agreed to take up bonds in connection with a government loan and has paid the first instalment. Scrip is principally associated with the issue of bonds or debentures.

Scrip Issue A capitalization of reserves by issuing fully paid-up shares free to present shareholders in proportion to their current holding.

Seller's Option Forward contract, which allows the seller to deliver the foreign currency on any date within the option period.

Selling Rate Rate at which a market maker will sell a foreign currency for a suitable maturity date.

Shipper Name of the exporter/consignor.

Short Bill A short bill is one which has only a few days to run to maturity, irrespective of the original tenor of the bill or a bill of exchange payable as soon as sighted or seen by the drawee.

Short Forward Date and Rate The term "short forward" can refer to periods of up to two months, although it tends to be used more and more for maturities of less than one month. Dealers may use the term "Shorts" as well.

Short Position It is position of a foreign exchange dealer when a dealer is short outright of a foreign currency.

Sling Loss Damage to goods by use of slings (Hooks).

Sous-Palan Clause The carrier reserves the right to unload the cargo to lighten the ship's cargo. This situation may arise out of port congestion.

Special Deposit An instrument of monetary policy, designed to restrict credit. The Bank of England may call upon all banks and financial institutions to deposit a percentage, usually 1%, of their total deposits with the Bank of England. This restricts the ability of the lending institutions to extend credit.

Speculation The purchase or sale of shares on an estimate of whether the share value will rise or fall, with the intention of making a quick profit, or avoiding a loss.

Speculator and Speculation Individual, an act of buying and selling a currency before the currency has to be paid for or delivered in the hope that a favourable exchange rate adjustment will take place.

Spot Generally the spot date falls two business days after the transaction date, though in some markets spot transactions may be executed for value next day.

Spot Deal (Transaction) Foreign currency purchase or sale effected for spot value.

Spot Rate The normal rate of exchange quoted in the foreign exchange markets, that is, the rate for transactions in which the funds are to be paid over in each centre two working days later.

Spot Rate (Exchange Rate) The spot rate is also the exchange rate of a currency and is the one against which appreciations and depreciations (devaluations and revaluations) will be calculated.

Spread Difference between the buying and selling rates, but also used to indicate the discounts or premiums between spot and forward.

Square Purchases and sales are in balance and thus the dealer has no position.

Stag A Stock Exchange expression for a person who applies for shares in any new company with the sole object of selling as soon as a premium is obtainable and never intending to hold or even fully subscribe for the shares.

Stale B/L Where a B/L is dated after the bill of exchange or received in the importer's country after the goods have arrived.

Straight B/L It is an American term for a bill of lading in which it is stated that the goods are consigned to a specified person.

Steam Ship B/L A Bill of Lading issued by Steam Ship owner (S.S.) for the cargo.

Steamer Arrival Date of the arrival of the steam ship.

Stockbroker One who purchases or sells stocks or shares for his clients on the Stock Exchange.

Stop-Loss Order Order given to ensure that, should a currency weaken by a certain percentage, a short position will be covered even though this involves taking a loss. "Realize Profit Orders" are less common.

Swap Transaction involving the simultaneous buying and selling of a currency for different maturities.

Swap Margin Discounts or premiums between the spot rate and the forward rates for a currency.

Telegraphic/Swift Transfer This is identical to Mail Transfer except that the instructions are conveyed by telex or cable or electronically. Transfers can also be made via the S.W.I.F.T. (Society for Worldwide Interbank Financial Telecommunications) network.

Tenant Right A right of the tenant of property, whether expressly stated or implied, such as a right to remove fixtures at the end of the tenancy, or to receive an allowance for seeds or fertilizer put on the land.

Tenor The term or meaning applied to a bill of exchange or financial instrument when it is payable on sight or a given number of days/months after the date of the instrument.

Term Bill A bill of exchange which is payable at the end of a period, as opposed to a bill payable at sight or on demand.

Thin Market When there is little activity in the market and even small orders will affect the rate structure.

Third Party B/L A B/L issued not by the ship owner but some other shipping company.

Through Bill of Lading It is a bill of lading, which provides (or ought to provide) for continuous responsibility of several railway and shipping undertakings from one place to another.

Token Money Coins where the value of the metal in them is less than the value attached to them by law, such as the cupro-nickel and bronze coins of the UK.

Trade Bill A bill of exchange drawn and accepted by commercial firms.

Tramp Shipping Freight or cargo vessel running on irregular line.

Trans-Shipment Transfer of cargo from one ship to another prior to reaching the destination.

Transaction Date Day on which a foreign exchange transaction is entered into.

Transaction Loss (or Profit) Real or opportunity loss or profit on a foreign exchange transaction covering the movement of goods or services or even to undo another foreign exchange transaction.

Translation Loss (or Profit) Estimated loss or profit resulting from the revaluation of foreign assets and liabilities for balance sheet purposes.

Treasury Bill Bills issued by the treasury in return for sums of money lent to the government by bankers, brokers and so on. They form part of the floating debt of the country.

Truck Way Bill A document issued by a Road Transporter for transportation of goods by a truck.

Two-Way Quotation When a dealer quotes both buying and selling rates for foreign exchange transactions.

Unclean B/L When the Bill of Lading indicates the packing of goods is defective or broken.

Undated Stock Gilt-edged security issued by the government on a perpetual basis and does not have a date by which it will be redeemed.

Under-Valuation An exchange rate is under-valued when it is below its purchasing power parity. The consequence of under-valuation is that goods produced in the under-valued country will be too cheap in the export markets.

Unitised Cargo Items such as motor vehicles, tractors and other machinery, which are delivered and accepted by the shipping company as units.

Usance Bill of Exchange It is a period of time between the date a bill of exchange is presented and the date it is paid. In the strict sense, the term means the time allowed by customs for the period of a bill of exchange in trade between two different countries. A bill of exchange drawn in one country and payable in another at a term which is governed by the custom or usage of such transactions.

Value Date Maturity date of a spot or forward contract.

Value Today Transactions executed for same-day settlement; sometimes also referred to as "cash transactions".

Wharfage Charges for storing goods at the wharf.

Wholesale Banking Borrowing or lending, usually in large sums, by big banks amongst themselves through the medium of the inter-bank market; dealing with other financial institutions, as opposed to retail banking which consists of the traditional course of business between a bank and its customer.

Yankee Bonds Dollar denominated bonds issued in the US by foreign banks and corporations. These bonds pay semi-annual interest, unlike Eurobonds, which pay annual interest, and are registered with Securities and Exchange Commission.

Yield Curve Comparison of the market return, or yield, of a security and its maturity. This usually is plotted on a graph showing the comparative yields of similar investments, such as bonds.

Z-Bond Long-term, deferred interest Collateralised Mortgage Obligation (CMO) bond that pays no interest until all prior bonds in a CMO bond offering have been retired. Z-Bond is similar to Zero Coupon bond.

Index

© The Author(s) 2019
T. Bhogal, A. Trivedi, *International Trade Finance*, Finance and Capital Markets Series,
https://doi.org/10.1007/978-3-030-24540-5

351

Printed by Printforce, the Netherlands